The Social Economy

Critically examining economic developments within the last sixty years, this book argues that a crisis in global social reproduction is altering existing understandings of work, labour and the economy.

The author of this original volume, Hasmet M. Uluorta, contends that the crisis in the global economy is triggering a potential paradigm shift from one defined under the rubric of Employment to an alternative theorized as Work. Discussing the Employment paradigm that formed the dominant mode of development after World War II through to the 1970s, the author considers the economic and political forces that resulted in its eventual decline.

Focusing on already existing practices of organizations and workers in Toronto, Canada, the book goes on to consider the shift to Work and the consequent rise in the social economy which has broken down conventional categories of work and leisure. The author concludes that the social economy presents fundamental challenges to understandings that underpinned the previous economic order.

Building on insights from a range of disciplines, *The Social Economy* will be of interest to students and scholars of international political economy, international relations, labour studies, sociology, and globalization studies.

Hasmet M. Uluorta is Visiting Assistant Professor at the Department of International Studies at the University of Miami. He is the former Associate Director of the Stanford Center on Ethics at Stanford University.

T0347412

Rethinking globalizations
Edited by Barry Gills
University of Newcastle, UK

This series is designed to break new ground in the literature on globalization and its academic and popular understanding. Rather than perpetuating or simply reacting to the economic understanding of globalization, this series seeks to capture the term and broaden its meaning to encompass a wide range of issues and disciplines and convey a sense of alternative possibilities for the future.

For Anne, whose aesthetics, labour and reflections make all possible

The Social Economy

Working alternatives in a globalizing era

Hasmet M. Uluorta

Routledge
Taylor & Francis Group

LONDON AND NEW YORK

First published 2009 by Routledge
2 Park Square, Milton Park, Abingdon, Oxon OX14 4RN

Simultaneously published in the USA and Canada
by Routledge
711 Third Avenue, New York, NY 10017

*Routledge is an imprint of the Taylor & Francis Group,
an informa business*

© 2009 Hasmet M. Uluorta

Typeset in Times New Roman by
Swales & Willis Ltd, Exeter, Devon

British Library Cataloguing in Publication Data
A catalogue record for this book is available from the British Library

Library of Congress Cataloging in Publication Data
A catalog record has been requested for this book

ISBN 13: 978–0–415–77593–9 (hbk)
ISBN 13: 978–0–203–88430–0 (ebk)
ISBN 13: 978-0-415-77593-9 (pbk)

Contents

Illustrations

Tables

Figures

Acknowledgements

This book is a heterotopic affair. It was written between immigration visas, life-changes, different cities and cafés as well as in and out of a variety of university settings. I wish to express my profound thanks to my family for their encouragement and understanding of the many challenges and sacrifices along the way. This project would not have been possible if it were not for the willingness of organizations and members of the Toronto social economy to participate. I thank them for their invaluable contribution. I remain grateful for the support I received from the Department of Political Science at York University, the Politics Department at the University of California, Santa Cruz, the Stanford Center on Ethics at Stanford University and to the International Studies Department at the University of Miami. As such this research is a result of a broad scholarly community situated across time and space but whose reflections and echoes filled my thoughts.

Dr Jan Nederveen Pieterse has been a constant source of intellectual stimulation, insisting on the acknowledgement of alternative development practices as well as the examination of the politics of alternative development. Dr Stephen Gill's insistence on and modelling of the pursuit to develop new theory without intimidation as a means to better explain current global structural reforms has been invaluable. Dr Lawrence Quill provided access and the necessary amusement for an understanding of political philosophy. Dr Barry Gills, editor of the Routledge *Rethinking Globalizations* book series, understood the significance of this project and supported its inclusion in this series.

This book would not exist however if it were not for two people: Dr Isabella Bakker and Anne Kim. As an instructor, mentor and friend Dr Bakker remained committed to this project by encouraging, prodding, editing, supporting and guiding me through to its completion. Anne Kim made everything possible with her care, scholarly engagements and skeptical belief in my theoretical conceptions. Her allowing me to monopolize conversations to discuss work, labour, multiactivity and the social economy as well as technical issues concerning web pages, databases and secure socket protocols has enriched this project beyond what I could have conceived on my own. Any misrepresentations or shortcomings with the ideas and arguments nonetheless are undoubtedly mine.

Abbreviations

BNA	British North America Act
CAD	Canadian Dollars
CCF	Cooperative Commonwealth Federation
CCRA	Canada Customs and Revenue Agency
EU	European Union
FNPW	Female Non-Paid Work
FPTPW	Female Part-Time Paid Work
FPW	Female Paid Work
FTPW	Full-Time Paid Work
HTML	Hypertext Markup Language
HTTPS	Hypertext Transfer Protocol over Secure Socket Layer
ICNPO	International Classification of Nonprofit Organizations
LETS	Local Exchange Trading Systems
NETS	New Employment Opportunities in the Third Sector
NPW	Non-Paid Work
PTPW	Part-Time Paid Work
PW	Paid Work
SSL	Secure Sockets Layer
US	United States
VSI	Voluntary Sector Initiative
WES	Workplace and Employee Survey

Working alternatives
An introduction

Nearly one-third of the labour force in the OECD is currently unemployed. Globally, official unemployment reached its highest recorded levels in 2003 at 185.9 million.[1] Besides unemployment, there is massive underemployment, a condition that many nations have identified in one way or another with catchy colloquialisms:

- overeducated and underemployed (Canada);
- the new underclass or digital divide (United States);
- the 40:30:30 society (United Kingdom);
- the two-thirds/one-third society (Germany);
- the two-speeds society, the socially excluded and socially expelled (France);
- the A-team and the B-team (Denmark).

In recent years, electoral platforms that have prioritized strategies to overcome high levels of unemployment and underemployment have resulted in success. These successes include Jean Chrétien's Liberal party in the 1993 Canadian elections; Gerhard Schröeder's 1998 Social Democrats and Angela Merkel's 2005 Christian Democratic Union in Germany; Luiz Inacio Lula da Silva's 2002 Workers' Party victory in Brazil; and Nicolas Sarkozy's 2007 Union for a Popular Movement victory in France. All of these political parties spent their campaigns talking about the employment issue; none of their victories solved the problem of unemployment and underemployment.

Scholarship has also turned to an examination of employment generation. One noted constellation of scholars proposes a transition to a knowledge economy as its solution. Proponents of this notion include scholars such as Robert Reich and Richard Florida, who maintain that the knowledge economy represents an unprecedented opportunity for employment generation with a global demand for high-waged jobs. For Reich, workers in this knowledge economy are referred to as 'symbolic analysts'.[2] For Florida, they comprise the emergent 'creative class'.[3] Regardless of what they call them, the encouragement of this form of employment, according to these scholars, is what policy-makers should focus on.

This contrasts sharply with alternative scholarship in the area of employment studies. Scholars such as Jeremy Rifkin, André Gorz, and Ulrich Beck do not believe in the salvation promised by the knowledge economy. Instead they posit that technological changes, rather than transforming employment (from industrial to knowledge work), will lead to the end of employment as it is currently understood.

According to Rifkin, the acceleration in new technologies today is triggering a crisis with no historical correlative.[4] To illustrate his point he describes the African American experience in the United States at the turn of the twentieth century, a time when technological changes in agriculture were quickly displacing traditional employment opportunities in the American south.[5] The difference between then and now, according to Rifkin, is that new forms of employment were being generated in the industrializing north and hence compensating for the losses in the south. This is not occurring today. Technology is still able to make labour redundant but it now does so in an era when our societies have been unable to generate new compensatory forms of employment.

André Gorz makes a similar argument but with theoretical distinctions. Gorz distinguishes for example between Marxist categories of abstracted and socially necessary labour. This approach enables him, unlike Rifkin, to provide a theory as to why technological change takes place and what the implications are for workers. Nevertheless, like Rifkin, he argues against the strategy for full employment championed by liberal scholarship and mainstream policy-makers. He argues instead for a greater distribution of existing employment that would thereby free individuals to pursue more socially meaningful pursuits. According to Gorz, these pursuits equal a shift away from capitalist to non-capitalist forms of employment, a means by which society may 'reclaim work' and hence free the individual from the subjectivity constraints imposed by capitalist social relations of production. In short Gorz theorizes the emancipation of the individual from the confines of alienated labour in the market economy and hence brings the role of the subject into the debate.

The subject is also highlighted in the work of Ulrich Beck, but through the lens of what he refers to as the emergence of global risk society. According to Beck, risk is the inability of the existing institutional order to foresee and control the consequences of industrial society.[6] In terms of employment, this global risk manifests as the 'Brazilification of the West' – the global growth of employment insecurity that occurs when precarious forms of employment (e.g., lack of full-time work, low wages, threat of worker reductions through capital flight) expand and are coupled with the rationing of social welfare provisions.[7]

According to Beck, the 'Brazilification of the West' can be detrimental for democracies. Increased risk triggers a decline in civic engagements and leads to the further hollowing out of nation-based democratic politics. However, it can also be transformative and unifying. According to Beck, risks that are simultaneously global and democratic are providing opportunities for a new form of democratic politics. People across boundaries are recognizing that they have a common problem and potentially a common solution. Experiences are becoming validated and, in this way, risk sharing is becoming the basis for new forms of collective action.[8]

However, much like Gorz and Rifkin, the way forward for Beck is not a return to the impossibility of full employment. It is the removal of the insecurity associated with currently precarious employment practices. In other words flexibility can serve as a solution to global risk society rather than as a trigger for its intensification. To illustrate his point, Beck posits two future scenarios that he believes would reinvigorate democracy and end the present crisis in employment.[9] The first involves the activation of paid civil labour within the national voluntary sector. The second activates this same force of paid labour but on a transnational basis. Both involve the displacement, but not the replacement, of the market economy by the voluntary sector.

The common denominator for both liberal and alternative theorists of the employment crisis is the assumption that the current crisis is an opportunity for alternative global employment futures. For Florida and Reich this opportunity lies within the knowledge economy and its proliferation of 'cultural creatives' and 'symbolic analysts'. Policy-makers and political elites have generally accepted this supply-side framing of the future of employment. However I would argue that it is, at best, utopian and, at worst, an ineffectual and therefore ultimately detrimental basis for policy formation. It is not that these new forms of employment are not being generated – they are – but in what numbers and to what extent? Can the knowledge economy really solve the current global crisis in employment? Scholars and policy-makers who support the liberal notion of a transition to a knowledge economy continue to base their solutions on a painfully simple and familiar question: how is it possible to generate employment? In this sense their focus remains converged on employment generation in the capitalist market economy and to a lesser extent within the state economy, and their solutions will only support and underwrite the current hegemonic capitalist market development that defines employment as paid work and nothing more.[10]

Alternative theorists, on the other hand, collectively call for a complete re-theorization of employment itself culminating in a demand for the better distribution of existing paid work (e.g., reduced working times) and for an increase in paid work in the voluntary sector. While I agree with these alternative re-theorizations of employment I believe that they still lack a full theorization of *alternative global working futures*. Specifically they do not theorize the distinctions between employment and labour and, as a result, fail to abandon the binary distinction between paid work (employment) and non-paid work in the market, state, and social economies. Their acceptance of this arbitrary distinction is significant because it also implies a tacit acceptance of the distinction between a salary or wage and a 'shadow wage',[11] 'guaranteed income'[12] or 'civic money'.[13]

More troubling though is that they remain in the realm of futurist literature by failing to adequately reflect on existing work practices. For example, alternative work theorizations silo labour expended in the market and voluntary sector in terms of either/or. But individuals do not work in either the market economy or the social economy. As discussed in Chapters 6–8, many individuals work across economies, expending their labour in both the market and social economies. This reality moves beyond the either/or theorization exemplified by Rifkin, Gorz and Beck. Boundaries become fuzzy; the work done in and through economies becomes blurred. In short, existing work practices do not confirm to either/or. Rather they conform more readily to both/and. Also Rifkin, Gorz and Beck's articulations assume that work exists out there, whether 'out there' is the market economy or the social economy. Missing is the work done within the household or other sites of labour production and consumption. As feminist scholarship points out the household is also a site of work. According to political economists Isabella Bakker and Stephen Gill, the basis of the market economy and all production is in fact reliant upon the work done within the household.[14]

Linked to this critique is the lack of agency that all of these conceptualizations present. Reich, Florida, Rifkin, Gorz and Beck all posit agency with capital. Like an all-powerful force, global capital swoops in to deterritorialize individuals, communities and nations. As passive objects we only know the power of capital as it manifests outside social and democratic control. Reich and Florida present a future without options – individuals and states must simply conform to the 'reality' of a knowledge economy or suffer at the hands of a vengeful deity. Rifkin, similarly, presents a future devoid of politics. For him, the future is one brought about by and limited to technological developments.

Gorz, unlike Rifkin, prioritizes the necessary struggle for the recovery of human subjectivity that post-Fordist capitalist accumulation denies. Yet his sympathetic discussion of the 'programmed society' posited by Alain Touraine presents a striking challenge to his own aim of reclaiming work and subjectivity.[15] Lost within this articulation is a focus on existing working alternatives and more broadly the political contestations and struggles that provide shape to this globalizing era.

Beck is the only theorist who truly foregrounds politics in his work by suggesting that the shift to global risk society presents an opening to a renewed politics that extends beyond legislatures and parliaments. In this conceptualization politics is activated in spheres that were previously ignored, such as the household. In a sense Beck echoes the feminist assertion that 'the personal is political'. Yet the precariousness of labour, the emergence of world risk society, and the resulting strategies to overcome this new human condition go beyond Beck's assertion of an emergent politics. Rather they point to an embedding of labour within the social through what I refer to as an already present consciousness of *being-in-the-world-with-others*.

This analysis of an emergent consciousness focuses explicitly on the agency of those who are already engaged in alternative working futures. Derived from the Heideggerian conceptualization of *dasein, being-in-the-world-with-others* refers to a state of being in which the individual is always already fully engaged in the social.[16] This challenges the atomistic disembedding of neo-liberal globalization and the individualism of global risk society by arguing that, in an era of intensifying globalization, individuals are constantly hybridizing with their perpetual others. In the face of employment insecurity and global risk society, it is this new consciousness rather than the end of solidarity that exemplifies already existing alternative working futures.

The critical analysis of working futures provided by Rifkin, Gorz and Beck cannot be discounted. Yet their alternative analyses of work are incomplete. They do not sufficiently address the distinctions between work, employment, and labour. They do not account for the household and the time spent performing other activities. Also, an alternative analysis of work does not require a utopian vision of a possible future. Analysis can and must focus on already existing practices and conceptions of working alternatives.

This book therefore provides a corrective to the utopian conceptualizations that characterize the theorizations put forward by Rifkin, Gorz and Beck. The utopian label arises from their assertion that a possible future can exist that combines both paid and voluntary work. An examination of already existing practices reveals that this future already exists, but not in the way envisioned. Existing examples reveal new practices and, potentially more important, new understandings of 'work'. The theorization of work and the individuals who engage in it cannot proceed in such discrete terms that describe some as working in the voluntary sector while others remain in the market economy. Instead, by taking existing working practices as a starting point, it becomes clear that individuals work across economies and within various activities within those economies. Stemming from the socially necessary work done in the household and continuing through to the voluntary, market and state economies, work therefore must be conceived as multiple and hybrid rather than singular and fixed.

In short, within the political economy of the everyday, practices already exist that challenge the hegemonic conceptions of work and economy. These practices reveal that the current crisis in employment is not necessarily that of numbers (number of jobs), technology, or paid/unpaid dialectics. Rather it is a crisis of a deeper fundamental nature – a crisis of social reproduction. 'The crisis,' Gramsci writes, referring to the capitalist crises of the 1930s, 'consists precisely in the fact that the old is dying and the new cannot be born'.[17] The resolution of the current crisis therefore cannot be found by fine-tuning the existing paradigm with the supply of 'cultural creatives' or the siphoning off of the excess of humanity to the voluntary sector.[18] The existing paradigm is constitutive of a crisis of social reproduction and it is only through this lens that a more thorough re-theorization of work is made possible.

Contextualizing social reproduction

The concept of social reproduction has been taken up most notably by political economists in the feminist tradition such as Isabella Bakker, Pat Armstrong and Hugh Armstrong, and Meg Luxton, and sociologists such as Pierre Bourdieu.[19] However, social reproduction remains a highly contested term. Feminist political economists define social reproduction as:

> both biological reproduction of the species ... and ongoing reproduction of the commodity labour power. In today's world involving social reproduction involves institutions, processes and social relations associated with the *creation and maintenance of communities* – and upon which, ultimately, all production and exchange rests. [original emphasis][20]

Central to a feminist understanding of social reproduction is the existence of a gendered division of labour that subordinates the reproductive work done in the household to work that is performed in the market and state economies. This bifurcation of work into paid/non-paid, public/private and productive/unproductive is arbitrary. As Meg Luxton and June Corman write, 'working-class households are those dependent on both the wages earned by one or more household members and the domestic labour that converts the wages into usable goods and services for household subsistence'.[21] In other words, social reproduction is based on the necessary symbiosis of both waged and unwaged labour. However, it is only waged labour that is valued as productive.

Scholars, such as Bakker, build on this theorization of social reproduction by unpacking the placement and association of gender in the economy. They utilize case studies to indicate that current global structural reforms are undermining the existing foundations of social reproduction (e.g., women's non-paid work, the welfare state, the environment) thereby constituting a crisis. As Bakker suggests, gender is becoming more muted and amplified as a result of the current global structural reforms.

These global structural reforms are driven by the hegemonic processes of what Stephen Gill refers to as disciplinary neo-liberalism.[22] Gill identifies three ways in which the social is subordinated to capital within disciplinary neo-liberalism:

1   **Politically.** Adherents of this model seek the submission of the state, society and labour to its utopian vision of 'free enterprise'. In terms of the state, this has meant the cutting of public expenditures, deregulation and the ideological positioning of the state as deficient (e.g., efficient allocation of capital). Society, in turn, has been made largely irrelevant as notions of the public or community good are effaced by the political project of privatization. Labour has also been impacted by the removal

of the historic compromise struck after World War II, exposing it to the unmediated power of capital.

2 **Economically.** This involves the introduction of neo-classical economics, which prioritizes the market economy as an objective manifestation. Disciplinary neo-liberalism is pragmatic and unequal in terms of the application and exposure to market forces. Anything that detracts from ensuring 'efficient market exchanges' (e.g., trade unions, unenforceable property laws) would by definition have to be eliminated.

3 **Historically and Spatially.** Gill situates disciplinary neo-liberalism within this era of intensifying globalization. This is signified by the use of 'neo' to indicate a new kind of liberalism. Global in scope, it is underpinned by the structural power of transnational capital and the United States.

Within disciplinary neo-liberalism, the feminization of labour extends beyond that of the gendered division of labour to the gendering of labour. This can be seen in the form of de-unionization, low-paid service sector employment, and the rise of part-time employment. This re-definition of gender is significant in that it clearly moves discussion away from gender roles to that of social construction and world orders in relation to production. It is a gendered 'harmonizing down' as the position of men deteriorates and the pressure on women to 'step up' increases. The crisis of social reproduction, therefore, becomes more readily an outcome of both the gendered division of labour (with value placed on paid work) and the feminization of work in the current global political economy. As such, emphasis within this literature is placed on the (re)production of the productive subject.

Janine Brodie adds to this literature on the crisis of social reproduction by linking it to subjectivity.[23] As she suggests, current restructuring is not merely an economic exercise with deeply gendered outcomes but is also constructive of a new subject or citizen. Brodie argues:

> [r]eprivatization discourse is increasingly framed in terms of a new defin-ition of citizenship which denies that the citizen can claim universal social rights from the state. The new common good is one which pro-motes efficiency and competition. In turn, the good citizen is one who recognizes the limits and liabilities of state intervention and, instead, works longer and harder in order to become self-reliant.[24]

Brodie's argument embeds the production of subjectivity within the political contestation that exists between social forces. In doing so, she draws specific attention to the role played by ideology in the construction of subjectivity.

Pierre Bourdieu also utilizes ideology in his theorization of social repro-duction.[25] Bourdieu's project, nevertheless, is dissimilar from that of feminist political economists in that his focus is on the structuring of social being. That is, Bourdieu conceptualizes social reproduction as the consistent ideational production of society rather than the contradictory material production of commodity labour. Social reproduction therefore is the tendency for fields (i.e., institutions), such as education, to reproduce existing social hierarchies through their ability to differentially reward those who accept their legitimacy. These fields are what Bourdieu refers to as the structured habitus or personal environment. The habitus is connected to the individual on both a conscious and subconscious level. As Bourdieu argues, '[t]he agent engaged in practice knows the world . . . too well, bound up with it; he inhabits it like a garment . . . he feels at home in the world because the world is also in him, in the form of the habitus'.[26]

The conceptualization of the habitus in relation to social reproduction is both the strength and limitation of Bourdieu's theorization. By conceiving the habitus as structured beyond economics, Bourdieu brings forward a varied and uneven field of cultural, economic, social and symbolic capital.[27] It is their uneven distribution and valuation that is said to reproduce the existing society. In reference to symbolic capital, for example, Bourdieu writes, 'the realistic, even resigned, or fatalistic, dispositions which lead members of the dominated classes to put up with objective conditions that would be judged intolerable or revolting by agents otherwise disposed . . . help to reproduce the conditions of oppression'.[28] Subordination therefore becomes a sort of rational coping strategy while at the same time reproducing the same social hierarchies.

Yet in this conceptualization Bourdieu produces a form of economic determinism not in the sense of base-superstructure dichotomies but by assuming that individual motivation is due to a neo-classical economic motivation (self-interest) and an anthropological conception (status). While the inclusion of status is a welcome development, economic motivations cannot be reduced to either of these classifications. Is engagement in non-paid work within the voluntary sector due to self-interest? Is there status to be gained by these sorts of engagements? The answer is undoubtedly yes, but only in some instances and for some individuals. Equally important are motivations stemming from a sense of community, responsibility, solidarity, hope, care and dependence, which is better understood as forming the consciousness of *being-in-the-world-with-others*.

This is precisely the point raised by political economy scholars who highlight the differentiated motivations for female non-paid work within the household. Yet their arguments often remain insufficient due to their emphasis on the household. With the burgeoning growth of non-governmental organizations, community groups, informal care networks and the like, the household is but one space within the larger social economy. These divergent motivations, however, are not inconsequential. They undermine the architecture of the existing institutional order that is predicated on the utopics of market economics. As such, they provide the material basis for social transformation.

For Bourdieu there is little chance of social transformation due to the arbitrary nature of social norms. Bourdieu provides an overly deterministic view of the potential for social transformation when he writes of the habitus as 'an acquired system of generative schemes objectively adjusted to the particular conditions in which it is constituted, the habitus engenders *all the thoughts, all the perceptions, and all the actions* consistent with those conditions *and no others*' (emphasis added).[29] Yet beyond indicating that it is elite-driven, this theorization cannot adequately indicate why cultural, economic, social and symbolic capital is structured to favour the elite minority over the majority. Are elite rule and dominant culture synonymous? Is the social economy also an equally important site for the creation of various forms of capital? Is it possible that the capital produced in the social economy may differ from that produced and controlled by the state or market economies? This theorization posits that transformation, if possible, is only achieved uni-directionally by adopting rather than altering or decentring the sources of social, cultural and economic capital.

Therefore, for Bourdieu, this inability to change the constitution of the various forms of capital leads to social reproduction – that is, reproduction of the status quo. Bourdieu is not interested in how institutions are themselves structured. Rather, he places significance on how institutions structure the social. In this sense social reproduction forms a seamless and virtuous circle. Political economy scholars, however, conceptualize social reproduction as a contingent process predicated on the specificities of a mode of *régulation* and regime of accumulation.[30] Subject to politics, social reproduction therefore is not assured and instead is open to contestation with the potential for transformation through social compromise and revolution.

The discussion in this book begins from this opening to contestation. This is an entirely different problematic from that defined by Bourdieu, and more readily identifiable yet differentiated from the project initiated by feminist political economy scholars. In contradistinction to Bourdieu, this discussion centres on alternatives since this project already assumes a crisis in social reproduction. It is due to this crisis that new and alternative development strategies are manifesting in the form of material practices and ideational re-orientations in the social economy. The starting point of this book therefore is the middle; it is an examination of the social economy as it is situated between what I refer to as the Employment paradigm and an emergent Work paradigm.

The crisis of social reproduction and the paradigm shift from Employment to Work

One of the central arguments of this book is that a paradigm shift is underway from Employment to Work. By employment I mean, 'an activity carried out: for someone else; in return for a wage; according to forms and time schedules laid down by the person paying the wage; and for a purpose not chosen by the worker'.[31] Employment is therefore an external imposition onto the self and easily located (i.e., factory floor, office). Employment within the same occupation, however, may have a differential impact on the self as the social relations of production may be varied. Nevertheless, the normalization of employment and the resultant social relations of production are a manufactured outcome of capitalist hegemony and constitutive of the Employment paradigm.

Work, conversely, is *what we do*. It is premised on a broader conceptualization of productivity, as production is conceived of as directed not solely for production and consumption but also for social reproduction. As such, work is not easily located on the factory floor or office but is instead dispersed throughout a multiplicity of sites within the social, state and market economies. In this sense there is no shortage of work to be done. Inclusive of the work done in the market economy and state economy, the Work paradigm expands labour and the ensuing social relations of production to include housework, environmental reclamation, elderly care, childcare, self work, neighbourhood revitalization and so on.

The paradigm of Employment is in Gramscian terms the 'old' paradigm: a period of time and a system of thought that associated labour with formal full-time employment, and subjectivity with that found in the employment-as-identity nexus. The new, on the other hand, may well be an emerging paradigm of Work that challenges the assumptions that demarcate labour with formal, full-time employment. As such, the new also addresses other forms of labour-power manifestations that are commonly overlooked and purposely negated by academics, policymakers and other stakeholders. Specifically, the focus of this work is on the production and reproduction of labour-power in its full manifestation as both paid and non-paid work.

These manifestations of labour-power do not fit within the current definitions of the wage-labourer. They are not part of the market or state economies. In many respects, they are not viewed as real. However, they are of equal social, cultural and economic significance particularly due to the way in which they contribute to social reproduction.

According to Karl Marx, all production is premised on labour-power, which he defines as 'the aggregate of those mental and physical capabilities existing in a human being, which he exercises whenever he produces a use-value of any description'.[32] In this sense, labour-power is imbued with agency; unlike dead labour it is variable. While Marx focused explicitly on the market economy, his definition is also amenable to the social economy. Applying his definition of labour-power to the social economy radicalizes both the term and the sector. Marx states, '[l]abour itself, in its immediate being, in its living existence, cannot be directly conceived as a commodity, but only labour-power, of which labour itself is the temporary manifestation'.[33] Labour-power, as a social relation, is therefore subject to politics. By focusing on labour, social output, irrespective of whether it takes place in the market or social economies, cannot be abstracted. In other words, the growth of the social economy cannot be attributed to technological innovation or increased free time (i.e., leisure). Rather, we learn that the growth of the social economy is due to its combination of both paid work and non-paid work.

The expenditure of labour-power within the social economy along with a popular engagement in multiactive work indicates a shift from Employment to the broader conceptualization of Work. This emergence of a new paradigm necessitates a rephrasing of the question asked earlier in this chapter. It is no longer, 'How is it possible to generate employment?', but 'How is it possible to ensure the (re)production of labour-power?' It is this expenditure that distinguishes labour from other commodities. It is the *capacity* to labour that forms the basis of the emerging Work paradigm.

Workers are currently alienated from their *capacity* to labour as well as a broad range of non-alienating activities. This is the central contradiction of the post-Employment era, to which it has no clear solution. The post-Employment era still places overwhelming emphasis on the market economy at the expense of the state and social economies. In doing so, it fails to consider how it is possible for workers to have the *capacity* to labour. Where does this *capacity* come from? How is it maintained?

In this book, I argue that the capacity to labour is located in the individual worker; it is derived not from the market but from the social. Foregrounding the social, in turn, contests the current hegemonic development model of disciplinary neo-liberalism. Starting from the capacity to labour, however, reveals that indeed another world is possible as it forms a counterpoint to the political, economic and spatial basis of disciplinary neo-liberalism. It is this situation in-between – that is, in-crisis – that I refer to as the post-employment era. Positioned after the possibility of the Employment paradigm it also precedes the institutionalization of the Work paradigm.

Case study: the social economy

The dramatic global growth of the social economy is significant as a site of this potential transition. In this book, I examine the work done in and through the social economy, focusing specifically on Canada and the Canadian experience within the global political economy.

The social economy does not have a single unifying definition. In fact the size, scope, temporality, purposes and impacts of the social economy are currently subject to considerable debate. Therefore, before proceeding it is important to delineate what I mean by this term. In broad terms, the social economy label is a reference point for a wide variety of activities that are carried out by diverse constellations of networks. These networks are both permanent and fleeting, signifying both social and economic impacts, but they are consistent in two respects: they work outside the market economy and state economy and for the purpose of ensuring social reproduction.

Common in Francophone locales, such as France, Belgium and Québec, the term 'social economy' is still relatively unfamiliar in Anglophone communities.[34] For example, within the pan-Canadian context (outside Québec), we are more likely to hear of activities that take place outside of the market economy and state economy defined as 'charities' or part of the 'voluntary' or 'non-profit' sectors. While these terms have their place, it is important to point out why they are deficient as proper classifications for the range of activities under discussion here. These deficiencies are discussed and summarized in Table 0.1.

Charity

Large institutions, such as Revenue Canada, predominantly use the term 'charity' as their classificatory basis for recognizing social economy organizations. However, this term conceals the embedded nature of the social economy as an economy in juxtaposition to the state economy and market economy. It also fails to capture the expansive role the social economy plays in addressing uneven capitalist development and its inevitable crises. Instead, the term charity conjures up the notion of a set of organizations that aid the temporarily and incidentally less fortunate out of altruism and piety. It also emphasizes the role of private donations without addressing the reality of this form of support – namely, that it is neither the sole nor major source of support for the sector.

Voluntary sector

The term 'voluntary sector' is the most commonly utilized term in the pan-Canadian context. However, the same criticisms generated for the term charity can be applied here. 'Voluntary sector' abstracts the social relations of production that take place within the sector. It hides from view the relationship that exists between waged and unwaged work. Instead, we are left with the impression that the liberal bourgeois individual bases her involvement in the social economy on choice. The term voluntary sector effectively decontextualizes and depoliticizes both the worker and the sector – the worker by defining his labour as volunteering, and the sector by casting it as an unimportant activity devoid of economic status.

Non-profit sector

The term 'non-profit sector' is an inadequate descriptor as it defines the sector explicitly through the lens of the market economy. Utilizing this term, the sector is the negation of the market economy – literally, a sector based on the absence of profit. This is misleading. The social economy sector is an economy that generates revenues, but it chooses to distribute its revenues differently. The distinction is therefore not in the generation of profit but in its distribution. While the market economy distributes its excess revenues to its shareholders and executives, the social economy distributes its revenues back into itself. This term also reaffirms the false dualism of economic and

Table 0.1 Critique of terms used in place of the social economy

Term	Critique
Charity	<ul><li>effaces all references to economy;</li><li>abstracts social relations of production;</li><li>voluntaristic;</li><li>temporary;</li><li>overemphasizes private donations.</li></ul>
Voluntary sector	<ul><li>effaces all references to economy;</li><li>abstracts social relations of production;</li><li>voluntaristic;</li><li>temporary.</li></ul>
Non-profit sector	<ul><li>effaces all references to economy;</li><li>abstracts social relations of production;</li><li>incorrect focus on profit rather than revenues and distribution;</li><li>functions as a negation of the market economy.</li></ul>

non-economic that maintains capitalist hegemony. In doing so, the sector is relegated to the position of an add-on.

Despite its lack of a single unified definition therefore, the term 'social economy' is most useful at this historical conjuncture. As a term that describes a separate yet juxtaposed economy, it can encompass the activities addressed by the terms *charity, voluntary,* and *non-profit* while still acknowledging its political context and social aims. It can also indicate, more clearly, why the sector is expanding.

The extensive and intensive growth of the social economy is a reflection of a cultural shift, underway in Canada and globally, that requires individuals to respond to the risks of the post-Employment era. This includes the embracing of a multiactivity lifestyle. Each work activity is now viewed as productive of the individual and his/her networked social relations. This is precisely where the social economy comes to the foreground, as production within it is centred on socially reproductive work. Table 0.2 further elucidates the definition of the social economy.

These characteristics identify the social economy as a diverse manifestation, as it is structured both formally and informally along a networked continuum ranging from the household to local and translocal organizations. This conceptualization of the social economy effaces the false binary that exists between such private undifferentiated spaces as the household, and public spaces of formal networks, such as those of non-profits. Instead, networks engaged in the direct production and distribution of goods and services for the purpose of ensuring social reproduction are viewed as elemental to the social economy.

Explicit in this conceptualization is that the social economy is juxtaposed alongside the market economy and state economy. Implicated by the other, it operates at arms' length from the market economy and state economy.

Table 0.2 Social economy characteristics

Fields	Characteristics
Structure	• formal, as social economy networks are institutionalized; • informal, as social economy networks come together temporarily as assemblages and then transform or disperse.
Network form	• households; • cooperatives; • charities; • voluntary organizations; • informal community-based organizations; • non-governmental organizations (NGOs).
Ownership	• self-governing; • governance and ownership premised on democratic participation models; • negotiated relations of production predicated on cooperation, conflict and compromise.
Activity	• direct involvement in the production and distribution of goods and services to a market most often to ensure social reproduction; • examples include care work within the household and environmental reclamation within communities.
Aims	• social reproduction; • economic activities, monetized or otherwise, seeking a viable rate of return on production and distribution without compromising social goals; • local capacity building; • enhancement of social values; • addressing emergent risks; • enrichment of the quality of life for both recipients and producers of goods and services
Productivity	• explicit fusion of paid and non-paid labour; • technologies and production techniques.
Profits	• may not be applicable due to non-commodification or legislative prohibition; • re-invested to expand quality and/or quantity of goods and services delivered; • distributed as profit sharing to stakeholders.
Economic status	• in juxtaposition to the market and state economies; • economies as co-evolutionary with each implicated by the other.

Likewise, the market economy and state economy operate at arms' length from the social economy and are similarly implicated by its activities. Examples of social economy activities include: care work, culture and recreation, education, research, health, social services, environment, development and advocacy.[35] More specifically, participants in the social economy are involved in a range of activities, such as childcare, international development, environmental protection, and participation in women's shelters and artist-run collectives to name but a few.

The social economy and work generation

While a precise accounting of organizations outside the household is difficult given definitional problems, a low estimate indicates 870,000 grassroots associations in Canada along with 175,000 registered charities and legally incorporated non-profit organizations.[36] Contributing 4.4 per cent to Canadian GDP and representing 6 per cent of employment, the social economy is a significant economic force.[37]

This importance is paralleled globally with both intensive and extensive expansion of the social economy. In Germany in 1995, the social economy employed 4.9 per cent of the workforce, contributing 3.9 per cent of GDP.[38] In Brazil during the same year, the social economy employed 2.2 per cent of the workforce, contributing 1.5 per cent of GDP.[39] While significant, these measures are likely to *understate* the true value of the social economy's contribution to social well-being. Not only do they artificially bifurcate labour into paid and non-paid (and then dispense with the latter), these figures fail to take into account the many intangible benefits that this sector provides, such as social capital and social solidarity.

Nevertheless, the rapid growth of the social economy has attracted growing interest in examining its size, scope and contribution to national economies and societies. Canada is no exception. In the past few years, there has been a dramatic growth in published research on the sector. Additionally, Canadian universities have developed programs of teaching and research focused on the non-profit or 'voluntary' sector, such as the Public Policy and the Third Sector programme at the School of Policy Studies at Queen's University; the Centre for Voluntary Sector Research and Development at Carleton University and the University of Ottawa; and the Applied Non-profit Studies programme at Mount Royal College in Calgary, Alberta.

Perhaps most significant though was the establishment in 2000 of the Voluntary Sector Initiative (VSI), a five-year, CA$94.6 million joint undertaking between the voluntary sector and the Canadian federal government. This reflects recognition of the role that the sector plays in providing goods and services that are important to Canadians.[40]

While this research is a welcome development and pertinent to gaining an understanding of the sector, it does not address the central challenge presented by the emergence and growth of the social economy. Specifically it fails to understand the significance of the social economy as triggering a paradigm shift from Employment to Work.

Book organization

Perspective and framework

Chapters 1 and 2 examine two epochal formations: the Employment paradigm and the Work paradigm. The Employment paradigm manifested as the dominant mode of development after World War II and lasted until the late 1970s. During this epoch, accumulation and *régulation* were reconciled by a set of socio-cultural compromises centred on an employment-as-identity nexus. This nexus was based on the successful construction of two subjectivities: the male-breadwinner and the female-carer.[41]

The Employment paradigm relied upon the metanarratives of full employment, growth, progress, science, nationalism and security to not only reinforce these subjectivities but also use them as the ideational basis for a hegemonic mode of development. In other words, the Employment paradigm structured its social relations and institutions on employment; its benefits and punishments followed the same lines.

With its objective of full employment and its ability to transfer the risks associated with capitalist production (away from the individual and toward the social), the Employment paradigm partially underwrote social reproduction and thereby undermined the social economy. However, during the 1970s, a number of contradictions emerged to challenge the Employment paradigm. Most critically, the employment-as-identity nexus began to unravel both economically and culturally.

Chapter 2 discusses this transition away from the Employment paradigm towards an epoch that is characterized by a crisis of hegemony. In the post-Employment era, otherwise referred to as the interregnum, the global economy is increasingly subject to risks that the existing institutional order cannot contain. But that does not mean the preceding order is inconsequential. Since the 1980s, disciplinary neo-liberalism has sought to reinvigorate the Employment paradigm's *employment-as-identity* nexus by explicitly prioritizing the market economy as the sole legitimate generator of wealth, employment, and therefore social reproduction. However, identities can no longer be contained within this hegemonic model of development, as employment no longer ensures both economic and ontological security.

The current global political economy is exemplified by a heightened polarization of life chances. Employment is increasingly subject to individualized risks. The results are high rates of unemployment, underemployment, (wage) inequality, social exclusion, asymmetrical inclusion and expulsion. Ontologically, the metanarratives of the Employment paradigm – growth, progress, science, security and full employment – are increasingly seen as points of contestation.

The combined processes of risk, individualization and reflexivity render the hegemonic discourse of market employment and its corollary, *employment-as-identity*, as implausible. The post-Employment era does not provide individuals with stable institutions. Rather, it throws individuals back onto themselves laden with a range of difficult choices. Since employment no longer inherently signifies social reproduction, individuals are compelled to engage their labour-power in a variety of sites. This goes beyond the limited confines of the market economy and even the broader flexibility of the state economy. Increasingly this includes the social economy, a sector that allows for reflexivity and multiactivity. Contemporary life is insisting on this reality. This reality is the transition to the Work paradigm.

Epistemological and ontological hurdles

The transition to the Work paradigm is not fully reflected in the politics and formation of current institutions. In Chapter 3, I argue that this is due to the predominance of Keynesian and neo-classical epistemologies of economy. A critical examination of how these dominant theories conceive of economy, and therefore employment generation, foregrounds the challenge the social economy presents to the hypothesized supremacy of the market and *homo economicus*. While the literature tends to view Keynesian and neo-classical economics as disparate theorizations, they are in fact similar, sharing four key tenets:

- both over-valorize the market economy and to a lesser extent the state economy;
- both overlook the social economy;
- both omit social reproduction as constitutive of economy;
- both hold the misconception that the household is a 'black box' separated out from the economy.

These shared tenets impede the ability of either theory to theorize the current paradigm shift to Work. These epistemological limitations however cannot be altered without addressing the ontological basis of these theories.

Chapter 4 examines the ontological basis of economy within the Employment and Work paradigms. Within the Employment paradigm, economy is an essentialized construct predicated on rationalism, dualism, and metanarrative. Each of these ontological stances is integral to the development of the epistemology of an essentialized economy that deterritorializes labour and reterritorializes it as employment. Within this paradigm, employment and its generation is a function entirely dependent upon and subordinate to the market economy.

The intensive and extensive growth of the social economy however challenges this assertion. First, it posits that there is no essence to economy. Employment is not demarcated by the supposed hegemony of the market economy. Rather, it is created by the juxtaposition of several economies – market, state and social. Second, labour is not contained within the categorization of employment. It floats within the broader conceptualization of work, as individuals manifest their labour multiactively in order to ensure social reproduction.

These alterations reveal that within the Work paradigm, the ontology of economy shifts from rationalism to reflexivity, dualism to *différance*, and metanarrative to heterotopia. Such an anti-essentialist ontology provides a multiplication of possibilities for alternative development strategies that focus on labour in its more holistic form. Such strategies challenge the disciplinary neo-liberal (and Keynesian) model's insistence on linking labour with employment.

Case study: the Toronto social economy

Chapter 5 tests the thesis of a transition to the Work paradigm by introducing the case study and methodology. The case study is based on both organizations and workers within the Toronto voluntary sector. It should be noted that within this study organizations are referred to as social economy rather than voluntary organizations since they conform to the social economy characteristics set out earlier within this chapter.

Methodologically, organizational representatives were asked to respond to a survey on work generation within the sector (see Appendix A). Questions were asked in reference to paid work, non-paid work and part-time paid work and were dispersed to executive directors. The organizational survey asked executive directors to describe work generation between 2000 and 2003. Additionally, the survey asked for medium-term work generation projections. Concurrently, workers within the social economy were asked to respond to a separate survey that focused on their experiences within the social economy, time management, and labour use (see Appendix B). Workers were asked how they valued the various forms of work they were engaged in and how they were able to manage the demands associated with work.

The utilization of two separate but linked surveys, directed at the Toronto social economy sector from both the organizational and labour perspectives, enabled the operationalization of the definition of the social economy set out earlier. The Organization Survey focused on work generation and structural limitations; the Worker Survey focused on the multiactive engagement of labour. In unison, both questioned how social reproduction could be ensured on a continuum from the household to the community.

Chapter 6 discusses the single and bivariant results of the Organization Survey. Focusing on the consumption of labour-power through work generation, overall findings support the hypothesis of a transition to the Work paradigm. However, upon closer inspection bivariant analysis reveals that the transition is highly uneven. Work generation within the interregnum is subject to an ideal-type organization that is local in scope, engaged in community benefit or welfare activities, small in size and founded within the timeframe of the post-Employment era. The success of these organizations, it is argued, is a result of their ability to respond quickly and without institutional lag to an ever-changing environment both in terms of emergent issues and claims as well as funding and financial circumstances.

Chapter 7 shifts the focus from organizations and the consumption of labour to individuals and the (re)production of labour-power. Findings from the Worker Survey, administered to both paid and non-paid workers in the Toronto social economy sample, are also supportive of the hypothesis of a transition to the Work paradigm. Respondents conceive of economy as a plural manifestation and base their engagement in a particular economy on an expanded notion of reflexivity.

However the analysis reveals that circumstances are much more compli-cated than that. Individuals are implicated by traces of both the Employment and Work paradigms. Compelled to enact their labour-power multiactively as part of the Work paradigm, individuals nevertheless remain connected to the prioritizing of paid work that dominated the Employment paradigm. The result is a schizophrenic subject who experiences the consequences of living in-between.

Afterword

It should be noted that this study is exploratory in nature and should be viewed as such. Rather than a comprehensive guide to the social economy, its impacts on the social, and subsequent transformations in work this book is an initial step that invites other researchers to engage in its expansion both within Canada and globally.

While the findings and conclusions could contribute to policy change, the objective of this book is to identify the emergence of a potential Work paradigm and to contextualize it within the global political economy. At issue therefore is the necessity to examine the contours of already existing prac-tices. Rather than revisiting the old and outdated discourses on employment and unemployment it is increasingly clear that the potential for a progressive transformation of the global political economy is no longer 'out there'. Instead, by formally acknowledging the material reality of the Work para-digm, reveals it is ever present in the daily (re)productive practices within the social. It is by making these practices visible that this project articulates the conceptual space necessary for the articulation of an already existing and working alternative development strategy.

To summarize, the overall aims of this book are:

1   To provide practical insights to encourage the continued implementation of alternative working practices;
2   To provide an innovative theoretical and empirical framework to analyze the paradigm shift from Employment to Work;
3   To provide a useful reference point for future research in this area by applying and refining this study's methodology.

1 The Employment paradigm

> [T]he theoretico-practical principle of hegemony has also epistemological sig-
> nificance. . . . The realisation of a hegemonic apparatus, in so far as it creates a
> new ideological terrain, determines a reform of consciousness and of methods
> of knowledge: it is a fact of knowledge, a philosophical fact.
>
> Antonio Gramsci[1]

The 1940s to the 1970s was a specific historical moment in capitalist development during which time an ascendant regime of accumulation, based on
intensive capitalist accumulation, was matched with an appropriate mode
of *régulation* to mitigate the capitalist crisis of the 1920s and 1930s. Mass
production techniques that utilized Taylorist and Fordist methodologies were
matched with the institutionalization of the Fordist (welfare) state. Gramsci
referred to this new historical epoch as 'Fordism and Americanism'.[2] I refer
to it here as the Employment paradigm.

However, the Employment paradigm was not merely a system of economic
or cultural production. It was also a system that constructed subjectivity,
becoming reliant upon those subjectivities for its own (re)production. In the
Althusserian sense, the Employment paradigm both hailed and interpellated
its subjects by configuring *being-in-the-world-with-others*.[3]

In the Employment paradigm, while identities were assumed to be natural,
they were instead reflections of a particular set of social arrangements structured around employment. In the Althusserian sense, familiarity with the
codes and associated metanarratives led to the naturalization of identities
reinforcing a sense of self while simultaneously contributing to the construction of the social order. For example, employees accepted managerial control
and new production methods in return for significant increases in their real
wages; farmers and other rural workers accepted the rule of the city in return
for stability in the prices of and demand for rural products; women were
expected to perform non-paid work in the household and provide care functions for the family; charity organizations and state governments structured
programmes and services for those whose identities failed to conform to the
paradigmatic dictates of employment.[4]

Table 1.1 Features of the Employment paradigm

Feature	Characteristics
Role of the state	<ul><li>Keynesian Fordist state;</li><li>demands management of economy;</li><li>political commitment to full employment;</li><li>provision of social services predicated on employment;</li><li>protection of 'social wage';</li><li>relatively closed national economy.</li></ul>
Labour processes	<ul><li>unskilled and semi-skilled workers;</li><li>single tasks;</li><li>wage levels generalized throughout the economy;</li><li>union representation of workers legitimated.</li></ul>
Production principles	<ul><li>highly specialized machinery dedicated to production of single products;</li><li>implementation of changes in production methods and new technologies mediated between government, labour and capital;</li><li>just-in-case production.</li></ul>
Modes of consumption	<ul><li>extensive product cycles;</li><li>standardized goods.</li></ul>
Spatial considerations	<ul><li>dispersed manufacturing plants;</li><li>growth of large industrial amalgamations.</li></ul>
Metanarratives	<ul><li>growth;</li><li>progress;</li><li>security;</li><li>nation-state.</li></ul>
International context	<ul><li>pax-Americana;</li><li>Bretton Woods System;</li><li>Liberal Internationalism;</li><li>Cold War;</li><li>decolonization;</li><li>regime of cheap energy.</li></ul>

In other words, the Employment paradigm depended on a set of socio-cultural compromises that were based on an *employment-as-identity* nexus.[5] This nexus was made possible by the rationalized execution of Taylorist production methods and discourses, the post-war Keynesian commitment to full employment, the hegemonic position of the United States, and a strict gender and collective compromise.[6]

Engineering the Employment paradigm's regime of accumulation

The regime of accumulation that is associated with the Employment paradigm was institutionalized during the capitalist crisis that took place at the turn of the twentieth century. Predicated on Taylorist management principles in tandem with the Fordist assembly line, capitalist industrialization transitioned to an intensive form of capital accumulation displacing its previous extensive form. The alteration was predicated upon the utilization of science and scientific management to advance capital's domination over labour. To this end, Frederick Winslow Taylor and Henry Ford conceived of and implemented new ways to enhance productivity by rationalizing labour and production processes.

Taylor used standardized factories, work schedules, and stopwatches to maximize labour's productive capacity. His central preoccupation was to rationalize the worker's body. Towards this aim, he watched their movements and timed each task. Utilizing science to alter the conception and organization of work, to conform to the interests of capital in opposition to labour, Taylor then economized the motion of work by reducing each task to a series of abstract, mathematically precise movements.

Taylor also extended his rationalization of the work process to management. He believed in a distinct difference, almost a species difference, between the person who worked and the 'man' who managed. As such, the conception of a task was differentiated from its execution. As he posited:

> [n]ow one of the very first requirements for a man who is fit to handle pig iron as a regular occupation is that he shall be so stupid and so phlegmatic that he more nearly resembles in his mental make-up the ox than any other type. The man who is mentally alert and intelligent is for this very reason entirely unsuited to what would, for him, be the grinding monotony of work of this character. Therefore the workman who is best suited to handling pig iron is unable to understand the real science of doing this class of work. He is so stupid that the word 'percentage' has no meaning to him, and he must consequently be trained by a man more intelligent than himself into the habit of working in accordance with the laws of this science before he can be successful.[7]

But management was not in itself a given category. In fact, Taylor defined two types of management: initiative or incentive management, and scientific or task management. The former recognized that knowledge was the prerogative of the worker. Therefore, it was the manager's role to provide incentives (i.e., money, working conditions, less hours, friendly manner, etc.) for production to occur. The latter assumed the superiority of scientific principles and the inherent superiority, and therefore responsibility, of managers over workers. As Taylor posited,

> [managers] cooperate heartily with the men so as to insure all of the work is being done in accordance with the principles of science which has been developed. [. . .] The management takes over all the work for which they are better fitted than the workmen, while in the past almost

all the work and the greater part of the responsibility were thrown upon the men.[8]

Taylorism therefore marked a shift to the technocratic management of work. Management was to develop a science for each element of work; use science in the selection, training, and development of the worker; cooperate with the worker as based on the extension of scientific principles; and share in the 'work' to be done – with the redistribution of work augmenting the skills that were the prerogative of management.

Taylor's rationalization of work represented a shift from *work* based on skill to *employment* based on 'science'.[9] By rationalizing the role of the worker and the role of the manager, he clearly defined the relations between the two: the (doing) worker on the factory floor under the watchful eye of the (knowing) manager. Under Taylorism, the worker no longer developed their own labour; work or more appropriately, employment, was now the exclusive prerogative of management.

Discussed in terms of class the industrial worker became a generalist, part of an undifferentiated labour-power that adhered to the dictates of management. As Isabella Bakker and Stephen Gill note, 'the social and power relations of capital reduced the creative capacities and potentials of workers to an instrumentality, with the effect that it transformed the advantages of human freedom and its objectification into means to accumulate profit'.[10] Reduced to an 'initiative' and bereft of any decision-making skills in relation to their own labour, the worker became no different from the machine.

Henry Ford built upon the Taylorist principles of division of labour and identity construction by combining them with the (modern) assembly line, a device that captured the imagination of capitalists throughout the industrializing world. As Charles Sabel writes,

> [b]y the time Henry Ford achieved a practical synthesis of nineteenth-century advances in mass-production techniques, his solution seemed a triumph of the inevitable. . . . Ford's ideas would fascinate the Bolsheviks and German Social Democrats, Louis Renault no less than Giovanni Agnelli. The first automobile factory in Czechoslovakia to use assembly-line techniques, built by Skoda in 1925, was called America.[11]

By 1913, the coordination of these two concepts allowed work to be conveyed to the worker thus enabling the movement of the assembly line to determine the speed of work. This resulted in significant productivity gains. For example, nearly one year after the installation of the conveyer belt system and the formation of work along an assembly line, the Ford Highland Park Plant could produce a car every 93 minutes.[12] However, the cost for workers was an increasing indeterminacy. Their roles in production were limited physically by their place on the assembly line and mentally by the tasks they were assigned by management.

The new regime of accumulation was not merely a shift in production techniques. It was also a change in the mode of life that demanded social adjustments. For example, scientific management and the assembly line required a disciplined workforce. Yet the imposition of the new regime of accumulation fueled worker resistance, both organized in the form of trade unions and unorganized in the form of worker absenteeism. Additionally, the increase in production not only required mass workers, but also mass consumers who could purchase the goods that were being produced. This necessarily included the working class, yet the reality of low wages undercut this possibility.

Ford responded to these contradictory elements with the introduction, in 1914, of the $5, eight-hour per day workweek. In doing so, Ford provided his employees with both the disposable income and leisure time they required to consume his mass produced commodities.[13] Sharing a fetish for bodily rationalization and disciplinarity with Taylor, Ford also ensured worker discipline with his $5 a day.[14]

While Ford's introduction of a new wage pact separated him out from other capitalists of his time, his rationale for such a pact kept him in step with his contemporaries. His aim was to reinforce employment as the central organizing element of the new industrial society. He joined other capitalists in ensuring this aim with the establishment of corporate welfare programmes and employee representation plans that cemented the employment relation by subordinating labour, the labour process, and the collective organizing efforts of labour to the domination of capital.

Following Ford, Alfred Sloan pushed the Employment paradigm to its next phase. According to Arthur Kuhn, Sloan 'marked the transition from an early entrepreneurial stage . . . to a corporate phase'.[15] He rationalized both labour and management. Production in this corporate phase was characterized by *just-in-case* production: goods were produced en masse and warehoused to accommodate projected need. Meanwhile, machinery utilized in the production process was based upon electro-magnetic technologies, which was highly specialized and dedicated to a single product. In the large Fordist industries this meant an ever-growing array of specialized but interchangeable components and accessories that could produce an assortment of goods on a large scale. The extensive product cycles coupled with the demand for standardized goods meant competitiveness was, in part, secured by economies of scale.

Manufacturing Canada

This new regime of accumulation had three critical impacts in the Canadian context. First, the need for economies of scale was met by a shift from East–West integration to North–South integration with the formation of a continental economy.[16] The 1920s witnessed massive American direct investment in the Canadian natural resource extraction industries and the manufacturing sector. The establishment by American corporations of branch plants in Canada ensured not only access to cost-advantageous inputs but also access to the larger markets within the British Empire including Canada.

Second, the intensification of resource-based industrialization triggered increased activation on the parts of provincial governments for economic governance, as the British North America Act (BNA) deferred jurisdiction to them.

Third, industrial inputs required wage labour as opposed to independent commodity production. This shifted economic growth from rural settings to urban agglomerations. The branch plant status of Canadian industrialization further compounded this form of spatially uneven development, as American corporations sought locations with geographical proximity to their US headquarters.

Beyond compounding spatially uneven development, this new regime of accumulation also exposed a greater number of workers to the risks of capitalist development. In response, in 1918, the manufacturing firm Massey-Harris established one of the first comprehensive welfare plans in Canada. In doing so, they became the generalized model for Canadian industrial development.[17] By 1928, the Ontario Department of Labour conducted a survey of 300 firms that employed a total of 185,187 individuals to report that a majority of firms had by this time instituted some form of corporate welfare scheme. For example, a majority of employees now had access to some form of medical services beyond those mandated by Workmen's Compensation; 49 firms employing 100,000 employees had a pension plan.[18]

However, benefits were only conceived in relation to employment. Throughout the mid-to-late 1920s, the Canadian business community remained fiercely opposed to the granting of welfare payments outside the employment relation and beyond the ad-hoc system of factory-by-factory compromises. According to the business community, benefits were granted for the sole purpose of ensuring the retention, motivation, and discipline of employees. This understanding of employment and benefit programmes is traceable to the prevailing notions of the day concerning unemployment and its remedies.[19]

In the 1920s, common consensus considered unemployment as an anomalous condition brought about by the improper decision-making of workers. The issue therefore was to ensure the distribution of labour, as employment was readily available. Public provision of any kind, it was argued, would serve as a disincentive for the unemployed to re-enter the labour market. As a representative of the Canadian Manufacturer's Association said, '[i]t is infinitely preferable that a man who is out of work should bestir himself and look for a new job, rather than sit down and twirl his hands and look for unemployment relief'.[20]

Nevertheless, incongruence between an intensive regime of accumulation and an underdeveloped mode of *régulation*, in the form of corporate welfarism, was exacerbated by both the growth of the trade union movement and the economic circumstances of the 1930s, which resulted in massive unemployment in Canada and throughout the world. By 1932, 20 per cent of the Canadian labour force was unemployed.[21] Without paid work, millions of workers and their families found themselves beyond any means of securing their basic existences. Since benefits were based upon ad-hoc arrangements made between employers and their employees, the mass of unemployed seeking remedy found this avenue closed to them.

Welfare payments to the poor outside employment were not a political priority at any level of government. The federal and provincial governments maintained that the BNA Act relegated jurisdiction to the municipal governments and were therefore reluctant to develop policy and administrative guidelines. Meanwhile, municipalities were wholly unequipped to deal with the mass of unemployed. Their guidelines regarding welfare were modeled on the nineteenth-century Poor Laws, which considered relief as a potential disincentive to gainful employment. 'Charities' were relied upon, but these were small in number and present only in the larger cities.[22] When the federal government did act, it did so to actively repress labour. It used its military power to control strikes and demonstrations, deport labour organizers, and establish relief camps in isolated areas of the nation.[23]

Relief for the unemployed in Canada was therefore geographically varied and entirely inadequate. Nevertheless, workers continued to challenge their circumstances through expanded membership in the trade union movement and the founding of political parties, such as the Cooperative Commonwealth Federation (CCF).[24]

The heightened levels of social unrest and worker agitation throughout the industrial capitalist nations, compounded by the commencement of World War II, coalesced to bring about the end to an era of 'reluctant welfarism' in Canada and throughout the international capitalist system.[25]

Engineering the Employment paradigm's mode of *régulation*

Intensive capitalist accumulation was salvaged and strengthened by the establishment of welfare states that aimed to ensure full employment as part of their political mandates. Internationally, the capitalist Employment paradigm was reinforced with the establishment of the Bretton Woods system under the hegemony of the United States. Collectively, these formed the institutionalization of the Employment paradigm's mode of *régulation*. Its theoretical basis was laid out in the tenets of Keynesian economics, but its practical application nationally was evidenced in the British Beveridge Report of 1942 and its Canadian correlative, the Marsh Report, which was released in 1943.[26]

Keynesian economics

Keynesian economics centres economic theory on employment generation. In this way, it establishes the Employment paradigm as the hegemonic mode of development.[27] Keynes sought the development of a new economic theory to save capitalism from the ill effects of mass unemployment, which he thought if left unchecked would result in social revolution.[28] As Keynes argued, the classic tenets of *laissez-faire* were not incorrect but 'belong to the days of fifty or a hundred years ago when trade unions were powerless, and when the economic juggernaut was allowed to crash along the highway of progress without obstruction and even with applause'.[29] In stating this, Keynes broke from the neo-classical orthodoxy by asserting that unemployment was the norm rather than the exception and that the social power of the now organized working classes had to be acknowledged.

By foregrounding employment, Keynes provided four key developments for the institutionalization of the Employment paradigm:

1. He altered the manner in which unemployment was conceived, shifting it from an individual pathology to a social outcome.
Keynes reasoned that the massive levels of unemployment seen during the 1930s could not be the result of individual errors or the failures of particular industries. Instead, he posited a social dimension to the problem by theorizing the economy as a whole rather than industry-by-industry, and the national economy's ability to put people to work over the individual.

2. He argued that unemployment arose from deficient aggregate demand.
Introducing the term 'effective demand' in Chapter 3 of the *General Theory*, Keynes posited that contrary to the established orthodoxy of neo-classical economics, the elimination of massive levels of unemployment required raising the equilibrium level of employment.[30] In a reversal of Say's Law, Keynes argued that demand generates supply up to the point of full employment. Effective demand, which is defined as demand backed by expenditure (i.e., consumption and investment), determined the level of output in the market economy and subsequently the level of employment. Keynes argued that in order to understand the level of output and therefore the rate of employment, there would have to be an understanding of what determines the level of consumption and investment in the economy as a whole. Market economy oscillations and subsequent changes in the rate of employment were subsequently attributed to three fundamental concepts: the propensity to consume, the marginal efficiency of capital, and the rate of interest.[31]

3. He conceptualized the state as both a 'neutral' arbiter between social classes and as a purchaser and producer of goods and services.
Keynesian economics replaced the assumed neo-classical view of the state as an external force upon the economy with one that saw the state as central to the economy's functioning. As arbiter, the state provided formal recognition to labour unions and legitimated collective bargaining processes. In terms of fiscal and monetary policies, government expenditure was the key to solving unemployment. According to Keynes, alterations in the interest rates were a wholly inefficient response to mass unemployment as investment decisions

went beyond those of calculating the cost of borrowing. The state alone was 'in a position to calculate . . . on long views and on the basis of the general social advantage, taking an ever greater responsibility for directly organizing investment'.[32]

4. He restored faith in the potential of the capitalist market system.
Keynesian economics accomplished this by intensifying and solidifying the social relations of production implemented during the early part of the twentieth century and forging the identity of the mass worker in mass national society.

The reports

The tenets of Keynesian economics were made manifest in the British government's commissioning of the 1942 Beveridge Report and the Canadian government's commissioning of the 1943 Marsh Report. The central thrust of both reports was the political objective of establishing a full employment economy that socialized the risks associated with breaks from employment. According to Beveridge, it was possible to divide the population into six classifications, 'employed workers, self-employed workers, housewives, all other adults of working age, children below and adults above the working age'.[33] As such, employment was to be the basis of a new social contract.

The Beveridge Report focused on the abolition of want, which Beveridge defined as the lack of income to obtain the means of a healthy subsistence.[34] The abolition of want was predicated on the full employment of (male) citizens. In this way social reproduction was partially underwritten through the family wage. The state was beholden to provide the opportunities of employment and was required to intervene periodically to ensure that the effects resulting from interruptions from employment would be compensated.[35]

In a similar vein, the Marsh Report also promoted the idea of a full employment society secured by a social welfare system. The Marsh Report though was more comprehensive than the Beveridge Report, as it covered issues such as a national employment programme, a supplementary occupational and training scheme, a comprehensive system of social insurance protection, medical care, children's allowances, and public assistance.[36] The comprehensiveness was not attributable to a more social model but instead was a result of both a generalized underdevelopment and a spatially uneven development of social welfare services in Canada as opposed to Britain.

The political economy of the Employment paradigm

In the post-World War II era, each nation found its own way to the Employment paradigm according to the unique structuring of its social forces, historical circumstances, and windows of opportunity. Nevertheless, the results across nations were similarly identified as indicative of a 'Golden Age', as state capitalism socialized class conflict on the basis of full (male) employment. On the international level the hegemonic positioning of the United States and the establishment of the Bretton Woods system buttressed the Employment paradigm.

Socializing Canada

In Canada, five key developments led to the implementation of the Employment paradigm during and after World War II.

1. World War II

The war required the Canadian government to heighten its coordination and production of social output. The state was able to successfully coordinate the economy with wage controls and a social security system that overtook the private industry-by-industry system that had previously prevailed.[37] However, its implementation of a social security system was marred by competing visions and biased attitudes toward the poor and unemployed.

The federal cabinet was divided on its forecasts of post-war economic conditions. Some within the governing Liberal party and the bureaucracy (e.g., the Department of Finance's Economic Advisory Committee) were convinced there would be a repeat of the massive unemployment and recession experienced after World War I. Others were convinced that a command economy, which had proved to be so productive during the war years, should be maintained. In the 1944 throne speech, these elements within the federal government, combined, called for the creation of a comprehensive national scheme of social security including family allowances and universal healthcare in order to ensure general prosperity.[38]

However others, such as Liberal Member of Parliament Clarence Decatur Howe (C.D. Howe), also known as the 'Minister of Everything', forecasted an economic boom with massive shortages of inputs including workers.[39] C.D. Howe and his sympathizers, including the Canadian Manufacturers' Association, demanded the removal of government from the economy and the reassertion of private industry as the means of economic development.

All of this took place against a background of biased attitudes towards the poor and unemployed. For example, the 1940 Unemployment Insurance Act provided benefits well below the take-home pay of earners. This made sense within an ideology that posited workers as slothful and undisciplined. Workers had to be compelled to rejoin the labour force rather than sit back on their laurels, replete with state benefits. Capital's concerns over the socialization of production also had to be alleviated.[40] The inadequacies of the legislation were masked, as mass unemployment was replaced with full civilian employment and military mobilization during the war.

2. The reports

The Beveridge and Marsh Reports cannot be viewed as separate within the Canadian context. Beveridge's appearances on the Canadian Broadcasting Corporation (CBC) radio programmes as well as numerous newspaper articles heightened the popularity of the Marsh Report. A poll, for example, conducted by the newspaper the *Toronto Daily Star* reported that 83 per cent of Canadians wished to see a similar plan adopted in Canada. Of those, 90 per cent said they would approve of such a plan even if it meant that the federal government would hold a greater concentration of powers.[41]

3. A sense of collective responsibility on the part of the Canadian public

The publication of the Reports and the experience of civilian workers and the mobilized public resulted in both a sense of collective responsibility and the promise of a better future. The simplicity of the message in the Reports – the abolition of want – struck a chord with a public who remembered the vagaries of the depression, where at one moment workers were being rounded up as hoodlums and threats to the state and in the very next being asked to serve and protect the nation. As Ian Mackenzie, the Minister of Pensions and National Health, stated when he introduced the Marsh Report, '[i]f we can pay for victory over the cures of Hitlerism, can we not also pay for victory over the scourge of disease, insecurity and poverty?'.[42] The public understood all too well the consequences of unemployment. Therefore, security against unemployment meant the post-war order would require a guarantee of some sort of employment.

4. The need on the part of established political parties to curtail the influence of a resurgent workers' movement

The Employment paradigm was institutionalized as the established political parties looked to curtail the influence of a resurgent workers' movement. By 1943, as the public increasingly realized that the war was won, support for the CCF surged. In 1943, the CCF formed the official opposition in Ontario and British Columbia and was gaining popularity throughout the country, posing a direct threat to the governing federal Liberal party.[43] Consequently, even though the Liberal government refused to support the Marsh Report, it introduced new social welfare legislation in the hopes of swaying the public away from the CCF.

With the leadership of C.D. Howe, who was the Minister of Reconstruction, employment in the private sector was foregrounded and the active welfare state was relegated to a residual role. According to Howe, the post-war objective was to maintain a high and stable level of employment and income. Employment, in the private sector, was therefore conceived as the basis for security. To this end, Howe and the Liberals looked to ensure that capital would be freed from any impediments, while acknowledging the public's demands for some form of social security.

It is in this sense that the welfare state in Canada is more appropriately described as the Fordist state. It is a descriptor I am sympathetic to, as employment was to be generated predominantly in the market economy; the welfare functions of the state were put in place in order to socialize risks generated within uneven capitalist development. However, the government was to maintain the dual role of large-scale employer and regulator in capitalist accumulation. Hence, employment was tied to increased growth and productivity in the national market economy. With the dual aims of (incomplete) social equity and economic growth positively linked, the Canadian Fordist nation-state promised increased productivity, profitability and investment as well as low levels of unemployment and a moderated income distribution.

5. *The post-war economic boom*

The economic boom that followed the war made entrenchment of the Employment paradigm possible. The upswing diffused the public's demands for broad-based security as advocated in the Marsh and Beveridge Reports and politically through the CCF. In doing so, (full male) employment became an effective form of class compromise legitimating the further intensification of accumulation in combination with an ad-hoc and inadequate residual welfare system.

International context

Internationally, the Employment paradigm was predicated on the rule of *pax-Americana*, as maintained by the institutionalization of the Bretton Woods system under the hegemony of the United States. Under the Bretton Woods system, the United States was the only nation-state on the gold standard, thus establishing the gold-exchange-rate. Since all other nation-states held most of their reserves in American dollars, their macroeconomic policies were limited to maintaining their currencies on a chosen exchange rate with the American dollar. As a result of this creditor position within the international system, the United States was effectively the only nation-state to have an 'autonomous' macroeconomic policy; its fiscal and monetary policy established the capitalist world system's monetary conditions.

Keynes, it should be noted, negotiated the creation of the Bretton Woods system as a way to overcome the unbalanced creditor position of the United States. Keynesian economics was an attempt to mitigate US dominance of the international system that emerged in the 1920s and sharpened in the 1940s, as Keynes viewed British unemployment to be a result of sterling's overvaluation against the US dollar.[44]

Close political and military cooperation also fostered market economic growth within the capitalist world system. Until the 1960s, the United States provided most nation-states with a secure anti-inflationary foundation while supplying them with an adequate amount of liquidity. The result was the prevention of deflationary contractions as was associated with the previous (pure) gold system under *pax-Britannica*. Beyond this, the United States provided public aid worth billions of dollars to its Cold War allies through the Marshall Plan[45] (Western Europe and Japan), the Truman Doctrine (Eastern Europe and the Middle East), and other related programmes (e.g., the creation of the Organization for European Economic Cooperation).[46]

Also provided were significant amounts of military aid totalling as much as US$2 trillion between 1950 and 1970, as well as the establishment of generous exchange rates coupled with low import tariffs to enable Western European and Japanese firms to compete with American firms even though they were not as competitive.[47] The result of such military Keynesianism was two-fold: it established a security regime on a national and international level predicated on creating a large demand for workers, which achieved the fulfillment of full employment commitments for domestic males within the capitalist world system.

Hailing the subject of the Employment paradigm

According to Louis Althusser, interpellation is the process by which ideology constitutes subjects by hailing them into the structure. It is also the process by which subjects (re)produce the ideology that constitutes them by identifying and accepting the hail. For example, Althusser illustrates this concept by presenting the image of a police officer who yells, ' "Hey you there!" The moment the individual recognizes the hail and turns around, he becomes a subject'.[48] He also validates the ideology hailing him by recognizing and affirming it. In other words, at the moment of realization, the individual in this example becomes a subject relative to the ideology of the law, as represented by the police officer, by both recognizing and submitting to it.

Yet this hailing is dependent upon spatial, temporal and contextual circumstances. The hailing of a police officer in different locations, times and circumstances evokes a differentiated response depending on an individual's situation and biography. The individual acts from a position of belief or cognizance of the hailing individual or institution, in other words, from a position within hegemony. If that belief or cognizance is not there, the cycle of interpellation is broken. In other words, the cycle of interpellation – that of hailing, recognition, and submission to ideology – is not a given. It is manufactured and subject to subversion.

As such, interpellation conforms to a consciousness of *being-in-the-world-with-others*. It conceives of the individual as always embedded within a web of social relations, past and present that must be considered and controlled. It is the individual's response to the hailing of others, including institutions, that continually instantiates them as a subject. This is significant for an understanding of epochs, such as the Employment paradigm, as it provides an explanation for the relationship between discourses and subjects.

A relatively unquestioning faith in the metanarratives of growth, progress, security and the nation-state formed the ontological basis for interpellation within the Employment paradigm. It provided the forged foundation for the legitimation of the Canadian Fordist state, whose initial political popularity would be implausible if not for the construction of risk as social rather than individual. This absorbed class, life-course, gender and inter-generational risks, thereby underwriting social reproduction. Furthermore, the Fordist state performed a crucial role in the perpetuation of the Employment paradigm by re-commodifying labour through its provision of mass education, healthcare, housing and other infrastructural benefits (i.e., roads). Such infrastructural investments assured a steady supply of employable labour to capitalist industry. It is important to note that universal healthcare emerged much later in the Canadian context than in the Western European Keynesian Fordist states. Full implementation occurred with the passage of hospital insurance in 1957 and medicare in 1968.[49]

Economic, social, and individual progress was intimately intertwined within the Employment paradigm. National mega-projects, both private and public, were the physical manifestation of progress, economic growth and security. However, these can be read in several ways: as the application of technological and social innovations to increase productivity and thereby intensify class exploitation, as the reconstruction of the nation-state, or as a means of distinguishing one nation-state's accomplishments from another's. In the Canadian context it could also be read as an intensification of branch plant industrialization, with Canadian industrial growth underpinned by the doubling of American direct investment between 1945 and 1952 and another doubling between 1955 and 1960.[50] They can also be read as the distinguishing of one social system's accomplishments from another's; the democratization of formerly exclusive standards of living; the hope for something better as well as a disciplining function defining not only the good life but providing explicit guidelines for its achievement.

Regardless, the good life, within the Employment paradigm, was unambiguous. Often referred to as the 'Diderot effect', it permeated everyday existence.[51] Its cultural expression was found in English with the identification of the 'Smiths/Joneses' as the generic mass man, woman and/or family of the Fordist nation-state. In terms of identity construction it defined *being-in-the-world-with-others* as it provided one with a tangible model of how one should manifest oneself. As Zygmunt Bauman argues, the phrase 'keeping up with the Joneses' points to the visibility of this way of *being*, as the Joneses not only enabled one to define oneself but for others to measure the success of that (social) identity construct.[52]

In this way material possession became a universal means of measuring and placing oneself within the social field. The type of neighbourhood, detached single dwelling home, and automobile coupled with the refrigerator, washer/dryer, and television were the symbolic manifestations on the individual level of the metanarratives of progress, growth, security and the nation-state. As Ulrich Beck poignantly asserts, '[b]oth the market character and the privateness guaranteed the integrative social character of this values system'.[53]

As a process of normalization the Employment paradigm points to conformity with identity possibilities rather than the assumed individualism of capitalist society. It is woven into Fordist production methods with standardized work, work-times, uniforms, and compensation. For example, only by securing an adequate income could a man become a 'man' – in other words, a 'good provider'. As such, for the (male) managerial classes this meant the internalization of job/career constraints and the execution of self-disciplining strategies in order to fit within the ordering structures of corporate reward and control systems.

The Employment paradigm also provided consensus on the boundaries between work and non-work and the subsequent gendered division of labour. Overall these disparate fields of identity construction, social identity, technological innovation, intensive capitalism, the expansion of the Fordist nation-state and normative discourses brought about a virtuous cycle of identity construction, Fordist accumulation and *régulation*.[54]

The mode of *régulation* supported the growth regime culturally, politically and legally by tying institutions into the relatively uniform metanarratives of nation-state, growth, progress and security. The Employment paradigm configured the subject by hailing and providing it with a corresponding set of measures that promised success. It also configured a socio-cultural compromise to the 'gender culture' and 'gender order' hence forming the dominant 'gender arrangements'.[55]

Gendering subjectivity: (re)production

In the Employment paradigm, all citizens were conceived of as working males. In economic terms it was the domicile of economic man – what Vilfredo Pareto referred to as *homo economicus*. Working male citizens had to earn a living in order to give life to the political rights and freedoms enacted through the Fordist nation-state. However, as Gramsci noted, Fordism did not stop at the factory gates.[56] Rather, it attempted to constitute the home and the most private and intimate spheres of the worker's life. This is particularly evident when analyzing the role of women during this era. As Harriet Fraad *et al.* aptly point out, '[f]or every knight in shining armor, there's a castle waiting to be cleaned'.[57] Enter the housewife, who emerged alongside the proletarian as one of the two characteristic labourers of capitalism.[58]

Within the Employment paradigm, there was strong societal encouragement of the housewife as an acceptable role for women. Promoted by publications, the emergent mass media, professionals (i.e., social workers, teachers, doctors) and various state institutions, women were socialized to take on the identity of primary family care provider. This role not only spoke about a forthcoming mode of *régulation* and regime of accumulation, but also of a socio-cultural order predicated on a strict worker and gendered identity construction that dominated the Employment paradigm.

Henry Ford himself encouraged this identification through his $5 a day wage package. Ford's wage package was granted to '[a]ll married men living with and taking good care of their families', single men aged 23 and over with 'proven thrifty habits', men aged less than 23, and women 'who are the sole support of some next-of-kin as blood relative'.[59] Consequently, the company refused to hire married women with employable husbands. In order to ensure compatibility Ford hired social investigators to visit homes and ensure compliance.

For those women who stayed home, their duties were transformed; Taylorism had forced its way into the household as an emancipatory strategy. Rational, explicit principles; scientific management; and an economy of motion would guide the modernization of the housewife. Yet the intended outcome of reduced labour was never fully realized. As Antonella Picchio states,

> [h]ousework's job is to restore a relation between production and reproduction that makes sense from the point of view of the people involved. Accumulation uses people as commodities, and the task of housework is to produce and restore them as people within the constraint of reproducing them as commodities.[60]

The labour necessary for household reproduction cannot be analyzed in instrumental terms, which, in part, explained why the incorporation of time-saving devices (i.e., washing machine, dishwasher) did not reduce labour-time expenditures.

Despite this, scientific management was thought to be an enabling factor for women. As the economy produced an ever-increasing array of domestic consumer goods and factory food products, the role of primary family care provider shifted increasingly into that of a family/household *manager*, supposedly freeing the woman from the 'traditional' ways of keeping house. She would now be able to better pursue the aims of maintaining a good home and providing intellectual enrichment for herself, her husband and her children. As Deborah Simonton points out, with scientific management,

> [w]omen controlled domestic finances, if not household accounts. They kept records, dealt with shopkeepers, merchants, insurance men and other administrators of public and private services which proliferated. Usually mothers liaised with teachers and officials, and were instrumental in choosing schools, although fathers often retained formal authority.[61]

Scientific management, fitting with the times, enabled an ideology of a re-invented domesticity. It provided a moral benchmark against which classes were able to judge themselves and measure their superiority over others. In other words, Taylorism enabled the existence of conformity not only in the workplace but also in the home and neighbourhood.

Taylorist rationalized principles also provided a basis for valuing women for their work outside a capitalist market structure. Women's non-paid domestic work, while important, was not regarded as making an independent (or productive) contribution worthy of social insurance. As Beveridge wrote, 'the great majority of married women must be regarded as occupied on work which is vital though non-paid, without which their husbands could not do their paid work and without which the nation could not continue'.[62] Women's work was therefore considered important as a supportive apparatus, always in relation to or in relation with. In short it simply was not considered to be part of the economy.

Such identity configurations were structured into the very foundations of the nation-state within the Employment paradigm. Ideas about women were strengthened by the construction of family metanarratives that cast men as employees or potential employees, heads of households or potential heads. Whereas men were incorporated into the Fordist state as individual citizens – that is, as workers who could contribute to social insurance, women were incorporated as members of families – that is, as wives and mothers. In other words, women's identities were constructed as *wife-mothers* or expected to become *wife-mothers*. In this way, women were dependants who made claims on the Fordist state's welfare provisions as members of an employee's household.

Beyond their relation to individual husbands and children, women were also bound by their identification with broader cultural interpretations of womanhood. This was evident within the French Fordist state, for example, as the state regularly incorporated images of women in accepted roles, such as that of the venerated mother, in patriotic rhetoric and propaganda.[63] This was in an effort to correct declining birth rates and thereby save the nation from immigrants.

This understanding of (patriotic) *wife-mothers* is also well established within the influential Beveridge model of the 'welfare' state. Beveridge argued in his report, '[i]n the next thirty years housewives as mothers have vital work to do in ensuring the adequate continuance of the British Race'.[64] It is important to note that Beveridge's conception of the identity of *wife-mothers* cannot be separated from his views on population and eugenics. Women were therefore supposed to save their husbands from 'losing touch with the emotional origins of a society in which work was the icon' or save their nation from the scourge of immigration.[65]

The gender compromise within the Employment paradigm was therefore manifest in the form of a male-breadwinner/female-carer model.[66] The explicit benefit of this model was the satisfaction of a system of social reproduction.

The state, far from being a benign institution, regulated the adjustment between processes of accumulation and social reproduction. Under capitalism and formalized within the Employment paradigm the labour required for social reproduction took the form of non-paid work within the household and community as a means to secure the reproduction of the population and specifically wage-labourers. Indeed, while it is possible to trace the gendered nature of this social order to nineteenth-century industrialization and earlier, the Fordist nation-state's institutionalization of the family wage, premised as it was on existing gendered assumptions, only served to intensify the gendered division of labour.[67]

However, an alternative reading of the Fordist state is as an institutional form that diminished social inequalities including gender inequalities.[68] The male-breadwinner model was never fair, but at least it was partly functional in that it underwrote social reproduction. Indeed the overemphasis on the universality of a male-breadwinner/female-carer model has tended to conflate two different realities: the identification of women as wives, recipients of social entitlements indirectly through their husbands; and the identification of women as mothers who receive social entitlements directly and in their own right.[69]

Yet men were presented with the possibility of constructing more of their personal biographies. While this potential was contingent on other disciplinary factors, such as race, class, and sexual orientation, the constraints for women were more impactful due to the lens of the strict gender binary of the Employment paradigm.

'The new methods of work,' said Gramsci 'are inseparable from a specific mode of living and thinking and feeling'.[70] The resulting social relations of production within the Employment paradigm, as Gramsci poignantly argued, were a hegemonic process. The institutionalization of Fordist social relations of production promised to ensure individual discipline through abundance, increased social goods in the form of consumer goods, the socialization of risks through welfare benefits, and national identity. This suggests that a broad-based paradigm shift would require a transformed consciousness, alternations in the social relations of production and a reconfiguration of the emotive dimensions of human life.

Following Gramsci, it could be argued that the regulation of wages in large corporate settings, despite gender inequalities, demarcated a certain advance over the previous system whereby the foreman and/or employer made work decisions premised on personal whim and/or sexual power. These social relations of production, this way of understanding *being-in-the-world*, were secured by democratic and political institutional mechanisms, such as trade unions, collective bargaining processes and the legal structures of the machinic assemblage of the newly emergent Fordist nation-state.

Afterword

In the 1960s, contradictions emerged that began to undermine the Employment paradigm. These included the decreasing productivity of the Fordist production model, increasing international competition, and raw materials shortages followed by high inflation, growing resistance to high taxes, and technological change. Additionally, the resurgence of previously displaced ideologies and the manifestation of new forms of consciousness were resulting in a crisis of meaning and further undermining the institutional order.

This crisis of hegemony has resulted in contestation over how this next mode of development should be constituted: as an improvised Employment paradigm or an emergent Work paradigm. This tension is the subject of the next chapter.

2 The Work paradigm

> When the other speaks, it is with the tongue of the nation, the intonation of a class, the rhetoric of a social position, the idiom of a subculture, the vocabulary of an age group. . . . To understand the other is to understand these laws and these codes as imperative for one's own understanding. But the other is also *other*. To recognize the other as other is to sense the imperative weighing on his or her thought. It is to sense its imperative force – a force that binds me also.
>
> Alphonso Lingis[1]

The asymmetrical power of transnational capital and the neo-liberal state in conjunction with the reassertion of the power and structural centrality of the United States has led to the termination of the Employment paradigm.[2] This has resulted in a grotesque polarization, globally, in the areas of employment, income, wealth, access, and life chances leading not only to a crisis of liberal democracy and a crisis of legitimacy for the institutions of global economic governance, but to a broader crisis of social reproduction.

A number of descriptors currently exist to illustrate this: the Brazilification of the North,[3] the emergence of the First World in the Third World, the emergence of the Third World in the First World,[4] the lost decade of development[5] and so on. Whereas this crisis phase of capitalist development is often normalized as 'globalization', I prefer to describe it as the interregnum: a post-Employment era between the paradigm of Employment and a yet-to-be instituted paradigm of Work.

As Gramsci wrote, '[t]he crisis consists precisely in the fact that the old is dying and the new cannot be born: in this interregnum, morbid phenomena of the most varied kind come to pass'.[6] In the post-Employment era, work in the form of paid work still retains its elemental character with the great bulk of humanity requiring it for social reproduction. Yet it does so at a time when the political commitment of capital and the neo-liberal state to full employment and the social wage has been appropriated from the social. Led by the United States and exampled in Canada, the Anglo-Saxon model has been held out as the model for global emulation. Central to this model is the assertion of market economy growth and market economy employment as the sole remedies to the dramatic levels of polarization seen throughout the globe. This assertion is dubious at best as employment only serves to intensify risks and the consequent crisis of social reproduction.[7]

However, within this context of uncontainable risk and crisis an emergent alternative development strategy predicated not on *employment* but *work* comes into view. The yet-to-be-instituted Work paradigm is not a normative or idealistic analytic.[8] Instead, it takes stock of existing socio-cultural practices already in motion within the social. The social may be defined as 'a shifting terrain of political struggle and public policy focused on individual and societal protection as well as the promotion of social cohesion and political stability'.[9]

The institutional lack precipitated by the termination of the Employment paradigm has triggered the activation of the social – not only as a means to ameliorate uneven capitalist development, but in order to realize alternative conceptions of global futures.[10] Within the interregnum existence is no longer predetermined but chosen; individuals are thrown back onto themselves necessitating reflexive engagement.[11] An organic social response has been the increased necessity to manifest individual labour-power in multiple fields of work that go well beyond employment.

These work fields include, but are not limited to, the following: family, house, political, self-improvement, school and voluntary. Exemplifying the emergence of the social economy, individuals are engaged multiactively and not simply in paid work in order to secure social reproduction. It is in this context that it is possible to make sense of the growth of the social economy as it circumvents the boundaries of the political and economic that have previously been located exclusively in the nation-state, the inter-state system and the market economy. This comes into view globally as indicators of a generative process of subpolitics and the formation of subpolitical networks.[12] It is by elaborating on these transformations that this chapter explores the contours of a paradigmatic shift between Employment and Work.

Transformative forces in the post-Employment era: capital, neo-liberalism and the United States

Capital

The unilateral withdrawal of capital from the social compromises that constituted the Employment paradigm has resulted in the reshaping of the social relations of production. Conforming to the hyper-power of capital, employment generation is relegated solely to the market economy and subject to structural and procedural disciplining. Structurally, the freeing of capital from national controls has resulted in the real and perceived heightening of planetary competition between locales in order to attract investment.[13]

Production within this phase of *just-in-time* capitalism involves the parceling out of the design and manufacturing aspects within global commodity chains. Employment, in turn, is subject to outsourcing or contracting out. This has resulted in enhanced mobility not just of manufacturing jobs but also, more recently, of high-skilled service jobs.

Employment within this context is rationalized through a global division of labour.[14] The creation of fear surrounding job losses for example with the threat of plant closures have been an effective strategy in de-unionizing Fordist industries (i.e., right-to-work states within the United States[15]) and increasing union accommodation.[16] This is reinforced in the South with the governmental creation of de-regulated export processing zones and *maquiladoras*. While actual mobility may be less than what is threatened by capital, the perception of mobility is often sufficient to ensure labour's acquiescence.

Central to the termination of the Employment paradigm are numerical and wage flexibility, and multitasking due to technological innovations. These are capitalist strategies employed independently and/or in combination to discipline labour. Numerical flexibility is the conferring, by both consent and coercion, to capital of the capacity to determine the necessary levels of labour required for production. Likewise wage flexibility confers capital with the capacity to determine wage levels, effectively eliminating the compromise of a social wage with labour. Finally, the introduction of technological innovations cannot be understood without an acknowledgement of the asymmetrical power of capital over labour.

The imposition of these strategies has resulted in a more fluid definition of employment. Employment is no longer equated with the standardized full-time worker. Rather, non-standard forms of employment are seen as elemental to capitalist cost savings and the assurance of 'full employment'. As such, there are now a polyphony of categories including part-time, permanent part-time, temporary, fixed-contract and self-employed. The OECD summarizes this reality in the following way:

> Obstacles to participation in economic life clearly need to be broken down. . . . One avenue being pursued is the removal of institutional impediments to other 'non-standard' forms of labour force participation, such as part-time work, week-end work, self-employment and home work, either through the removal of regulatory constraints (as in the United States and the United Kingdom) or through the renegotiation of collectively-bargained constraints. A policy choice has to be made here. . . . The 'permanent job' as an entitlement to a secure income in return for performing the same unchanging tasks is increasingly inappropriate in societies which seek to mobilise their full talents in response to evolving technologies and markets.[17]

It later adds: 'access to work should also be facilitated by a variety of services and flexible working arrangements such as part-time jobs'.[18] Non-standard work has been the most predominate form of employment expansion within the OECD. In Canada, one in five workers in 2003 were involved in part-time paid work, significantly higher than the one in ten in 1976.[19] Similarly, between 1997 and 2002, temporary jobs increased by 31 per cent while permanent full-time paid work and part-time paid work increased by 12 per cent.[20]

The increase in non-standardized work terminates the Employment paradigm. The conditions trade unions won under the standardized mass-production factory regime cannot be maintained in a world of individualized, non-standard arrangements. While some non-standardized workers have union representation, this flexibility discourse creates new structures of inequality. Disproportionately represented by women, part-time paid work is concentrated in the service sector at the lower paying occupational levels, such as food services, cleaning and retail trade.[21] Wage flexibility has also resulted in the elimination of the social wage as workers are exposed to global wage competition. For example, in Canada the average hourly wage of temporary employees in 2003 was $13.94CAD as compared with $18.65CAD for permanent employees.[22]

Within jobs, functional flexibility requires workers to be multitaskers. Matched to their machines, i.e., their computers, workers are expected to complete multiple functions simultaneously. The ability to execute more than one task simultaneously renders workers, once again, as generalists. However, it also increases firm productivity.[23] This is in contradistinction to the Fordist assembly-line worker, as exemplified in Charlie Chaplin's *Modern Times*, who spent his day completing a single task.

It is important to note that the structural and procedural disciplining that has taken place in the post-Employment era has been facilitated by changes in information technologies. However, the critical element of these changes, indicative of the termination of the Employment paradigm, is that advances resulting from technological developments have not been shared out with workers. Instead, technological innovation leading to worker lay-offs is couched as a necessity for competitiveness and the well-being of the worker.

The gains have remained concentrated with capital and in CEO earnings. An oft-mentioned example of this circumstance is the dramatic growth of the American retailer Wal-Mart. Wal-Mart has overtaken General Motors as the largest employer in the United States. On average, it pays its workers $7.50USD per hour, with no defined benefit pension and inadequate health care, totaling approximately $18,000USD per annum.[24] This can be compared with the members of the Walton family who occupy places 6–10 of Forbes' annual World's Richest People list at $20 billion each.[25]

However, Wal-Mart is not exceptional. According to the UNDP, the world's richest 1 per cent receive as much income as the poorest 57 per cent.[26] The income gap between the world's richest 20 per cent and poorest 20 per cent rose from 30:1 in 1960, to 60:1 in 1990, to 74:1 in 1999, and is projected to reach 100:1 in 2015.[27] With these escalating inequalities capital has been able to restore profit levels thereby terminating its crisis of profitability.

The neo-liberal state form

Emanating from the Anglo-Saxon nations, the basis of support for the Employment paradigm has been transformed with the promotion of neo-liberal ideology. This model of capitalist development seeks to guarantee the realigned power of capital over the social, effectively terminating the political commitment to full employment. A positive account of this transformation is the Competition State[28] and the Schumpeterian workfare state.[29] Both posit a radical alteration in the state's commitment to employment.

The Competition State thesis highlights this alteration in state form, as the active state is replaced by a residual state whose primary macro-economic concern is the control of inflation. National policy preferences ensuring full employment are replaced by policies augmenting competitiveness in international terms. Innovation and flexibility are viewed as central to this political project, as these are viewed as forming the basis of competitive adaptability. In the Canadian context, evidence of the Competition State thesis materializes with the formation of 'Team Canada'.[30] Initiated in 1994, Prime Minister Chrétien put it this way,

> [t]eam Canada is proof of our country's commitment to trade. And it is proof that we understand the single most important fact of the world of today: that more trade means jobs. Jobs and opportunity. Growth in our economy. A better future for our children. Prosperity at home and abroad.[31]

In other words, employment is to be generated by market economy growth. Within this liberal economic view, growth is unrestricted providing a veritable win-win for all. In this sporting analogy, the state and capital are indistinguishable, forming a singular unit with a single objective: to champion economic growth through trade. This is the only game in town ensuring employment and security. However, the sporting analogy is telling in that it makes explicit that competitiveness is built-in with Team Canada vs. Team USA, Germany, Brazil etc.[32]

Bob Jessop agrees that the internationalization of the economy has presented increasing constraints on the state. However, for Jessop, the issue is not that of globalization but the transition from Fordism to post-Fordism or after-Fordism. Jessop posits that it is only through a change in both the regime of accumulation and the mode of *régulation* that a new mode of development is possible. According to Jessop, the Schumpeterian workfare state provides this possibility as it,

> . . . promotes product, process, organizational, and market innovation; the

enhancement of the structural competitiveness of open economies mainly through supply-side intervention; and the subordination of social policy to the demands of labour market flexibility and structural competitiveness.[33]

Domestic full employment is downplayed in favour of international competitiveness, and redistributive welfare rights take second place to a productivist reordering of social policy. In this sense the Schumpeterian workfare state marks a clear break from the Keynesian Fordist state.

This manifested in Canada with the termination of provincial welfare programs and their replacement with workfare programs.[34] In Ontario, workfare legislation is known by the pleasant moniker *Ontario Works*.[35] The stated purpose of the act is to accomplish the following:

1   Recognize individual responsibility and promote self-reliance through employment;
2   Provide temporary financial assistance to those most in need while they satisfy obligations to become and stay employed;
3   Effectively serve people needing assistance;
4   Be accountable to the taxpayers of Ontario.

The shift from welfare to workfare stated within Schumpeterian workfare state theorization and exampled with this legislation points to the centrality of employment while simultaneously shifting the burden of employment from a social and therefore political responsibility to an individual one predicated on market circumstances. Consequently, the state's concern is not for the welfare of the unemployed individual, but the utilization of the state's coercive powers to push him back into employment through workfare.

To summarize, these theorizations highlight three disciplinary developments that signify the abandonment of the Employment paradigm by the neo-liberal state. First, since the market is viewed as the sole legitimate means of employment generation, market discipline is imposed. Since states are subject to threats of short-term capital flight, this is in part an external imposition. The mobility of capital undermines the nation's ability to undertake policies that threaten investor confidence.[36] Domestically, this is reinforced as large financial firms and transnational corporations demand financial liberalization.

Second, social discipline is imposed with the reprivatization of the social, through policies such as workfare, in order to enforce a mythical ideal of self-reliance. Conforming more readily to the social Darwinian notion of survival of the fittest, as opposed to the 'hand up, not a hand out' heralded by US President Clinton, gainful employment forms the basis of this transition.[37]

Third, discipline based on global othering encourages and facilitates the construction of a global social Darwinism. At issue, for example in Canada, is not simply the heightened rhetoric of the competitive threats emerging from South and East Asia, but the potential of a free fall into a 'Third World' or global South status. In this sense, the state is complicit in the construction of poverty both domestically and globally as 'other'. Poverty becomes an inevitable outcome if adherence to the state's (and capital's) dictates is not forthcoming.[38] In this way, the disciplining of the global South provides positive feedback mechanisms for capital and the states' agenda to dismantle the Employment paradigm.

The United States

Termination of the Employment paradigm was a political project directed by the United States and conducted globally in an attempt to reassert US economic and geopolitical hegemony. The structural centrality of the United States to the global system, specifically its economic and military power, provides the United States with the necessary regime (re)producing capacities. Economically, the US economy is twice the size of the world's second largest economy, Japan, and spends nearly as much on R&D as the next seven richest nations combined. More importantly, utilization of the US dollar as the global currency has enabled the United States to be the globe's *de facto* central banker. Militarily, the United States defense budget ($399 billion USD) is equal to the combined spending of the next 25 largest defense spenders.[39]

The Nixon administration's unilateral withdrawal in 1973 from the fixed currency system established within the Bretton Woods system effectively dislodged the Employment paradigm. Faced with competitive challenges from Western Europe and Japan, the United States imposed competitive devaluations of its currency.[40] In doing so, the US signaled an end to the post-war Employment paradigm policies that supported the growth and stabilization of these economies. As the dollar remained inconvertible, the 'floating dollar standard' served both to insulate the United States from the negative effects of its growing balance of payments constraints and to trigger commodity speculation, which further exacerbated growing imbalances within the global economy.

The summary dismissal of the Employment paradigm came in 1979 with a change in US monetary policy. Imposition of an interest rate shock by the US Federal Reserve transformed policy from a focus on employment and growth to the containment of inflation. This, combined with the (military Keynesian) expansionary policies of the Reagan administration, reaffirmed the supremacy of the United States. Wealth was again transferred back into USD and flowed in terms of investments and outcome from the explosive levels of debt denominated in USD, which cannot be separated out from the imposition of high rates of interest charged on that debt. The impact was the further removal of emergent competitive threats globally and particularly from the South.[41] These nations were forced to subordinate policies of employment generation and replace them with fiscal austerity measures in order to finance their foreign debts.

Emerging in the 1980s and 1990s was a new regime of financial discipline based within the Washington Consensus, which consisted of the US administration, US Congress, the IMF, World Bank, and a collection of think-tanks and academics.[42] The Washington Consensus formally eliminates the arbitrary bifurcation between 'development economics' and economics. In its place a universal model of (economic development) is put forward. While there was disagreement within the consensus over how 'shock therapy' in the form of Structural Adjustment Policies (SAPs) should be applied (i.e., Russia in the 1990s), dissent was limited to the speed and policy order – not over whether SAPs were required.[43]

Gill describes this as 'new constitutionalism', which has functioned to enable the United States to deepen and manage neo-liberal globalization.[44] New constitutionalism institutionalizes disciplinary neo-liberal concepts and practices at the global level. Fundamental to this framework of global governance and to the subsequent termination of the Employment paradigm was the US imposition of financial deregulation on the rest of the world. By making them susceptible to speculative attacks on their currencies, national governments were disciplined and policies that underwrote the Employment paradigm were effectively relegated to the dustbin of history.

Employment capitalism and the structuring of the Anglo-Saxon model

The legitimacy of the Anglo-Saxon model is predicated on its reputation as an employment generator. Specifically, this reputation focuses on the Anglo-Saxon model's successful transition to a knowledge economy with its requisite generation of high-quality knowledge economy jobs.[45] According to Figure 2.1, this is illustrated by the characteristic decrease in the 'official' unemployment rate of all neo-liberal states. Of note is the significant decline

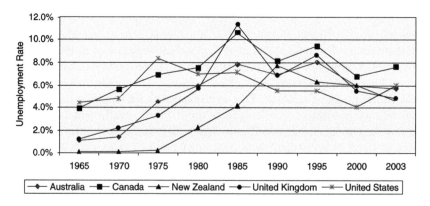

Figure 2.1 Neo-liberal model unemployment rates.

in the unemployment rate of the United States, which fell from a high of 8.3 per cent in 1975 to a low of 4 per cent in 2000.

Proponents of the Anglo-Saxon model have argued that the basis of the model's success is its sole reliance on the market economy and its spurring of the necessary 'animal instincts of entrepreneurs'. Rhetoric characteristic of this position points to wage subordination and decreased regulation as integral to the proper operation of the market. Such rhetoric has formed the ideological basis for purporting the American and, more broadly, neo-liberal model as the model for global emulation.[46]

Complications with the Anglo-Saxon model of development

However, unemployment reduction has not been uniform across nations within the Anglo-Saxon model. As Figure 2.1 illustrates, unemployment in Canada has remained significantly higher than in the United States. The oft-cited cause of this discrepancy is over-regulation in Canada.[47] However, according to the OECD, '[c]ompetitive forces are, in general, strong in Canada, in large part because most barriers to international trade have been dismantled, and administrative and economic regulations inhibiting competition are amongst the lowest in the OECD'.[48]

Also, as Figure 2.2 indicates, nations such as Austria, Denmark and South Korea have lower unemployment while having greater regulation than that instituted in Canada. To further complicate this rationale, the accusation of over-regulation fails to account for the 4.4 per cent employment growth in Canada between 2001 and 2004 as compared with a mere 0.6 per cent growth

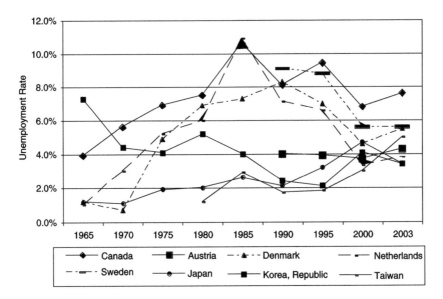

Figure 2.2 Regulation and employment generation.

in the United States over the same period.[49] In short, the assumed correlation between governmental regulation and levels of employment is not as straightforward as proponents of this model claim.

Hidden unemployment

The 'official' unemployment rate also functions to disguise and artificially lower the true unemployment rate in these economies. For example, as Figure 2.3 reveals, the official unemployment rate in the United States fails to incorporate marginally attached (i.e., temporary) and part-time workers who cannot find full-time paid work. A far more accurate measure of unemployment is an alternative measure known as the 'U-6 Special Unemployment Rate'. The U-6 rate includes the standard unemployment rate as well as the numbers for those who are marginally attached or involuntarily employed as part-time workers.

However, the U-6 Unemployment Rate also understates the true rate of unemployment in the United States by not taking into account the numbers of incarcerated individuals and those claiming disability or active membership in the National Guard or US Reserves. In 2002, the United States had an incarceration rate of 2,166,260.[50] Since prisoners are drawn from a segment of the population with generally high rates of unemployment, the impact of their inclusion in the unemployment rate raises it by 1.5 per cent.[51]

In terms of disability claimants, studies indicate a 60 per cent increase in the Social Security Disability Insurance income programme between 1984 and 2001 to a total of 5,300,000.[52] The increase is attributable to a combination of low skilled workers exiting the paid labour market in order to collect higher incomes through the programme, and the easing of eligibility criteria. The increase in disability claimants corresponds to a further 0.5 per cent increase in the unemployment rate.

Lastly, the recent dramatic increase in Reservists and National Guard members serving in Iraq and Afghanistan numbers approximately 58,000. This raises the unemployment rate by 0.04 per cent. Combined, these measures

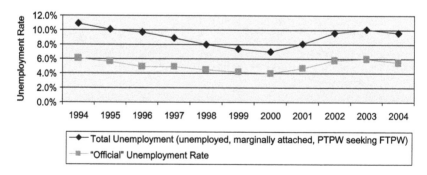

Figure 2.3 'Official' versus 'U-6' unemployment rates.

total an approximate increase of 2.04 per cent in the unemployment rate raising the official rate in 2004 to 7.54 per cent and the U-6 rate closer to 11.64 per cent.[53]

The reality of the knowledge economy

The claim of a transition to a knowledge economy is also highly dubious. The protagonist of this new economy is the knowledge worker or as Robert Reich describes them the 'symbolic analysts'[54] or as Richard Florida posits the 'creative class'.[55] The argument for increasing focus on the knowledge worker relied on statistics that portrayed the positions taken up by knowledge workers as the fastest growing forms of employment in the 'new economy'.[56] However, the focus was based on percentage growth, which masked the actual numbers of total employment.

Examining the employment projections indicated by the United States Bureau of Labor Statistics from 2000 to 2010 reveals that the largest growth in occupations is not in the much vaunted 'knowledge worker' occupations, but in low wage occupations, such as retail sales, cashiers, janitors, (fast) food preparation, food servers and security guards. Of the thirty occupational classifications representing 43 million workers, the Department of Labor's employment projection statistics reveal that 15 million people, representing 35 per cent of employment generation, will be in these low-wage, dead-end, service-sector jobs.[57] Additionally, using data from the 1995 Current Population Survey approximately one in seven jobs in the United States suffers on three levels: low pay, no access to health insurance, and no pension benefits.[58]

Canada presents a similar pattern of overall employment generation. Much of the focus between 1991 and 2001 has been on the 32.9 per cent increase in demand for occupations requiring a university education.[59] This percentage increase, like that in the United States, has formed the ideological basis for the 'common sense' assertion of a supposed transition to a knowledge economy. However, these high skilled knowledge jobs only account for 2.5 million jobs, or 16 per cent of all occupations in Canada.[60] As Figure 2.4 illustrates, the great bulk of employment remains in the low-end, service sector jobs that require a high school diploma or less. Numerically, this conforms to 6.5 million occupations or 42 per cent of all paid work.[61]

With more than one in four workers engaged in sales and service occupations, these forms of employment are indicative of high levels of precariousness in the Canadian neo-liberal model. Wages in these occupations are the lowest within the paid labour market, averaging $12.34CAD per hour in 2003.[62] Labour market precariousness is exasperated by the growth in the number of people working in non-standard forms of paid work. For example, one in five workers are categorized as part-time workers – significantly higher than the one in ten reported in 1976.[63] Unemployment is also exacerbated along ethnic, regional and age lines.[64] The unemployment rate of First

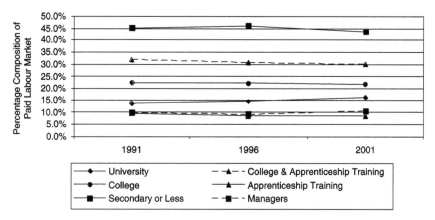

Figure 2.4 Educational requirements and the composition of the Canadian paid
labour market.

Nations peoples has remained significantly higher than the rest of the
Canadian population.[65]

The result of the neo-liberal model's deregulation through wage flexibility,
declining trade unionism and weakened employee protections has led to
both higher rates of employment and a pear-shaped income distribution.[66]
Will Hutton, describing this in terms of the United Kingdom, posits that the
continuation of these trends will result in a 40:30:30 society:[67]

- 40 per cent of the population will have reasonably secure full-time paid
  work or self-employment and their prosperity will be reinforced by
  technological progress;
- 30 per cent will struggle in the secondary labour market in an attempt to
  retain some stake in the economy and over their life courses;
- 30 per cent will more or less be socially excluded, a term Alain Lipietz
  reappraises as socially 'expelled'.[68]

The widening of income inequalities within the neo-liberal model poses
threats to social cohesion, thus redirecting resources into processes of social
control.

The Work paradigm

The termination of the Employment paradigm has triggered a crisis in social
reproduction from the personal to the planetary. The unintended consequence of this termination has been the global activation of the social.

Social responses are two-fold. First, individuals are thrown back onto themselves with the burgeoning of risks, necessitating the reflexive engagement of
individual labour-power. Second, these labour processes are in themselves

social and constitutive of new 'we' orientations within newly forming sub-political networks. These subpolitical networks emphasize that 'we' are inextricably bound up with the world and others rather than simply existing as autonomous entities among other independent bodies in the world.[69]

Together, these responses can be seen as the nascent beginnings of a Work paradigm predicated on the intensive and extensive growth of the social economy. Explicitly requiring the individual to embrace a multiactive life-style, the Work paradigm locates labour-power manifestations across differentiated work sites as opposed to being contained within the paid labour market. As each activity necessitates the manifestation of labour, work is viewed as irreducibly productive of both the individual and their networked relations. This necessary dispersal of labour-power beyond the realm of paid work discredits the hegemonic discourses that promote the market economy and employment within it. Assertions that credit the market economy as the panacea to the burgeoning of risks and the crisis of social reproduction are revealed as one-dimensional, inadequate and implausible.

Subjectivity in the post-Employment era

To reiterate the argument thus far the Employment paradigm, as described in Chapter 1, was largely based on the employment-as-identity nexus. As individuals were forged together with their occupations, within the gendered terrain of male public employment and female housework, ontological security was gained *vis-à-vis* collective lifestyles and the socialization of risks that arose from capitalist development. Yet the termination of the Employment paradigm by capital, the neo-liberal state, and the United States has resulted in the exposure of the social to risk. Previous metanarratives of the nation-state, science, progress, growth, full employment, the work ethic, family, and gender roles are now points of contestation in the current interregnum between Employment and Work.

The side effect of this current interregnum is that individuals are increasingly forced into rule-finding reflexive judgment situations. For example, households may have to choose between lesser paying male full-time paid work and higher paying female full-time paid work. In this way, the assignment of gender roles, societal interactions, the division of household labour and more broadly issues of power are potentially reconfigured. The institutionalization of reflexivity that this example points to transforms both the structure of contemporary society and individual self-identity. This process is called individualization.

For Anthony Giddens, individualization is a socio-psychological adaptation, which is fundamentally linked to a process of detraditionalization.[70] It is emancipatory as the individual becomes free to address his needs in ways he prefers. This understanding of individualization conforms to methodological individualism as it prioritizes personal freedom and choice. In other words, this definition fits with the conception of the liberal individual.

Ulrich Beck also discusses the individualization thesis. However, his discussion is reminiscent of the pessimism associated with the Frankfurt School.[71] For Beck, risk is a different kind of ontological insecurity; it is not a side effect of detraditionalization. Beck, and it is a conceptualization I favour, views risk as overdetermined and rife with complexity. Dismissing Giddens' utopian reading of risk society, Beck argues that expert systems may offer solutions by further developing expert knowledge about particular risks (their causes and the best way to deal with them) but in doing so they are inherently contributing to an amplification of risk. This complexity precludes the possibility of effective control by any overarching system.[72] Consequently the individual is not the liberal individual described by Giddens; identity cannot be reduced to self-reflection, understanding, and the development of a life project. Instead, identity is about issues of belonging, expression, performance, identification and communication with others; it is inherently social as it is always with-others.

In either case, individualization necessitates the *construction* and performance of an identity for ourselves, as biographies are no longer inherited signifiers. Within the post-Employment era, it is implausible to assume that identity can be constructed by one's employment or lack thereof. With the absence of institutional structures, whether they are the Fordist welfare state or extended family support mechanisms, individuals are forced to adapt by splintering themselves into multiple roles that necessitate labour-power in their manufacture.

These roles go beyond that of the male-breadwinner and female-carer model idealized in the Fordist welfare state. Different milieus assert different identities, which proceed to produce subjects, modes of calculation, the subsequent politics of a particular space-place and forms of labour-power. As such, identity is more readily viewed as a space-time distribution of hybrid and dialogical sub-contexts, constantly being copied, revised, enunciated and performed into a self-scripted semblance of a biography.

In struggling to come to terms with one's own biography, we see that one's life is in constant movement; it is a traveling life both literally and metaphorically – a nomadic life as people are 'place polygamous'.[73] This is critical within the Work paradigm as it conforms more readily to the multiactive manifestation of labour-power across work places. The imposition of neoliberal policies along with the transport and technological revolutions increasingly means that individuals are made (virtually) present in the processes and machinations of global capital. Disciplinary neo-liberal policies enacted locally (e.g., through municipal and provincial level governments) and enforced more remotely (e.g., through international financial institutions) increasingly impact individuals compelling the multiactive engagement of their labour-power. Ruth Pearson highlights this, for instance, in her study of Cuban households, as they are compelled to adopt new strategies to contend with structural reforms imposed after the collapse of the Soviet Union and the continuing US embargo.[74]

The notion of remote occurrences having dramatic impacts on other locales and of distanced power imposing developmental dictates is not new to capitalism and/or imperialism. History is replete with examples, including that of South Asian weavers being impacted by decisions emanating from the imperial centre of Britain. Nevertheless this phase of globalization is more extensive and intensive in form and function. Pearson's study however suggests that by examining the daily responses to structural reforms, new strategies of resistance can come to the foreground.

Theorization of the Work paradigm and issues of labour-power therefore cannot be limited solely to class motivation. As strategy, such a limitation serves to alienate rather than combine and thereby undermines the potential transformative capacity of a paradigm shift. In practical terms, class does not fit the structure of the social economy and instead is mapped onto it. Social economy actors coalesce around issues that are impacted by class but this may or may not be central to the issues and claims raised. Examples include organizations focused on issues of ecology, multiculturalism, gender and sexuality. This does not discount class since individuals engage in various forms of work in order to address certain identity structures – including that of class. Rather, the issues of how and by whom labour-power is defined, enacted and valorized are what is central to analysis and emancipatory strategies.

Therefore, the more pertinent issue is the following: how is it possible to conceive and valorize labour-power manifestations in their necessary holistic forms as opposed to the dichotomous valorizing of paid work versus its others? This is precisely the issue that comes to the fore when we recognize, within the post-Employment era, that woman cannot exist exclusively as a carer. She is also self-employed, a volunteer and engaged in self-improvement work. Likewise, man is no longer solely an employee but also a carer, an activist and a student. These divergent identity structures necessitate the manifestation of labour-power specific to each role and should be complemented by a theorization that connects one to each other.

Multiactive labour-power

Multiactive work is activity of divergent intensities and durations that corresponds to identity structures that conform, conflict and complicate one another. This can include family, house, school, self, political and voluntary work.[75] Within the Employment paradigm the narrative is simple. Work in the form of formal paid work, or employment, is the central organizing dynamic of the social. Other forms of work, such as volunteering and housework, are relegated to non-work status. If they are made visible they are immediately subordinated to paid work. They are productive of the individual and indispensable to social reproduction, but this is not accounted for within the simple narrative of the Employment paradigm.

The post-Employment era presents a new dilemma. The everyday reality of multiple forms of work has invariably garnered increasing attention within the discursive constraints of 'work–life balances'. In Canada, numerous studies have examined work–life balance as individuals increasingly identify high levels of stress and strain associated with the complexities of conducting their labour-power across these fields.[76] Defined as 'role overload', the studies document a significant increase in individuals 'feeling overwhelmed, overloaded or stressed by the pressures of multiple roles'.[77] Between 1991 and 2001, national surveys in Canada indicate an 11 per cent increase (from 47 per cent to 58 per cent) in high levels of stress associated with role overload.[78]

While the acknowledgement of multiactive labour-power is a welcome development, the framing of the issue as that of work–life balances reduces the level of analysis to that of time management. Strategies to overcome the problem come across as mechanistic and economistic. Life is conceived within these articulations as that belonging to Giddens' liberal individual. By responding to the risks of contemporary life as that of goal overload, life is reduced to a goal-oriented rationalistic product. In this sense, the critical issue is that of management. As the manager of one's life the question posed therefore is: how can I better manage my time in order to fulfill my responsibilities? As a result, these studies fail to address the more important subjective evaluations accorded to the manifestation of multiactive labour-power, namely meaning and value. Foregrounded is the social conception of the individual as inherently *being-in-the-world-with-others*.

Commentators, such as Ray Pahl, provide an examination of multiactive labour-power manifestation precisely in terms of intersubjective evaluations. Pahl argues that with the decline of the old male-dominated career paths that demanded a person to completely invest himself in his paid work, our understanding of success is changing from one emphasizing individual power, control and wealth to one emphasizing a 'balance' between paid work and non-paid work, such as 'parenting, caring, education or retraining, being unemployed, taking rests between jobs and so on'.[79]

Peter Meiksins and Peter Whalley take this one step further by trying to discover how individuals balance both meaningful work and meaningful lives. They interviewed technical professionals – engineers, computer professionals, and technical writers – who, within this context of overwork, 'have managed to find a way around the institutional structures that frame the "normal" work career'.[80] They conclude that the rationale for reducing working time extends beyond that of the most often cited reason, childcare, to a complexity of reasons, such as lifestyle.

This trend is also supported, for example, with evidence of downshifting, voluntary simplicity, simple living and slow speed living. Juliet Schor provides a quantitative study of the trend for voluntary downshifting. She defines it as 'a phenomenon in which individuals choose to reduce their working hours (and generally, in consequence, their income and consumption levels) in the pursuit of non-material goals such as leisure time, better family relationships, and reduced stress'.[81] She identifies five types of down-shifting: income, spending, hours, pace of life, and geographic, pointing out that nearly 19 per cent of all adult Americans made a voluntary life-style change to downshifting.[82] Another 12 per cent of Americans were involuntarily downshifted, that is, they had their incomes reduced through no choice of their own. However, 24 per cent of these said it was a blessing in disguise.

This research has been critiqued for its focus on 'privileged workers' such as the high-technology workers. It has also been critiqued for its non-systemic basis. For example, Robert Frank points out in reference to downshifting, '[t]o the extent that choices that are smart for one are dumb for all, individual action, by itself, simply won't be enough'.[83] While these critiques are import-ant for pointing to the centrality of structure and structural change, they prematurely dismiss the political potential of these activities as indications of a paradigm transition from Employment to Work.

Such a transition combines economic classes on the basis of risk and refle-xive modernization.[84] Pay, and consequently paid work, is displaced as the sole or preeminent criteria determining labour-power manifestation. Rachel Dwyer for example, extends Schor's work by providing quantitative support of voluntary downshifting where a loss of pay is an acknowledged and accepted outcome.[85] This research concludes that other values and measures beyond economic utility must be included in understanding labour-power manifestation in the post-Employment era. In doing so, Dwyer captures a different ethos emblematic of the Work paradigm. In the words of former French Prime Minster Lionel Jospin, '[w]e need time to live'.[86] This provides an apt declaration of this emergent alternative positioning. The economistic view of living is replaced with an aesthetic one, whereby work–life *beauty* can replace work–life *balance* as an equally appropriate means to understanding multiactive labour-power.

Needing the social

The issue is not the importance or unimportance of paid work. This is to mistake the argument. Instead, it is that paid work is an increasingly insufficient criterion for addressing social reproduction. As stated earlier, the need for paid work remains elemental to the existence of the great bulk of humanity within capitalist social relations. However, the social economy is increasingly relied upon as a supplementary and alternative economy in the post-Employment era, as it is more capable of addressing both individual and social needs.

Individual need necessitates the coming together of individuals into social networks, as social reproduction is plausible only in relation with-others. Individuals and their labour-power are not synonymous with the fiction of Robinson Crusoe (minus Friday) – self-reliant and autonomous. Instead labour, as a process and in terms of its product, is entirely social. Individuals and their labour-power are inextricably networked in relations of dependence, mutuality, responsibility and solidarity. In short, individuals come together to perform their labour as they are irreducibly engaged in this social world.

This understanding of labour is evident within the household, for example, as family work. Children and the elderly are dependent on the care of others. However, the dynamic of life-course events necessitates alternating the provision of labour. As such, individuals shift from a dependence on the labour of others in childhood to being responsible for others in their adulthood to again being dependent on the care of others in old age.

On a broader level, Local Exchange Trading Networks (LETS) provide an example of the individual's need of the social beyond the parameters of the family network. Increasingly widespread after the mid-1990s, LETS allow for the alternative exchange of goods and services beyond that of monetary relations.[87] This involves either the bartering of services through the exchange of labour or by the creation of mechanisms such as time-dollars to enable a wider reciprocity economy. This enables cash-poor individuals and communities the possibility of accessing goods and services that would otherwise be out of reach.[88] LETS are a sophisticated means of rewarding reciprocity and civic engagement. Explicitly centred on mutuality and solidarity, they shield individuals and communities from the risks of the market economy by connecting individual labour-power to the broader social economy.

The Toronto Dollar, developed in 1998, is an example of a LET system. Individuals can either purchase Toronto Dollars by converting their CAD (on a one-to-one basis) or receiving them as payment for community service. This currency can then be used to purchase goods and services from participating retailers and community organizations as well as other individuals. The dollars can also be traded back into CAD, but with a 10 per cent loss. This provides an incentive to maintain the alternative currency and ensure the reproduction of the system. The transaction cost provides additional means for generating income to fund community activities and services or to compensate volunteer workers for their labour-power contributions.

Social needs also underpin social economy intensification and expansion. The transformative forces discussed earlier have simultaneously undermined the protective institutions of the Employment paradigm and proved incapable of establishing a new mode of development. It is within this context of escalating crisis that the social economy is activated.

This shift toward the social economy is outside and beyond the representative institutions of the political and economic system of nation-states, and the market economy defines this movement towards more temporally and spatially dispersed networks as subpolitics.[89] Its clearest manifestation is in the emergence of an interconnectivity between the new social movements and the social economy, both of which acknowledge the relationships between economy, environment, politics and society.

Increasingly engaged on multiple scales and durations, subpolitical networks challenge the ideological ordering and institutionalization of power within societies. The struggles are not only concerned with issues of how economic and social resources are controlled and distributed in society, they are also over the power to give meaning to the world by defining who the legitimate participants are, what the issues are, and what the available alternatives might be. In other words, the struggles that new social movement and social economy actors engage in are for both identity and resources.

The social economy, like the new social movements, explicitly confronts the assumptions and assertions of a neo-liberal vision of economy as derived from the transformative forces discussed earlier. For example, the demand for and the implementation of strategies that prioritize social entrepreneurship, socially responsible productivity, as well as the insistence on prioritizing endogenous development all counter the dominant neo-liberal economic orthodoxy of market-led growth.

Desire and **being-in-the-world-with-others**

Social economy growth nevertheless cannot be delimited solely to that of individual and social need. If it did we could conclude, for example, that individuals participate in LETS due to a lack of market access; that social movements organizing around the issue of civil rights do so due to a lack of racial and gender equality; that communities form neighbourhood watches because of a lack of safety. While these assessments may seem, on the surface, to be appropriate, they are largely dependent on the assumption that this coming together is rational, reactionary and defensive in nature. Missing is a theorization of collective desire based on a consciousness of *being-in-the-world-with-others*.

Gilles Deleuze and Felix Guattari posit that desire depends not on a lack, but on the lack of a lack. In other words, collective desire is productive as it is socially connective.[90] Endlessly spreading and generating newly created relations between and amongst individuals, groups and communities in the form of subpolitical networks, collective desire frees up territorialities for the construction of new alternative social arrangements. As Deleuze and Guattari state, '[i]ts [capitalism's] gaps are everywhere, forever giving rise to the displaced limits of capitalism. . . . But it is certainly the problem of the marginalized: to plug all these lines of escape into a revolutionary plateau'.[91]

The individual participating in the local LETS exemplifies this as she participates in order to realize a different world predicated not on monetary exchange and exploitation, but on reciprocity and solidarity. The civil rights movement expanded not only because those affected demonstrated, but also because others engaged in the movement as an act of solidarity. Neighbourhood watch participants organize not only due to fear, but also with the knowledge that the community is theirs to construct. These are all examples of a social consciousness of *being-in-the-world-with-others*.

For Heidegger, this is the beginning as existence commences with the social. The individual is always already in a state of *being-in-the-world* (*dasein*), a co-constitutive relationship of mutual effect.[92] As such, she does not have to break through to the world from an encapsulated solipsistic self (e.g., homo economicus). The term 'world' in this conceptualization is not a synonym for the earth, but a reflexively organized unencumbered relation between selves and things that are both surrounding us and produced by us. However, missing but implicit in Heidegger's phrase is Heidegger's subject. It is not Descarte's 'I', split from its object, but rather an existing connectivity of *being-with*. Thus *being-in-the-world-with-others* is a condition that dilutes the subject, constantly hybridizing it with its perpetual others. The addition of *with-others* brings to the foreground yet another connectivity, transforming Heidegger's disembodied and ahistorical category of *being-in-the-world* into a political subject within the dialectic of institutions and embodiment.

This conception of acting in the world, and the consciousness it is based upon, conflicts with orthodox economic theorizations by forming an unresolved paradox. Such theorizations hold that there is a stark choice between collectivism and individualism, with individualism propelling the economic system.[93] Yet this modernist dichotomy presents a false choice as evidenced in our examples. As Beck fittingly points out, '[t]hinking of oneself and living for others, once considered a contradiction in terms, is revealed as an internal connection.'[94] As rationality becomes a principle of reflexivity, we cannot choose a world without other people. The side effects of the post-Employment era increasingly force us to choose how it is that we respond to this primary relatedness. Engagement and isolation are each responses to *being-in-the-world-with-others.*[95]

Afterword

The termination of the Employment paradigm by the transformative forces of capital, the neo-liberal state and the United States has triggered a crisis in social reproduction. In this interregnum, employment is no longer capable of providing ontological and social security. Rather, it arguably exacerbates the crisis by failing to address emergent risks and the broad requirements of social reproduction. Nevertheless, employment remains central within a hegemonic vision of development. While the institutional structure of the current global political economy no longer adheres to a political mandate for full employment, employment is still valorized as the organizing dynamic.

Socially, individuals increasingly bear the risks associated with the post-Employment era. This has resulted in an alteration in subjectivity. Labour is no longer associated strictly with paid work.[96] Rather, it is manifested multi-actively and always contingent. Needs are identified within the individual yet resolved in the social. Politics is linked increasingly with social values and meaning systems.

The disjunction between institutional and individual responses to the post-Employment era has triggered the growth of the social economy, an economy that accommodates the reflexive nature of a society that is engaged enough to challenge its institutions, traditions and experts. As discussed above, this challenge stems not simply from an institutional or collective level but also from an individual level. The growth of the social economy in the post-Employment era illustrates how reflexive *do-it-yourself* biographies can activate the *do-it-yourself* sector. It also reveals how the identity that orients action in the world spills over into a generalizable account of *being-in-the-world-with-others*.

Yet the social shift to the Work paradigm as evidenced through the emergence of the social economy raises key questions: how is it possible that the issue remains that of employment and unemployment on the institutional level? How is it possible that only labour-power in the form of paid work is still valorized? Answering these questions is the subject of the following chapter, which examines the epistemology of economics.

3   Unpacking economy

What is left outside the confines of rational discourse is the very issue that stands a chance of making the discourse rational and perhaps even practically effective: the political issue of democratic control over technology and expertise, their purposes and their desirable limits – the issue of politics as self-management and collectively made choices.

Zygmunt Bauman[1]

As the foundations of economic orthodoxy, the theoretical constellations of Keynesian and neo-classical economics are often discussed as structuring disparate understandings of economy.[2] This is largely predicated on their dissimilar conceptualizations of unemployment and consequent employment generation strategies, such as Keynesian economics' focus on demand stimulus versus neo-classical economics' focus on supply-side initiatives.[3] However, such examples obfuscate as much as inform on what these mainstream theorizations posit as the 'limits of the possible'.[4] The dominance of Keynesian and neo-classical economics in constructing how economy is understood serves to facilitate capital and the state's hyper-power within the interregnum. In this sense, they are both complicit in exposing and amplifying risks within the social.

Therefore, rather than viewing Keynesian and neo-classical economics as contrasting dualisms, I argue that they are in fact essentially similar in that they share four epistemological shortcomings. First, both overvalorize the market economy (and to a lesser extent the state economy). For neo-classical economics, the market economy is conceived as an objective manifestation, which requires adherence to laws that exist outside any social determination. This conceptualization, in turn, renders labour solely as employment within the market economy and subject to its objective workings. For Keynesian economics, the market economy remains the preeminent means of achieving efficient outcomes. Deficiency therefore is not to be found in the market but in human psychology. The state consequently is required to manage aggregate demand in order to ensure the proper functioning of the market.

Second, the complete dismissal of the social economy by both Keynesian and neo-classical economics precludes the possibility of conceiving economy as made up of social, market and state economies. Reversing this would undermine the classification of labour solely as employment and instead point to the possibility of multiactive labour-power manifestations across economies. Such a reversal would displace the centrality of production to that of social reproduction. This forms the third omission, as both Keynesian and neo-classical economics are complicit in a discursive omission of social reproduction as the constitutive basis of economy.

Bringing this together is the conceptualization, both internally and externally, of the household as a 'black-box'. This is the fourth shortcoming of both Keynesian and neo-classical economics. The two theorizations present a misconception of the household as a space devoid of surplus-value extraction that impacts and is impactful on economy. Forming the basic unit of economic analysis, the household is significant for understanding working economies. Defined within the social economy, households are not only sites for the reproduction of wage-labour but also sites of non-capitalist class processes. The structuring therefore of social relations, the strategies utilized, and the labour required to reproduce the household are a molecular formation of the broader workings of economy and society.

Amplified by a universalistic top-down approach to economic and social development, these shared epistemological tenets impede the ability of either Keynesian or neo-classical economics to theorize and support the shift underway within the social to a Work paradigm.

Conceiving labour: economy as objective manifestation

Both neo-classical and Keynesian economics undertheorize the co-constitution and interrelationship between and through the social, governmental and market economies. Within both theories, the terms *market* and *economy* are constituted in a metonymic relationship where one (the market) implicitly evokes the other (the economy). The market is therefore the saviour of the economic day, the sole producer of welfare in society. In Keynesian terms it is consumption and investment within the market economy that is productive of welfare. As hero nevertheless, the market economy therefore presents the sole possibility for the realization of several metanarratives, including modernization, transformation, progress, unconstrained growth, employment and security to name a few.

Excluded from both definitions therefore is the social, the arena of social and political struggle. Epistemologically, Keynesian and neo-classical economics posit the (market) economy as forming and operating outside the realm of the social. The inclusion of other potential sectors, such as the social economy, is therefore implausible, as these would drain the market's capacity to generate the optimal allocation of scarce goods. Therefore, the social and political claims that arise to form the social economy are omitted from these calculations of economy. However, as described in Chapter 2, labour is inherently a social process.

Despite the circumscribing of the individual's labour-power to that of paid work/employment, the social is inextricably present within both neo-classical and Keynesian economics in the form of the wage-labourer. Therefore, in order to understand how either theorization views economy, this chapter examines how neo-classical and Keynesian economics understand labour and segregate this process from social existence in the form of employment generation.

Employment generation within neo-classical economics

The stated objective of the neo-classical approach is to study the allocation of scarce resources between competing wants. Toward this aim, neo-classical economics views the market as the most optimal mechanism for the allocation of scarce goods to maximize the welfare of society. The basis of this understanding is the market principles of supply and demand, perfect competition, and equilibrium. According to neo-classical economics, it is only when each individual acts in a selfish manner, maximizing individual self-interest with supply equal to demand, that society will have more wealth available to it.[5] For example, Vilfredo Pareto, like Léon Walras before him, attempted to show that a perfectly competitive market economy would achieve its optimal level of economic justice when the allocation of resources could not be changed to make anyone better off without hurting someone else in the process. This efficiency criterion of the market economy, referred to as Pareto-optimality, argued that if further improvements could not make anyone worse off, then the position was sub-optimal and gains from trade were possible.

Neo-classical explanations of unemployment flow from this abstracted universal model centring on the workings of the labour market and the concept of 'natural unemployment'. Therefore, unemployment, as understood within neo-classical economics, is untenable in the long-term. This infeasibility is predicated on the market's natural tendency towards equilibrium.[6] In other words, if the labour market is allowed to work in the sense that wages are flexible, labour is mobile, skills are matched etc., there should be no unintended unemployment.

This stems, in part, from Jean-Baptiste Say and his postulate, Say's Law, which argues that supply always equals demand.[7] The economy always moves toward equilibrium because all produced commodities create national income in the form of their value. Therefore, total supply is equal in value to the money or means received in payment for producing that supply.

Neo-classical theory does, however, posit that the economy will encounter some level of unemployment, as a certain portion of the workforce will either refuse to accept lower wages and prefer to spend their time searching for higher wage jobs or refuse to move to areas where jobs exist.[8] These forms of unemployment are referred to as 'frictional' and it is in this sense that unemployment within neo-classical economics is entirely voluntary. If, however, unemployment is higher than this natural level over the long-term (and not simply due to cyclical movements of the economy) it is because of 'rigidities' and 'inflexibilities' in the labour market most commonly associated with government and/or trade union interference.[9]

Employment generation within Keynesian economics

The overarching objective of Keynesian economics, on the other hand, is to reveal the actual workings of the market economy as compared with the hypothesized neo-classical ideal. Keynes lived in an era of social turmoil. He witnessed the rise of working class movements, the Bolshevik revolution, the Great Depression and the rise and defeat of Fascism. These manifestations revealed the fragility of the capitalist system economically, politically and socially. What became increasingly clear to him was the lack of a clear institutional pattern for the management of class relations.

Given this, Keynes argues that the classic tenets of *laissez-faire* are not incorrect but, 'belong to the days of fifty or a hundred years ago when trade unions were powerless, and when the economic juggernaut was allowed to crash along the highway of progress without obstruction and even with applause'.[10] In other words, Keynesian economics is an attempt to include historical and social considerations into economics as it looks to maintain and perpetuate capitalism and capitalist social relations with regard to new challenges posed by social conflict. In doing so, Keynesian economics addresses power – the power of the now organized working classes.

Highlighting the flaws of the 'unfettered' market economy, Keynesian economics maintains that involuntary unemployment and long-term unemployment are not only possible but also representative of the norm. Keynes' criticism of classical theory focuses on its inability to theorize the persistence of unemployment and to formulate consistent strategies for its reduction. This Keynesian understanding of an ever-present condition of unemployment is centred on aggregate output. This is in contradistinction to neo-classical economics' understanding of un/employment, which focuses on supply creating demand. In other words, while neo-classical economics argues that employment determines real output in society, Keynesian economics reverses this and argues that spending determines real output and *thus* employment. By making this shift, unemployment becomes an inevitable outcome of the market economy, as modern economies are thought to produce an aggregate real demand below full output. In short, employment generation within Keynesian theorization stems from aggregate demand within the market economy.

The basis of this understanding of the constancy of unemployment is premised on several Keynesian innovations, including demand-determined equilibrium; the ineffectiveness of price flexibility to resolve unemployment;

the introduction of liquidity preference; radical uncertainty; and the acknow-ledgement of the working class as a potential negation of the system. The focus on aggregates signifies a methodological distinction between neo-classical and Keynesian economics. Also, unlike neo-classical economics, which takes the particular and generalizes it to the universal, Keynesian eco-nomics takes the particular and aggregates it in juxtaposition with other functions to form an aggregated universal.[11]

In this way, the fulfillment of the Fordist nation-state's political aim of full employment can only be fulfilled with increasing investment, which within Keynesian economics is thought to be directly linked to consumption. Yet the need for investment decreases over time as investment outpaces con-sumption (linked to consumption lag). The combined result is a decline of new capital demand in the capital market. According to Keynesian econom-ics, the reason for the decline lies in our inability to foresee the future of demand. This uncertainty again leads to a decrease in investment.

It is important to note that Keynesian economics does not state that there is an imperfection in the market economy. Rather, the Keynesian framework grounds its understanding of economy in an assumption about human psychology.[12] According to Keynesian economics, the ailment is not to be found in the structure of the market economy, but in our own imperfect human nature. This human lack triggers a reduction in investment, as those with capital fear a loss. By choosing instead to hold their money, they act as a catalyst for idle money on the one hand and idle workers on the other.

In this sense, the agenda of Keynesian economics is to remove a fear of the future and restore confidence to the market economy. Michael Hardt and Antonio Negri provide an insightful comment when they identify the fear that Keynes is at pains to undermine. Keynesian economics is, they argue, an attempt, 'to cancel out the future by prolonging the present'.[13] The fear is the collapse of the market economy and the potential catastrophe represented by the working class. Employment strategies therefore stem from demand stimu-lus with the introduction of the state economy as a stabilizing and enhancing force for the market economy.

In this way the future is fixed in the present. Stabilization and enhancement are made possible as the nation-state acts as planner, employer, arbiter between social classes, and an instrument (using government fiscal and mon-etary policy) to help temper market economy cycles. What is critical is that intervention is no longer a question of political convenience; rather, it is a technical necessity.

Conceiving labour: economy as social manifestation

Both Keynesian and neo-classical economics are *capitalocentric*, as the market economy exists a priori and is self-constituting and hegemonic. This epistemological positioning curtails a transition to a Work paradigm, as it eliminates the existence or challenges presented by the social economy. This challenge occurs on two levels. On a definitional level, the capitalocentric nature of Keynesian and neo-classical economics insists that non-capitalist forms, such as the social economy, remain the market economy's feminized 'other' – hidden and therefore unacknowledged.[14] Inclusion of the social economy would therefore not only serve to acknowledge its role as an economy, but also function to re-embed the market economy as a socially constructed and constituted institution. On an operational level, explicit utilization of both paid and non-paid labour within the social economy melts away the hypothesized exceptionalism of paid work/employment inside the labour market. Analyzed within the context of market, state and social economies labour-power manifests as work distributed through workscapes.

Market, state, and social economies

The unquestioning faith placed in the market and the market mechanism forces both neo-classical and Keynesian economics to approach uneven development as exogenous to capitalism. In both cases, the full maximization of society's welfare is to be attained solely via the market economy by way of adjustments on either the demand or supply side. These adjustments tend to concentrate solely on commodities (goods and services), which are bought and sold in the market economy. Wealth generation, therefore, in both Keynesian and neo-classical economics, is solely generated within the market economy and measured by the Keynesian statistical innovation of the Gross National Product.[15] Yet this presents a partial understanding of the complexity of the social-economic field by engendering a false classificatory regime of productivist (market economy) and non-productivistic sectors (social economy).

Within neo-classical and Keynesian economics the expansion of non-productivist sectors, such as the social economy, are permitted through increases in productivist sectors. As John Kenneth Galbraith argues, '[a] strong and stable economy and the opportunity it provides are thus central to the good society'.[16] This sentiment is underscored in the exposition of Baumol's cost-disease, which assumes that in the long run productivity grows on average much faster in manufacturing than in most services.[17] Understanding economy in this manner precludes the possibility of theorizing the reverse, that non-productivist sectors enable the possibility of expanding productivist sectors. It also denies the possibility that the classificatory schema itself may contribute to an incomplete and false understanding of economy.

This classificatory regime is itself historically contingent. Changes in the constitutive notions of productivity and efficiency reveal that definitions are driven more by institutionalized social forces than supposed objectivity. For example, the Fordist family wage, inclusive of the male-breadwinner wage coupled with family allowances, was seen as a way to ensure productivity toward the generation of workers. This historical compromise was a central element of the Employment paradigm. Within the post-Employment era the social economy has taken on this role with the formation of labour re-training organizations and community regeneration projects. As Mark Granovetter suggests, the 'productivist sector' cannot function without the social sector.[18] At issue therefore is how much social and cultural capital flows from the social economy to underpin the possibility of market economy productivity.

This discussion does not, by extension, necessitate the elimination of the market economy and its replacement with that of an unknown social economy. The aim is not to reverse Galbraith's position and assume the 'good society' and then productivity. It is more precisely to displace the metonymic understanding of economy as solely constitutive of the market. In doing so, the epistemology that presumes market economy exceptionalism is open to challenge.

An example of this challenge is to shift the definition of capital from singularly constitutive of (objective) finance/industrial capital to a hybridized one with financial/industrial, social, and cultural capital. These latter forms of capital are an explicit component of the social economy, but have also been increasingly identified as operating within the market economy. Such a hybrid definition of capital allows for a clearer explanation of the social economy since the extensive and intensive growth of the social economy within the post-Employment era is indicative of the interrelatedness of the market, state, and social economies.[19]

Figure 3.1 is an adaptation of an illustration developed by Diane Elson.[20] It attempts to illustrate how each economy is productive of social outputs. However, each economy functions within different logics, constraints and dynamics. Elson categorizes these economic dynamics as circuits set in motion by underlying values. The social economy is defined, in these terms, as constitutive of the 'provisioning circuit' that not only reproduces an available workforce but also provides intangible 'provisioning values' such as ethical behaviours.[21] Elson posits that the market economy is constitutive of the 'goods and services circuit' that is underpinned by 'commercial values'.[22] The state economy, in turn, is constitutive of the 'tax and benefit circuit' premised on 'regulatory values'.[23] Indicated by the directional arrow leading towards social output, the resulting output is then re-introduced within the other economies. Labour reproduction is an explicit example of output. Less explicit examples are issues of trust, sociability and ethics. The arrows emanating from social output back to the three economies indicate this process.

The primary distinction between Figure 3.1 and Elson's illustration is the explicit manner in which the interrelatedness of the three economies is indicated. In Figure 3.1, the interrelatedness between economies is expressed through the use of overlapping forms.

To restate the argument, the dramatic growth of the social economy challenges the epistemological positioning within Keynesian and neo-classical economics of a metonymic relationship between economy and market.

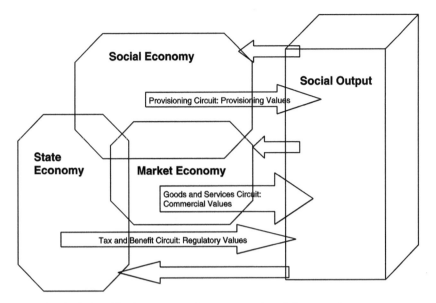

Figure 3.1 Relationships between market, state, and social economies.

Economy is more accurately conceived in plural, constitutive of market, state and social economies. Each economy is productive in and of itself as well as of the other economies. For example, each economy satisfies different needs and therefore enables claims on social output. The state provides collective needs, the market provides private needs, and the social provides (local and translocal) community needs. The lack of provision by one economy can only be offset by the transference of risk onto the others. In brief, work strategies must acknowledge and incorporate all three economies as sites of possible work generation as they are always *in-relation-with*.

Multiactive labour-power: from Employment to Work

The dynamism and productivity of the social economy presents an insurmountable challenge to both Keynesian and neo-classical economics since providing a full accounting of it requires the explicit acknowledgement of both paid and non-paid labour. This requires a radical alteration in the conceptualization of work since reclaiming work, as constitutive of both paid and non-paid labour-power expenditure runs in stark contrast to the historical ascendancy of capitalist social relations.

Keynesian and neo-classical economics conceive of work exclusively as wage-labour traded within the labour market – in other words, as employment. An individual's participation in work is predicated entirely on his choosing between it and non-work, which in this conceptualization is equated to leisure. Such a conceptualization inhibits the ability of Keynesian and neo-classical economics to theorize the Work paradigm since it denies the possibility of different forms of work outside the labour market and assumes activities to be exclusive of one another.

Feminist scholars have long provided a significant challenge to this bifurcated conceptualization of work/non-work.[24] Arguing that the 'labour of love' was indeed work, these scholars identified orthodox economic definitions of work as incomplete and socially produced.[25] For example, (female) non-paid work, in the form of housework, was defined in terms of (male) paid employment. As a result, it was deemed non-economic and inconsequential to the functioning of economy. However, by extending the articulation of work beyond mere paid work, we can reveal a multiplicity of work possibilities outside that of the labour market. These include activities within family, house, school, self, political and voluntary sites.

In other words, an individual's labour-power cannot be siloed within a particular form of work activity (e.g., housework, paid work) nor can it be situated exclusively within a particular economy. Rather, as depicted in Figure 3.2, labour-power floats between different *workscapes*, sites of contingent yet differentiated activity.

Within this conceptualization, how work is constituted, by whom, for what purposes and with what intensities/durations, are factors that are embedded in and defined by the specifics of the social relations within which they are situated. This challenges the exclusivity of the labour market as separated and abstracted from the social. Workscapes instead highlight the connectivity of work to the social as well as the connected nature of work to the physical world.

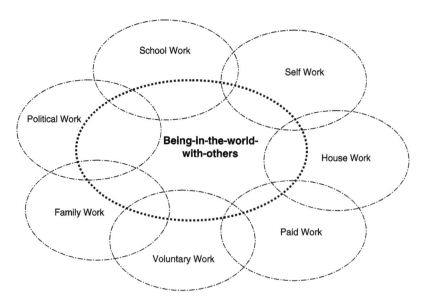

Figure 3.2 Workscapes.

The intensification of the individual's labour-power expenditure in one economy (e.g., illness of family member, work-related travel) necessitates a broad recalibration of expenditures in other economies and/or other work activities (e.g., paid work, family work, business trips, laundry). This is not simply an issue of achieving a work-life balance, but of social meanings and values. Paid work takes precedence not because of anything innate to the market economy, but as a result of the value system established within it.

Additionally, paid work and non-paid work are not mutually exclusive. For example, family, house and school work can all manifest as paid work. This may come in the form of parents/guardians paying their children to do housework or their schoolwork, or corporations encouraging their employees to engage in voluntary work as part of their employment. It could also be accomplished with the issuing of 'Toronto Dollars', as discussed in Chapter 2, to those who engage in volunteer work. It is important to note the interconnections between multiple forms of work rather than their exclusivity.

Compelled in the post-Employment era to manifest their labour-power multiactively, individuals, with their existing social practices, dispute the discrete categorizations present within Keynesian and neo-classical economics. Multiactive engagement within the social suggests that we can no longer categorize according to paid work and leisure. Instead, work done is productive of the individual and his networked social relations; work done forms the basis of social reproduction.

Labouring for social reproduction

It was the Physiocrat, François Quesnay, who first asked how it was possible for a collection of individuals associated solely by contract to be able to reproduce themselves and their social structures in such a way that the same individuals and classes would reappear after a cycle of production and circulation of commodities.[26] The question is misguided in that it assumes the regularity of a never-changing cycle. Karl Marx, following Quesnay, showed how crucial the transformations in the economic process are for both the reproduction of the system as well as its subversion. As Marx pointed out, the process of reproduction brings everything back – money, commodity and production – to the starting point. But this return, according to Marx, is not guaranteed since in reproducing itself capitalism also reproduces its contradictions.

Marx identifies two primary and interrelated contradictions that demarcate capitalism as inherently unstable and prone to systematic crises. The first is the creation and enforcement of the private ownership of the means of production. This is generative of two distinct and hierarchical class identities in the social relations of production: the capitalist and the worker. Second, the private ownership of the means of production generates competition between capitalists necessitating the constant revolutionizing of the means of production. For Marx, capitalist control over the rate of exploitation is both economic and social; it is in this process that capital conceives of labour as any other commodity. The worker, therefore, is subject to rationalizing, as it is only his labour-power that is required by capital (e.g., wage reduction, replaced by machine or other labourers). As a result, the produced category of worker, that is, someone who is compelled to sell his labour as the sole means of reproduction, is faced with a new reality under capitalist social relations – a contradiction between his social reproduction and that of capitalist reproduction.

Isabella Bakker defines social reproduction as 'the daily and generational reproduction of the commodity labour-power and the social processes and human relations associated with the creation and maintenance of the communities upon which all production and exchange rests'.[27] Neither neo-classical nor Keynesian economics can fully accept this definition, as neither can truly understand the concept.

In neo-classical economics, reproduction is not considered since time is seen as theoretically exogenous. With past, present and future bound to the dictates of an ever-present 'now', overproduction and crises are deemed implausible and the need to theorize reproduction nullified. Keynesian economics takes a more nuanced view of reproduction since it is capable of theorizing time. In doing so it posits that the market economy is unable to maximize its welfare function due to a deficiency in effective demand. By opening the possibility of overproduction, Keynesian economics posits a limited role for reproduction – that it serves only to ensure that the market economy is able to reach Pareto-optimality.

The absence of social reproduction as a theoretical construct within Keynesian and neo-classical economics reveals the implicit subject position of economy within these theorizations. Economy is theorized from the subject position of power. It confers capital as the basis of economy and its active agent. In other words, capital produces and labour consumes. However, this fails to acknowledge the cyclical nature of production and consumption, which is part of the larger dynamic of reproduction. It also means that 'there has been little or no discussion of reproduction as a central factor in economic crisis or its resolution in current analytical approaches'.[28]

Pearson discusses the centrality of reproduction by focusing on structural reforms within the Cuban economy. Her conclusions, however, are applicable to structural reforms more generally. She argues,

> [i]t is also important that the design of strategies of economic transformation should bear in mind the centrality of reproductive work to the economic system and recognize that the future legitimacy of the regime will be nurtured or destroyed by the quality of reproduction as well as the rewards from production.[29]

The social economy also presents a challenge to this understanding of economy as it aims to compensate, in some instances, and transform, in others, the deficiencies of spatially uneven capitalist development. For example, Antonella Picchio identifies a key shortcoming in Marx's analysis of reproduction, which is applicable to our understanding of the re-emergence of the social economy.[30] According to Picchio, Marx emphasizes the production and accumulation of profit rather than the broader processes of *social* reproduction. In doing so, Marxian analysis discounts other sites of social reproduction, including the state and social economy.

Marx's insight nevertheless is the reversal of the basis of the market economy from that of capital to that of the worker. Specifically, it is the moment when the worker engages their labour in the form of labour-power that the market economy is set in motion. It is the produced subject therefore of the worker that forms the basis of capitalism. Emancipatory strategies have therefore considered the worker as central to the overturning of capitalist social relations. Extending Marx's insights to the social economy replaces the centrality of labour-power to the workings of this economy, and this economy to the functioning of economy in its totality. In terms of the former, the functioning of the social economy is dependent upon individuals transforming their potential energy into labour-power within social economy organizations. In doing so, the social economy is activated. In terms of the latter, it is the activation of the social economy that functions to both ameliorate and compensate for the deficiencies of the market economy.

Folbre also provides a counterpoint to Marx, focusing on the costs of social reproduction that are associated with the bearing, raising, socialization, and education of children.[31] Through her analysis, she reveals that the focus on waged workers, as exemplified by both neo-classical and Keynesian economics, undermines the reproductive role played by subjects within the social economy. She also exposes the gendered implications of such a construct in terms of societal and economic valorization.[32] Additionally she reveals the omission of the reproductive work done in other locations, which enables the 'naturalization' of a false binary of productive and unproductive sites of economy. According to Folbre, social reproduction is an economic activity and should therefore be accounted for within political economy. The gendering of these processes, she argues, has resulted in the subordination of women and their socially reproductive labour.

Folbre nevertheless presents a disparate understanding of social reproduction than that provided to us by both Picchio and Bakker.[33] All three are concerned with biological, generational and daily reproduction, the individualized processes involved as well as the gendered nature of these processes. Overlooked, however, in Folbre's discussion is the manner in which social reproduction is the basis of capitalist processes of production and accumulation.

To this end, both Picchio and Bakker merge Marx's discussion of simple and expanded reproduction with the role played by the nation-state and the family in the labour market.[34] Picchio underscores this understanding with her discussion of housework and its relation to capitalist production and accumulation. She stresses,

> [h]ousework is not merely a combination of tasks necessary for the daily reproduction of households and for the physical and psychological life of the members. Housework's job is to restore a relation between production and reproduction that makes sense from the point of view of the people involved. It is expected that within the family, through women and their housework, the alienated relation that structures the system of production and the social system will be reversed and its conflicts absorbed. Housework serves the well-being of people, whereas the production of commodities is geared to the accumulation of capital. Accumulation uses people as commodities, and the task of housework is to produce and restore them as people within the constraint of reproducing them as commodities. That is what makes this work so endless in spite of all the changes which have occurred in the household and in the technological and occupational structure of the waged labour market.[35]

Furthermore, Marx's theorization provides a theoretical abstraction of the social whole (i.e., the capitalist system, class divisions) as representative of individuated processes. In doing so it disallows individuality, which is critical and elemental to the theorization of social reproduction, and the regenerative processes of the social economy and its correspondence with the emergence of the Work paradigm.

Marx's analysis focused on the material practices and social relations present in capitalist production. His analysis theorized the specificity of these relations with the end result being an analysis of class relations. The analysis of class relations did not exist prior to Marx's naming of it as such. In other words, classificatory identity schemes are not a priori, but are instead constructed and performed in relation with others.

Social reproduction: the Employment paradigm

The role of the state and market economy in social reproduction was most visible within the Employment paradigm. The Keynesian Fordist state attempted to stabilize social reproduction with the political mandate of full employment, consequent macroeconomic policies, a variety of social welfare policies and a gender compromise. In this way, the Keynesian Fordist state assumed the responsibility for coping with a number of economic and social risks (e.g., unemployment, poverty, sickness, education, infrastructure) while women in the household carried out the remainder of the reproductive processes.

However the state played a far smaller role in the reproduction of labour. In broad terms, the Keynesian Fordist state, national capitalist economic growth, collective bargaining, effective demand, norms of mass consumption,

and the gender compromise combined into a virtuous circle of production, accumulation and reproduction thereby stabilizing this new mode of
development.

While the Fordist state's welfare policies were enacted at the local and
subnational level (i.e., provinces, wards etc.) its standards and policies were
normally developed and enforced at the national level. The effect, in many
instances, was to de-politicize social reproduction and to subordinate these
processes to those of capitalist accumulation. The politicization of unemployment in Canada during the 1920s and 1930s serves as an example. By
removing jurisdiction from local authorities the Canadian government
ensured that potential remedies for unemployment would stay at the federal
level. In doing so, unemployment was given formal acknowledgement and the
means for addressing employment generation were transferred to the federal
government. In this way unemployment was figuratively removed from the
streets and placed in the halls of government. Furthermore, both capitalist
accumulation and social reproduction were de-politicized as they were sub-
jected to technocratic governance. As Keynes's biographer, Robert Skidelsky
concludes, '[t]he task he (Keynes) set out to do was to reconstruct the capitalist social order on the basis of improved technical management'.[36] This
included what would later be referred to as the Keynesian levers: monetary
(e.g., interest rates), fiscal (e.g., tax policy) and other active government
policies (e.g., active labour markets).

In this sense, Keynesian economics is a scientific attempt to socialize risk
associated with the paid labour market. It endeavours to remove a fear of the
future and restore confidence in the capitalist system thereby returning it to
the acceptable belief that results and consequences must match expectations.
Employment strategies within Keynesian economics, therefore, stem from
demand stimulus with the introduction of the state (and the state economy)
as a stabilizing and enhancing force for the predominant market economy. In
this way the future is fixed in the present.

Stabilization and enhancement are made possible due to the role of the
nation-state as planner, employer, arbiter between social classes, and instrument (using government fiscal and monetary policy) to help temper capitalist
cycles. Intervention is no longer a question of political convenience, but a
technical necessity. This is exemplified by the enactment of unemployment
insurance in Canada. As John Taylor argues,

> [f]or the unemployed, financial responsibility was divided among the
> federal government, employers, and a large portion of the work force, in
> the form of an insurance plan that was class neutral. It could not become
> a focus for class politics, since theoretically almost everyone was both a
> contributor and a potential beneficiary. It removed the question of relief
> from the local level, where it had created the most political difficulties.
> And with some resistance from the provinces at the outset, confined
> management of the entire program to the federal government.[37]

As the socialization of risk clearly indicates, aspects of social reproduction were undertaken by the emergent Fordist state, in line with Keynesian principles, while other aspects remained privatized in the gendered constitution of social reproduction within the household. Squeezed out by the institutionalization of Keynesian economics within the Fordist nation-state was the social economy. Juan Carpi argues,

> [n]ot only were the reasons for its (the social economy's) very existence (unemployment, insecurity, poverty, monopoly prices, etc.) seen to have become overcome to a great extent, but *exit* and *voice*, especially the latter, turned out to be effective and sufficient ways for workers to have influence on the social and economic process.[38]

The remaining social economy actors soon began replicating the dominant organizational attributes within the Employment paradigm, including increased scale, centralization, increased hierarchical organizational form, technocratic management, and service rationalization.[39]

Social reproduction: the post-Employment era

It is with the crisis of the Employment paradigm and the transition to a yet-to-be-constituted Work paradigm that the social economy comes to the foreground as both a hegemonic and grassroots strategy. Adherents of disciplinary neo-liberalism, with their political programme of global structural reforms, have called for a return to the predominance of the 'market' mechanism. Built into this is the neo-classical assumption that the market tends toward equilibrium, hence staving off crises.

Yet as Bakker points out this transformation includes a 'strategic silence', which assumes that women will take up the slack when the nation-state withdraws from its role in social reproduction.[40] They have not. They cannot. The result has been a global crisis of social reproduction. There is also an increasing recognition, even by adherents of disciplinary neo-liberalism, of the limits of the market.[41]

It is in this context that the social economy has been rediscovered. For policymakers and supporters of current global structural reforms the social economy is viewed as a means to ameliorate the crises by facilitating a move towards a fully marketized global political economy. In other words, the social economy is more often viewed as a subordinated tributary whose function is to enhance the commodification of individuals in order to reintegrate them as workers in the global capitalist economy. This, as discussed above, is directly traceable to historical developments and the hegemonic positioning of neo-classical theorizations. The concentration on accumulation has made processes of social reproduction unintelligible to mainstream understandings of economy.[42]

Nevertheless, as indicated in the previous chapter, the crisis of the

Employment paradigm has situated us in the interregnum of a post-Employment era. It is due to this crisis that the social economy and its role are foregrounded within a much broader definition of social reproduction. The limits to disciplinary neo-liberalism and the turbulence of unregulated economic globalization are increasingly unmistakable. This is evidenced by the increasing number of agencies – ranging from employment clubs to after-school childcare clubs to international NGOs – that function as facilitating organizations for the reproduction of societal aims.

However, the crisis of social reproduction within the context of the post-Employment era points to more than just the social reproduction of labour as a commodity. It also points to issues such as biospheric reproduction and alternative democratic governance and structures. In terms of the former, social economy enterprises have capitalized on new market niches such as ecological goods.[43] Social entrepreneurs interested in ecological sustainability have pointed to new business practices as well as products that incorporate social reproduction.[44] By doing so, such enterprises and entrepreneurs again challenge the neo-classical distinction between production, accumulation and reproduction. In terms of the latter, social economy enterprises speak to the emergence of an alternative movement, which not only seeks these goods but also seeks alternative democratic economic organizations to provide them.

This signifies the close connection between the social economy and sub-political networks. This close association is a strategic instrument in the augmentation of *being-in-the-world-with-others*. It points to the emancipatory potential of individualization as the social economy incorporates processes of de-alienation, social change and the production of new reflexive lifestyles. In this sense the social economy becomes an emergent global social force as the problems and challenges of reflexive modernization make its organizational forms the privileged instruments of an emergent paradigm of Work.

Its ability to accommodate new subpolitical networks while controlling its own productive processes enables the social economy to insert new values into economy. This is evident in its ability to seamlessly connect the individual with the global through the fabric of the social. This is evidenced at its most basic level in the household.

Bringing it all together at home

The household is critical to both Keynesian and neo-classical understandings of economy as a basic unit of consumption. For example, Keynesian economics explains household demand by examining changes in money income, while also considering the role of the state in protecting the household from market volatility. Neo-classical economics, on the other hand, explains household demand by examining substitution effects that result from relative price changes. Within both theorizations, the household is both subordinate to and interactive with the market economy.

However, both approaches to the household are limited and unsophisticated. This becomes increasingly apparent when the household is viewed as part of the social economy, a relationship that many scholars have already articulated.[45] This relationship is convincing as the household fits within the list of identificatory characteristics for the social economy developed in the introductory chapter. It is formal, private, non-profit distributing, self-governing and voluntary. As such, it is not only a site of consumption, but also a site of provisioning, contradiction and contestation. In short, it is an economy.

By viewing the household solely as a site of consumption, I argue that neither Keynesian nor neo-classical economics are able to fully appreciate the household as a site of economic activity. The household is also a site for the production of labour. Pat Armstrong and Hugh Armstrong identify four types of work that ensure this production of future commodity-labour: housework, child care, tension management and sexual relationships.[46] However, in order for the household to produce the future commodity of labour-power it must be outside the boundaries of capitalism. The inability of Keynesian and neo-classical economics to theorize this inherently limits them from fully considering the possibilities required for a transition to a Work paradigm.

Household: Keynesian and neo-classical economics

Within mainstream economic perspectives the household is viewed as an undifferentiated rational actor – the 'black-box'. Keynesians, for example, assume that the household is a unitary actor, which acts on mutually agreeable trade-offs. Gary S. Becker extends the neo-classical rational actor approach to the household arguing that these principles explain household outcomes. He states,

> [I]ncreasing returns from specialized human capital is a powerful force creating a division of labor in the allocation of time and investment in human capital between married men and married women. . . . Hence, married women have lower hourly earnings than married men with the same market human capital, and they economize on the effort expended on market work by seeking less demanding jobs.[47]

Within both theorizations there is no room within this understanding for contradiction, contestation or provisioning. The importance of this mistheorization, for our discussion, is that these theorizations base their economic models on a non-existent household.

A closer examination of households reveals a more complex and divergent site. Households base their decisions on a number of factors, including market rationalities, power relations, societal expectations, gender roles, class, ethnicity, culture, habit, provisioning, altruism, dignity and imprecise information. Work strategies, therefore, are selected based on diverse and often contradictory motivations that go beyond the simple profit-maximizing behaviours of *homo economicus*.

Implicit in these mainstream theorizations is a theory of identity and subjectivity. Both Keynesian and neo-classical economics view members of a family as either independent autonomous individuals (i.e., adult males and females) or as passive non-persons (i.e., adult females and children) who can be subsumed by someone else's preferences (i.e., children) or by existing constraints.

Julie Nelson deviates from this assumption by asking how we would identify the family if we viewed family members as both individuals and as being embedded in relationships.[48] In pondering this question we engage in a more relational understanding of family that conforms to a consciousness of *being-in-the-world-with-others*. This consciousness insists that individuals engage in a continuum of separation and connection. Independence, for example, alters over time throughout the many changes that take place in a family. Children are restricted in their ability to exercise their individuality when young, but gain greater degrees of independence as situations permit. The same is true of adult family members as they age, with elderly family members often becoming increasingly dependent upon their children.

This introduces us to two dialectical concepts that are overlooked in mainstream economic approaches: economic responsibility and economic dependence.[49] Encapsulated by the notion of provisioning, these concepts introduce another rationality to economic decision-making that goes well beyond those of profit-maximization and utility-based theorizations. For example, many of the decisions made by caretakers are not done for personal gain, but out of a sense of responsibility (to children, for example) and as a result of dependence (by the elderly, for example). Provisioning rather than production or consumption forms the starting point of economic analysis. Power defines social provisioning as the process by which society organizes itself to produce and reproduce material life.[50]

Keynesian and neo-classical economics attempt to provide market or state solutions to social crises. Yet the household is constitutive of and reliant upon the social economy – thereby requiring a social solution. By assuming that wealth is only generated in the market economy, social provision is considered a cost rather than being viewed as productive. This becomes especially critical to young families and single parents who may not live close to family relations. The lack of adequate childcare provision results in the withdrawal of many from the market sector, thereby subjecting families to undue poverty and disallowing their contributions and innovative capacities to the wider society.

These examples highlight some of the complexities associated with the household and household work strategies. This is not to say that the market economy is premised on rational individualism and the household is premised on altruism. It is instead an attempt to shine light on the complexities of action and inaction in economy.

Household: social economy

Amartya Sen has argued that the household is an arena of 'cooperative-conflict'.[51] On the one hand, partners have an interest in cooperating to increase their quality of life above what it would be in the absence of the other partner. On the other hand, conflict of interest arises over how the consumption gains from cooperation are to be distributed, and over the way work is allocated. The household, then, is more aptly thought of as a site of economy.

Understanding that the household has divergent and often contradictory rationalities opens up the possibility that the economy can be based on other logics, hence broadening the range of possible working strategies. The importance of the household is not questioned in either Keynesian or neo-classical economics. What is questioned is the form households take and the implication this has for theorizing the relation between the household and the larger society and economy.

Keynes argued that if the government is to be effective it should not concern itself with 'those activities which private individuals are already fulfilling', but attend to 'those functions which fall outside the private sphere of the individual, to those decisions that are made by no one if the state does not make them'.[52] Implicit in the Keynesian model is the conceptualization that the household consists of a single bread-winner in the public sphere and a domestic labourer in the private sphere. This is the gendered arrangement, described in Chapter 1, that formed the basis of the Employment paradigm. It was assumed that caregivers were married women who were dependent on their husbands and their waged-labour. As such, women's 'work' remained non-paid while men's 'employment' received remuneration in the form of money and social status. This, to some degree, explains why Beveridge and other framers of Keynesian Fordist states saw no difficulty in tying benefits to employment rather than to caring responsibilities.

In part, due to the current restructuring and disciplinary neo-liberal ideology that is underpinning it, women are increasingly entering the cash labour market while the domestic labour requirements remain.[53] In some instances the result is an incomplete reversal of gender roles, as women are employable and men become unemployed.[54] In others, it has resulted in the globalization of reproductive services with women from the South and former Eastern bloc coming to work in the OECD nations as caretakers (i.e., nannies) for privileged OECD families and their children.[55] The results of these transformations have been discussed as the double or triple burden and increasingly as the crisis of reproduction, as the male-breadwinner/female-carer model is terminated. The large number of lone parent families; the high level of male unemployment; the increased dependence of households on female earnings from employment; and the demands of women to find other ways, including waged-labour, to gain greater meaning, independence and personal sustainability have only exacerbated it.

The labour required to sustain the household therefore is a significant issue. Men, women and children are increasingly reliant on wage-labour and the inability of the institutional order to address the gap this creates within the household has placed households under significant strain. Strategies put forward thus far to address these realities are at best unrealistic and marginal. For example, the employment of Southern women as nannies is not a solution to the demands placed upon the household. It is a limited response in terms of economic feasibility and, more importantly, calls into question issues of human rights, equity, justice and quality of life for all stakeholders in this relation. Another response, daycare strategies, as advocated by many Third Way governments (i.e., Britain, Canada) has been too piecemeal and ill-considered to have a real and lasting effect on families. Again, we are left with either a market solution or a state solution to social crises. Yet the household is constitutive of and reliant upon the social economy – thereby requiring a social solution.

In summary, the black-box view of the household has obscured the complex and contradictory nature of this institution. This is especially critical in this post-Employment era with its global restructuring of economy and work. Processes outside the pricing mechanism, such as those that take place in the household, have not been fully explored due to their unconsidered nature. As such, their social impact has never been fully integrated into the framework of economic understandings.

Afterword

Both neo-classical and Keynesian economics posit a single socio-economic development strategy that is to be universally applied. In other words, the metanarrative (economy) and the actor (market) are already known; the paramount concern is the fulfillment of the narrative. Therefore the economy retains a temporal element, as enactment rather than constitution becomes the focus.

Neo-classical economics theorizes the economy as a transcendental phenomenon that requires it to be unlocked outside time. The market economy is ever-present in this conception. Keynesian economics does not dispute the future of an ever-present market economy, but assumes a need to intervene on its behalf to get to that future. Economy, prescribed in these terms, delimits labour solely to paid work in the market economy and, to a lesser extent, the state economy. Work done, whether paid or non-paid, within the social economy is not considered. As such, Keynesian and neo-classical economics can only postulate a one-size-fits-all national and global strategy of employment generation in the market economy. Implementation of their requisite employment generation strategies is viewed as the application of objective rationality, of nothing short of truth. Impediments to the implementation become its opposite – irrational and false. This irrationality is then associated with political manoeuvring in avoidance of economic realities with the standardized question of 'How can we afford to pay for this?'[56] In other words, the implicit assumption that enables the asking of this question is the presumed productive and nonproductive dichotomy. The market economy in this equation is productive; the remainder are nonproductive.

However, the dualistic episteme of neo-classical and Keynesian economics is incapable of explaining the growth and significance of the social economy. Specifically, how is it possible to explain the production of tangible goods and services as well as intangibles within the social economy? How is it possible to account for the increased labour-power manifestations within the social economy? Additionally, how is it possible to arbitrarily delimit labour solely as employment when individuals engage their labour-power throughout workscapes? How, if individuals are engaged in workscapes is it possible to delimit economy to production and consumption and not reproduction? The unpacking of economy reveals these as critical issues to the workings of and consequently an understanding of economy.

The answer to these questions is to be found by examining the ontological basis of economics. The unpacking of economy reveals both neo-classical and Keynesian economics as premising their understandings of economy on an essentialized ontology. In short, the economy is known; it has fundamental laws and functions. In this conceptualization knower–known relations are formed whereby certain subject positions, such as CEOs and economists, are viewed as bearers of knowledge and therefore constituting legitimate claims. The others, in contrast, are relegated to the status of the uninformed and consequently marginalized in the process and outcome. It is the essentialized ontology that enables universal strategies to be formulated, planned and implemented at the centre behind closed doors with the input of 'relevant' experts and policy-makers. The essentialized ontology also defines the others as they are marginalized and/or provided with minimal consultation in the process of economic policy formulation, which reinforces economy as an objective rather than social manifestation.

Yet as knowledge, innovation and social relations increasingly underpin reflexive development in the post-Employment era, the interrelations between these others, such as those in the social economy, as well as their relationships with the state and market economies requires a different ontology of economy.

The discussion therefore must necessarily shift to ontology, as an add-and-stir approach to the emergence of the social economy will fail to absorb the full potential of the transition it represents from employment to work. The emergence of the social economy shows that current theorizations of economy describe only a partial fragment of it. Therefore, the assumption of a known economy or an essentialized economy with a set of given properties is precluded. Instead, an unessential ontology is required to form a metaphoric bridge within this interregnum from the post-Employment era to the yet-to-be-realized paradigm of Work.

As this chapter has demonstrated, economy is always *in-relation-with*. It is co-constituted by state, market and social. Chapter 4 therefore asks, 'What constitutes the identity of economy?' In asking this, a general framework emerges that then allows for the formation of the shorthand referred to in discourse as economy. What also emerges in this questioning is the possibility of an alternative ontology that conforms more readily to the ideas developed in this chapter that economy is constitutive of state, market and social. It is with the development of an unessential ontology of economy that new alternative strategies emerge based on process rather than product, and spaces are opened for a transition to the Work paradigm. This is the aim of the next chapter.

4 Unessential economy

The symbolic – i.e., overdetermined – character of social relations . . . implies that they lack any immanent law . . . Society and social agents lack any essence, and their regularities merely consist of the relative and precarious forms of fixation which accompany the establishment of a certain order.

Laclau and Mouffe[1]

The aim of this chapter is to assess the ontological basis of economic theory within the tension of two paradigms: the Employment paradigm as described in Chapter 1 and the emergence of the Work paradigm as described in Chapter 2. Theory is never objective. It is as Robert Cox aptly put it, 'always for someone and for some purpose'.[2] Within the Employment paradigm, economy was shaped by three ontological categories: rationalism, dualism and metanarrative. Each of these ontological stances was integral to the epistemological development of an essentialized economy that deterritorialized *work* and reterritorialized it as *employment* in order to secure capitalist hegemony.[3] In other words, employment is a produced reality associated with the broader history of capitalist development. Similarly the gendered division of labour that produced the male-breadwinner and female-carer model was not an objective outcome but a produced one associated with the Employment paradigm.

Within this ontology, *work*, understood as *employment*, was a function entirely dependent upon and subordinate to an essentialized economy – the market economy, a (global) capitalist economy that delimits employment generation to the level of 'problem solving'.[4]

However, the emergence of the social economy within the post-Employment era challenges and displaces the assertion of an essentialized economy that has fixed social meanings and positions. First, the social economy disputes the privilege garnered towards the market economy as the single legitimate site of production. Second, it challenges the privileged position of the market economy as the sole originator of employment. Third, the utilization of both paid work and non-paid work in the production of the social economy challenges the primacy of employment as triggering the paradigm shift from Employment to Work.

Economy, therefore, is increasingly exposed as an empty signifier. It does not contain an essence and instead its definition is subject to alteration. It is not immutable but instead predicated on an ontology that produces immutability as an effect. The question that arises therefore is the following: if, as argued here, the ontological basis of economy within the Employment paradigm is constituted by a specific ontology, what is the ontological basis for the Work paradigm?

In response to this question, what is revealed is that ontology shifts as per the required paradigm. It shifts from an essentialized economy marked by rationalism, dualism and metanarrative to an unessential economy increasingly demarcated by reflexivity, *différance* and heterotopia. In other words, the Work paradigm posits that economy has no essence and, as such, is not essential. In doing so, the Work paradigm broadens the parameters of discussion from one demarcated by the supposed hegemony of the market economy to one in which the possibility of juxtaposed economies exists. Within such a forum, the market economy is toppled from its privileged position and located alongside the social economy (and state economy) as simply another form of economy.

Since economy is no longer the end result of a constitutive identity, it can no longer be understood without understanding the relations *between* economies. On a deeper level, the lack of a singular economic logic allows developmental strategy to shift from mere problem-solving to the conceptualization of new social imaginaries.

It is with these theoretical ruptures that it is possible to put forward the beginnings of an alternative conceptual framework for theorizing economy within the Work paradigm. Implicit in this discussion is the position that it is not possible to view the logics within this new framework as separate. Indeed, in the course of this chapter, it uncovers the overlapping nature of this discussion not only in terms of an understanding of the ontological underpinnings within each paradigm, but also across them.

From rationalism to reflexivity

The transition from the Employment paradigm to the Work paradigm is characterized by risk. Contradictions within and between the regime of accumulation and the mode of *régulation* are constitutive of a crisis of reproduction as economic, social, political and ecological risks remain beyond the control and protection of the existing institutional order. As discussed in Chapter 2, this inability to control risk signifies both catastrophe and possibility. Modernism, with its assumption of a utopian society based on rationalism, cries catastrophe; postmodernism, with its vision of a dystopic utopia, claims possibility. Thrust in between these two ontological camps is a single refuge: an alternative rationality based on the broader conceptualization of reflexivity.

The possibilities and the means for establishing a new mode of development are intimately related to the subsuming of rationalism by reflexivity. The withdrawal of the Employment paradigm and the onset of risks in the post-Employment era have forced individuals to take their lives into their own hands.[5] The processes they use are composed of both individualization and assemblage – individualization to assess the reality of individual needs and desires, and assemblage to coalesce the needs and have them met. We can see the implications of these processes in the extension and intensification of the social economy.

However, the ontological hub of the social economy is a consciousness of *being-in-the-world-with-others*. As such, reflexivity within the Work paradigm is not simply an example of the splintering of rationality to various subjects (as in nested games or new institutional economics). Rather, it is centred on non-knowing. It transcends the fixed notion of a single rationality to include the possibility of multiple rationalities, such as local, indigenous, and experiential knowledge, as well as affect and emotion.[6] The coalescing of claims within the social economy constitutes new 'we' orientations that collide with other discourses and practices. Each orientation presumes its own authority over identifying the bearers of knowledge, and assessing the action that should be taken to address risks in the global political economy.

Locating the ontology of an essentialized economy

While reflexivity grows as a critical force in the post-Employment era, rationalism remains the ontological foundation of economic orthodoxy. This doctrine is grounded on the assumption that the subject – be it the individual, social classes, states, or society in general – has a consistent set of objectives and preferences and acts instrumentally to achieve those ends. In other words, the subject has reason (for reason signifies method and system); it denotes science, technology and, as such, serves as a principle or foundation of order and control.[7] As Michel Foucault emphasizes, reason has given rise to ever-greater levels of discipline and surveillance over the individual to the point where discipline has become internally driven.[8]

The argument for rationalism is grounded on the Cartesian thesis that human beings are made up of two distinct substances: one thinking, and the other corporeal. As Descartes asserted,

> I became aware that, while I decided thus to think that everything was false, it followed necessarily that I who thought thus must be something: and observing that this truth: *I think therefore I am*, was so certain and so evident that all the most extravagant suppositions of the skeptics were not capable of shaking it, I judged that I could accept it without scruple. ... I thereby concluded that I was a substance, of which the whole essence or nature consists in thinking, and which, in order to exist, needs no place and depends on no material thing; so that this 'I', that

is to say, the mind, by which I am what I am, is entirely distinct from the body, and even that it is easier to know than the body. [original emphasis][9]

In this view, economic thought is independent of the body and discretely located within a system of dualities that includes mind/body, rational/irrational. By following this system of dualistic mapping to its logical conclusions, we can search for a 'method' that will gain us access to the universal truths behind the economy and the established grand narratives of the Employment paradigm.

These truths are independent of the researcher and are therefore objective. Yet they also produce the researcher as the rightful bearer of knowledge. In terms of methodology, the claim of objectivity allows for a single approach to access the truth, which is fitting, as the sciences taken together were nothing less than the very unity of human reason itself. The discovery of these economic truths by experts establishes the basis of the Employment paradigm's metanarratives of progress, emancipation and power.[10]

Max Weber argued that the development of the market economy and the nation-state marked the institutionalization of rationalism and the scientific method.[11] Capitalism required technocratic administrative structures to impose predictability and stability on the chaotic (market) economy. Central to the establishment of this technocratic structure was the development of statistical and mathematical models. The collection of data by technocratic administrative structures not only provided information (thereby reducing uncertainty and enhancing predictability), but also acted, in itself, as part of the technology of power in the modern nation-state.[12]

Weber's discussion of Protestantism exemplifies this trajectory with its emphasis on the solidification of privatization, individualization and a concern for marketplace salvation. Enhancement and intensification of the (market) economy required that both social relations and technical production be rendered calculative, impersonal and predictive.

Keynesian economics and the rational economy

The Keynesian revolution popularized the idea that technocratic control and management of both the national and international economy were feasible (i.e., Bretton Woods system). Keynes' invention of macroeconomics led directly to the expansion of national economic statistics and economic modeling and was influential in the development of econometrics.[13] This demand for commensurability and calculability within Keynesian economics runs counter to the position of reflexivity, which has theoretical and institutional ramifications for conceptualizing the social economy.[14]

In its application Keynesian economics manifested as hydraulic Keynesianism, also known as the Neo-classical Synthesis, as it conceptualized the economy in Newtonian fashion as a universal machine. This is an apt metaphor as it lends itself to rational inquiry and intervention on the part of the bearers of knowledge.

Economist Victoria Chick has argued that this is a misunderstanding of Keynes' methodology.[15] Instead, she posits that his methodology is more readily analogous to a film composed of stills. As indicated in Figure 4.1, each still systematically relates to what has gone before and after.

While Chick's distinction is important to note, due to its epistemological implications, it does not challenge the contention that rationalism is central within Keynesian economics. Conceptualizing the nation-state, with its national economy, as a passive feminine object of inquiry Keynesian economics inclusive of hydraulic Keynesianism, foregrounds the role played by omniscient technocrats.[16] Technocratic administration implies an economy that is knowable, predictable and, as a consequence, highly stable. However, the object of technocratic analysis, the nation and the national economy, is viewed as a distinct entity that is naturally and inherently unstable. What is

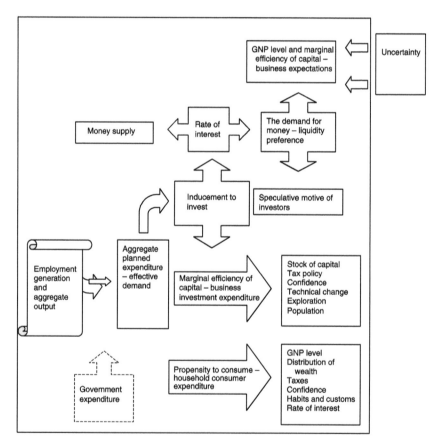

Figure 4.1 Basis for employment generation in Keynesian economics.

Adapted from Wright 1962, 68 and Snowdon *et al.* 1994, p. 67

critical, therefore, is that intervention is no longer a question of political convenience, but a technical necessity since modern economies are thought to produce an aggregate real demand below full output. It is only with the technocrats' rational intervention *vis-à-vis* the Keynesian levers that order and social cohesion may be fashioned.

Neo-classical economics and the rational economy

Neo-classical economics also retains the nation-state and the national economy as an economic unit of analysis. However, it views the market economy as the sole vehicle to ameliorate economic instability and restore order and social cohesion. As described in Chapter 3, according to neo-classical economics, it is only when individuals act selfishly, thus maximizing their individual self-interest, and with supply equalling demand in all markets, that society will have more wealth available to it.

The neo-classical assumption that no individuals, neither sellers nor buyers, can alter the price of commodities enables the market economy to be viewed as not only the sole generator of value, but also as the most efficient institution for the maximization of welfare. Implicit in this understanding is the objectivity and hence rationality of the market.[17]

Methodologically these assumptions combine to make the economy appear knowable and accessible through deductive reasoning, which is centred on the metaphor of 'rational man' – also known as *homo economicus*. Void of contingent obligations and responsibilities, *homo economicus* is motivated solely by self-interest and guided on the basis of contractual social relations. In other words it is assumed that as rational actors, individuals, regardless of geographical location, race, ethnicity, class, gender, etc., maintain a neo-classical model of the economy in their heads when making decisions. In this way, individuals are thought to conform to the metanarrative of rationality or, more specifically, to market economy rationality.

This theorization of economy is based on the assumption that humans naturally approach economic opportunities as sets of rational choices. This emphasis on choice relates to the Cartesian dichotomy between embodiment and rationality. But what determines this detached rationality natural to all humans? According to neo-classical economics, this question is not worth asking. Rationality is an essentialized component of human nature and thus assumed.[18] Mathematically modeled as preference curves, the choices or preferences of *homo economicus* are used within neo-classical economics to help explain almost all economic phenomena. This includes the demand and supply of all commodities and resources in the economy.

By way of the social economy: Keynesian and neo-classical economics

Within both the dominant discourses of neo-classical economics and Keynesian economics, what underpins the objective method that has granted proponents access to their universal economic truths is the mapping of rationalism to the Cartesian dualism of mind/body. Economic knowledge is circumscribed; knowledge bearers are designated. As such the market economy, replete with rational form and function, is the sole site of economy.

But within the post-Employment era, the claims of different groups coalescing into the social economy are increasingly colliding with the essentialized discourses and practices of economy. To this end, in claiming their own authority over knowledge and the direction of the global political economy, the social economy is presenting a formidable challenge to dualistic ontology. For example, by conforming explicitly to a consciousness of *being-in-the-world-with-others*, household production can only be characterized by reflexive rather than rationalist engagement. This post-rationalist sentiment challenges rationalist accounts of domestic labour as failing to address motivations such as care and self-fulfillment. Rationalism, as sole cause and explanation, is simply incapable of bearing the weight associated with the provisioning motivations and values that emanate from the social economy. Rationalism is not discounted in this articulation but is situated as one factor amongst others in the process of production.

From dualism to *différance*

The ontological hub of the social economy is a consciousness of *being-in-the-world-with-others*. This presents an alternative to the dualistic ontology of the Employment paradigm. As described in Chapter 2, this consciousness forms the basis of meaning within the post-Employment era as increasing globalization necessitates not only the crossing and erasure of borders, but also the constancy of Otherness. In other words, as risks increasingly manifest as global, the post-Employment era is increasingly marked by its inability to constrain *différance*.

Within economic discourses of the Employment paradigm, meanings arise from dualisms and categorizations. This is not a neutral logic used to divide two equal but opposing terms; the relation is one of hierarchy, non-reversibility and non-reciprocity. Singularity of meaning relies on the self-presence of meaning, which can only be constructed within the binary pairing of presence and absence.

Derrida refers to this as *logocentrism*, which occurs when a term, truth or logic is conceived as existing in itself as a foundation.[19] *Logocentrism*, then, is bound up with the notion of presence and seeks foundations/origins in a series of 'present' poles in dualities. Each of the 'privileged' concepts involves a notion of presence and is treated as a centring and grounding force. As Derrida states, 'one of the two terms governs the other (axiologically, logically, etc.) or has the upper hand'.[20] While the first term assumes the priority, the second becomes a complication, a negation or a disruption of the first. Examples of *logocentrism* include the following pairings: rational/irrational, objective/subjective, male/female, productive/unproductive, private/public, mind/body, nature/culture and market economy/social economy. Within this binary structure the privileged term defines its 'Other' and gains positive value and self-presence as a result. The 'Other', or marginalized term, such as the social economy, is then established as lacking self-presence or positive qualities of its own.

Dualism and economy

Dualistic episteme is expressed according to three rules. The first is the principle of identity (if anything is A, it is A). This principle underlines mainstream economic theories that view economy solely as a (global) capitalist economy. For example, the market economy exists as a monolith; the social economy is subsumed as Other – insufficient or absent. According to Gibson-Graham, this is an example of *capitalocentrism* as 'other forms of economy are often understood primarily with reference to capitalism'.[21]

The second rule of dualistic episteme is the principle of contradiction (nothing can be both A and Not-A). In other words, the economy cannot be both social and market. This conforms to the third rule of the excluded middle (anything and everything must be *either* A *or* Not-A). It is in this way that economic discourse within the Employment paradigm subordinates one term (social economy), and enables the hegemony of another (market economy). Each pairing, along with their hierarchical significances, then claims to describe the real world and constitute truth.

This process is not benign. These hierarchical categorizations reflect the power of the dominant community to enmesh and even render invisible the subordinated half of each duality. According to Foucault, such powers form the process of *normalization* – a form of both identity construction and knowledge construction, the basis of transcendental truths.[22] He states, '[t]he perpetual penalty that traverses all points and supervises every instant in the disciplinary institutions compares, differentiates, homogenizes, excludes. In short, it *normalizes*' [original emphasis].[23] Capital, therefore produces while labour consumes. The result of this understanding of economy is a limitation of strategies, as other possible actors and spaces are left outside theorization and hence policymaking priorities.

Différance *and economy*

As Derrida correctly points out, words and concepts are complicated and in a differential relation as marked by *différance*.[24] The term *différance* is more applicable than the term 'difference' since the French verb *différer* means both 'to differ' and 'to defer'. With the displacement of a single letter, Derrida is able to release a word to new meanings without obscuring the trace of the other meanings in its past. This is similar to Ferdinand de Saussure's notions that language is based on a system of differences rather than a collection of meaningful terms that pre-exist it.[25] For our purposes, the significance of this displacement lies in the realization that meaning (i.e., truth) relies on *différance*.

Différance challenges dualistic epistemology by using displacement to invert the hierarchy between presence and absence. Put simply, in order for something to be present, it must have the quality that supposedly belongs to its opposite – absence. Thus, instead of defining absence in terms of presence, as *its* negative, we can treat presence as the effect of a generalized absence, or of *différance*. For example, the word 'economy' is always inhabited by the traces of words and conceptualizations that have not been spoken. These may include production, labour, capital, money, public and so on. Economy works as a signifier only because of those traces.

As Scott Lash points out, *différance* is primordial; there is no understanding of self without the Other.[26] This is not the replication of binaries. Thinking in terms of *différance* moves us deeper into our understandings of variation; it is a process towards positionality, which opens concepts to increasing points of disturbance. Yet we cannot view *différance* without reflexivity; the signifier in this ontological frame only becomes complete in its ambiguity. That is, the signifier cannot have a direct relation to the signified. The signifier is larger than the definition provided by the discourse used to describe it. Instead the signifier moves to another, endlessly shifting and sliding.

It is this ambiguity, this surface of uncertainty, that is effaced in the conceptualization of economy in both neo-classical and Keynesian economics. Language, whether written or oral, is a representation and cannot be the object it wishes to describe. The ambiguity of economy and its overdetermination within both neo-classical and Keynesian economics are effaced with some success, but the containment of meaning within both conceptualizations is only temporary. The Employment paradigm is precisely this moment in time; the crisis of its termination represents the movement away.

Resolving the contradictions within the mode of *régulation* and the regime of accumulation therefore necessitates an appropriate economic epistemology that conforms to the post-Employment era. This does not place us in a position of political paralysis. In fact, it opens the parameters of the possible since what becomes clear is that utterance, of any form, is positioning. This is the critical tension identified in Derrida's usage of *différance* – to differ and to defer. It renders positionality and politics visible, but also, more importantly, the reflexivity that will characterize the Work paradigm.

Economy therefore is neither as complete nor as predetermined as Keynesian and neo-classical economics would have us believe. Instead, it is contingent and deeply political in its determinations. If that is the case, then what would a non-dualistic economic epistemology entail? What is a discourse about economy premised on within the tension identified in *différance*? Such questions suggest that analysis will always fall short of finding the ultimate causes of events. 'Truth' is elusive; it requires the constancy of inquiry. Such questions also suggest the necessity of a relational approach to conceptualizing economy so that we can recognize important elements of interconnectivity that go into the construction of economy and the re-imagination of the either/or constructions of binary thinking.

It is in this ambiguity that reflexivity comes into play. The space between self and Other, of *différance* then, is the space of reflexivity. It is the space into which meaning has to be reaffirmed, as there is no transcendental truth, no anchoring term. Instead what is left is an irreducible ontology that views economies as being 'constituted by billions of happy or unhappy encounters . . . consisting of multitudinous paths which intersect'.[27] This is what I mean when I say that *différance* is the separate representation of self/other. The market economy/social economy duality is exploded and in its place is the relational understanding of economy.

Implicating social economy **différance**

A representational inquiry might therefore ask the question: how important is the social economy to the constitution of the market economy? A relational understanding would posit this inquiry in a different manner: how is it possible to theorize the market and social economies? This may appear to be a subtle modification, but it is significant nonetheless. In the first example, the anchoring term is the market economy – the subject of inquiry. The subordination of the social economy to the market economy precludes the possibility of reversing or transgressing the relation. While each is assumed to be autonomous of the other, this dualistic privileging thwarts the possibility of fully elaborating the social economy as an economy. Its functioning is relegated to that of a market economy assistant.

Conversely, the second question allows both terms to float in relation to one another. With the privileging sentiment removed, each gains space from the other while keeping their interdependence intact. In relation to the market economy, the social economy is now independent and unencumbered. As distinct economies, production and labour processes can now be explored with the understanding that function, crisis and innovation may emerge from one or both and impact the other.

This negates the centrifugal view that agency emanates from the market economy outwards and makes it possible to conceptualize work generation in and through these economies of *différance*. This does not imply that inter-relatedness will lead to happiness, understanding or respect for the 'Other', simply that inequalities can only be addressed when they have been adequately recognized – when power has been mapped.

This understanding of *différance* complicates the discussion of the Employment and Work paradigms. As Foucault emphasized, by proceeding with dualistic thinking we face the danger of being caught in a truth regime.[28] However, deferral, a movement away from duality, is not as easy as it seems. There is neither beginning nor end and, in this sense, no neutral 'space' to make a deferral. We are constantly stuck in the middle navigating between two meanings. Indeed, we cannot step out of one truth regime without stepping into another. But this does not mean that one cannot proceed – a common criticism of the deconstructive method. We may have to switch from one division to another to another in a reflexive mediation, but in this way economic truths remain juxtaposed rather than transcendental. *Différance* forces us to work harder, to situate ourselves within the terrain of the unknown. In other words, *différance* locates us ontologically within heterotopia.

From metanarratives to heterotopia

> The essential political problem for the intellectual is . . . the political, economic, institutional régime of the production of truth. It's not a matter of emancipating truth from every system of power (which would be a chimera, for truth is already power) but of detaching the power of truth from the forms of hegemony, social, economic and cultural, within which it operates at the present time. The political question . . . is truth itself.
>
> Michel Foucault[29]

Metanarratives are central to the economic epistemology of the Employment paradigm since their function is to assemble the assumed hegemony of the market economy. Constructing the market economy as a self-regulating system, economic orthodoxy confers on it the Enlightenment aims of progress, truth and emancipation.[30] The objective nature of the market economy within this conceptualization provides a general, supervening pattern of meaning, explanation and direction upon the heterogeneous ways in which people think and act. In other words, orthodox economic metanarratives privilege the objective background over the social foreground. Economic truths are immutable and universal.

Gramsci considered this construction to be constitutive of hegemony. As a deeply contingent and political process, hegemony refers to the creation of political alliances under the leadership of a particular class who represent their interests as universal interests. In this sense, hegemony is conditional; it cannot be assumed. It is conditional upon the ability of a class to establish and to represent its own structural needs as a unifying force in the form of the 'collective will'.

This is rendered possible through the establishment of metanarratives. For example, the orthodox metanarrative of growth within the Employment paradigm enabled the dominant classes to exercise state power.[31] Gramsci's understanding of society as politically based rather than objectively determined opens the doors to understanding specificity versus deterministic economic laws.

Economy as ~~metanarrative~~[32]

The question therefore arises: What if these metanarratives of economy with their universalizing truths were abandoned? What would emerge? Ontologically, this locates us in the reflexive tension of *différance*, which characterizes the emergent consciousness of *being-in-the-world-with-others*. This is not, as argued elsewhere, the equivalent of relativism nor an apolitical positioning. Instead, from an epistemological sensibility, it is the emergence of alterity – a rejection of the Enlightenment ontology that defines knowledge as constituted by identity: either absolute or relative.

To answer these questions therefore, the idea of a complete and separate identity called the market economy would have to be discarded. Since no identity can be fully constituted, 'economy' is not a valid object with set 'truths'. There is no such thing as economy if, by economy, we mean a fully fixed and defined totality. Rather, the totality of the economy is a site of multiple forms of economy whose relations with each other are only partial and folded into one another. Replacing the complete and separate identity called the market economy would therefore be a hybrid and nomadic economic identity. This strategically expands the range of possible hegemonic centres and counterpoints.

This new nomadic economic identity complicates hegemony further by pluralizing it, revealing multiple hierarchies as constantly negotiated and originating from multiple sites. In this light, it is possible to see contemporary discourses of market hegemony as enacting a disciplinary force upon other forms of economy; it requires their subordination as a condition of market dominance. Placing the social economy in relation with the market economy is therefore a political strategy as inquiry focuses on the construction of meaning and its consequences. The Employment paradigm's horizon recedes to the background and in its place emerges a patchwork of situated knowledges and scattered hegemonies.[33] We see the landscape of the everyday, of multiple orderings, and epistemic communities making discernible the complexity of hegemony as it is enacted at various nodal points within the Work paradigm.[34]

This anti-essentialist strategy reveals that if there is no underlying essence to the market economy, then it must adapt to (be constituted by) other forms of economy just as they must adapt to (be constituted by) it. The result is a multiplication of the possibilities and the opening of a thousand lines of flight for the articulation of alternative development strategies. As Gibson-Graham states, '[a]t the same time, recontextualizing capitalism in a discourse of economic plurality destabilizes its presumptive hegemony'.[35] The landscape has shifted from that of a flat surface leading to the horizon of discovery and market utopia to that of a crumpled surface of economic heterotopia.

Economy as heterotopia

According to Foucault, utopia reduces the everyday diversity of society into a homogenous vision based on a given set of norms and power relationships. In other words, utopias, in a sense, are sites with no real place. Neo-classical and Keynesian economics are utopian sites in that they have a generalized relation, an inverted analogy with the real space of economy. In this manner, they present economy in either a perfected form or turned upside down. In any case, both provide us with fundamentally unreal spaces or, as Foucault asserts, merely abstract representations of the political interests of groups competing for control.

Heterotopias, on the other hand, are

> ... real places – places that do exist and that are formed in the very founding of society – which are something like counter-sites, a kind of effectively enacted utopia in which the real sites, all the other real sites that can be found within the culture, are simultaneously represented, contested, and inverted.[36]

In other words, heterotopic spaces act as spaces for the means of alternative orderings, which come to be seen in contrast to others. This does not mean heterotopias exist a priori but rather, that they are constituted through the very ordering of the things they helped to create.[37] The social economy is emblematic of a heterotopic space as it is a site in which all things displaced, marginal, rejected or ambivalent are represented. These representations become the basis for alternative modes of ordering that have the effect of offering contrasts to the dominant representation of the economic order.

We cannot consider the establishment of economic metanarratives within the Employment paradigm without also reflecting on flux and contingency. As Foucault elaborates,

> [t]he real scandal of Galileo's work lay not so much in his discovery, or rediscovery, that the earth revolved around the sun, but in his constitution of an infinitely open space. In such a space the place of the Middle Ages turned out to be dissolved, as it were; a thing's place was no longer anything but a point in its movement, just as the stability of a thing was only its movement indefinitely slowed down.[38]

Momentary stability paradoxically sets the utopian horizon of economic orthodoxy into the realm of the unreal as it remains within 'site' but perpetually receding. Heterotopia, on the other hand, contextualizes the alternative potentials of the social economy. It locates this marginal space within the paradox of momentary stability since these spaces are not merely sites of disruption but also of ordering. As Keith Hetherington states, 'no matter how much we wish to be free, we will always create conditions of ordering if not order itself'.[39] He goes on to conclude, '[e]qually, in devising conditions of social order we will always create positions of freedom from which to resist that order if not freedom from order'.[40] In other words, the market economy utopia is unattainable precisely because its presence is attributable to the end of resistance.

It is in this sense that Foucault's notion of heterotopia becomes appropriate in this era of *in-différance*. Heterotopia, for Foucault, is not only concerned with acts of resistance and transgression, but also with issues of ordering and control. Nevertheless, alternative challenges to the present ordering of economy and society must view marginal spaces as critical to the development of new imaginaries. Heterotopic spaces are sites established through dissonant spatial relations that challenge the spaces of representation as well as the modes of representation within society.[41] The significance of discussing heterotopias in relation to economic ontology lies in juxtaposition. Heterotopias signify not through resemblance (one thing being used to resemble another), but through similitude (a match or counterpart of another). In other words, they are established between signifier and signified rather than directly to a referent.

Therefore, it is from the standpoint of the market economy that the social economy can be seen as heterotopic. This was expressed in Chapter 3, as each economy was deemed to initiate different circuits predicated on different values. Consequently, heterotopia cannot exist within an episteme of identification – of self/other. It can only exist in relation (*in-différance*), in the relationship between sites as seen from the outside. This relational articulation, along with the ambiguity associated with heterotopia, means that heterotopic spaces can be both marginal and central – marginal in the sense of being 'alternative' to mainstream practices, and central in the sense that they become central to those who inhabit them. However, it should be noted that heterotopias are not solely about resistance and the establishment of alternative strategies. They are also about ordering identities within conditions of uncertainty. As Foucault recognized, we cannot separate freedom from order nor vice-versa. Rather, the two categories, like all categories, are folded into one another. As indicated by his writings on prisons and mental institutions, heterotopic spaces can be sites of social control in the desire for a perfect order.

Despite this tension, heterotopias are always sites of things displaced, marginal, novel, rejected or ambivalent. In fact, it is through their juxtaposition with the spaces around them that the foreground collage comes to be seen as heterotopic.

Heterotopic social economy

The conceptual power of heterotopia lies in its ambiguity – that it can be a site of order just as much as a site of resistance. Hetherington refers to it this way: 'this ambivalence contained in the idea of heterotopia [is] both the castles of the Marquis de Sade and Franz Kafka'.[42] The subversion of metanarratives by heterotopia leaves us with a more nuanced and complicated vista of conflicting sites and contested truths of economy. Simultaneously this view opens new sites and acknowledges new agents for transformative politics.

In terms of economic epistemology, Foucault's definition of heterotopia provides a useful means for undertaking an analysis of the nature of the social economy in relation to traditional definitions of economy. The space of the social economy, especially its manifestation as a feminized-Other within a discourse that presumes the hegemony of the market economy, more closely resembles Foucault's description of a heterotopia of deviation than the timeless homogenized space assumed by mainstream economic theorizations.

However, the social economy should not be viewed as a romanticized Other – as a transgressive space to be celebrated because it allows the marginal to find their voices within its confines. Instead it should be noted due to the condition of difference and *in-différance*, which makes it indispensable to economic theorizations. The social economy is an obligatory point of passage constituted through different ordering practices. It exposes conditions of difference that open up a new perspective on previous economic discourses and their faults. In other words, it is the emerging post-modernity within the social economy that marks it out as a heterotopia, not the conditions of transgression in themselves.

Afterword

The discursive conceptualizations and practices of the Employment paradigm not only theorized market economy hegemony, but also actively reaffirmed this construction. In doing so, they essentialized the economy as synonymous with the market and rendered those practices outside its norm, namely the non-capitalist practices of the social economy, invisible. However, the recent extensive and intensive growth of the social economy, within the post-Employment era, challenges this produced invisibility. This chapter has posited that acknowledgement of the social economy and its economic productivity reveals that there is no underlying essence to the market economy. The removal of economy as founded upon transcendental objective truths renders its constituent elements open to alterity. This destabilization, at a practical level, not only opens economy to other sites of production but also renders the ontology that enables an objective definition of economy as lacking.

An unessential economy based on the ontological stances of reflexivity, *différance* and heterotopia forms the basis of an alternative conceptualization that conforms to the Work paradigm. First, the assumed rationalism is displaced by reflexivity. Individual and institutional social economy involvement is more readily conceptualized as reflexive engagement. Care, altruism and self-fulfillment, for example, are just as likely as rationalism to explain economic action. An economic ontology predicated on reflexivity, therefore, challenges the very core of mainstream economic theory. Answers to questions such as why the social economy is expanding and why individuals choose to engage their labour-power in the social economy, are radically altered when reflexivity, rather than rationalism, is taken as the starting point of economic analysis.

Second, the shift from dualism to *différance* undermines the essentialist conception of economy as representational. The consequence of severing the market economy from its 'others' is the enabling of a hegemonic construction of capitalism as the sole and therefore necessary means of production. This has been hastened in the post-Employment era with the collapse of the Socialist bloc, the re-assertion of American hegemony, implementation of disciplinary neo-liberalism and the oversimplified articulation of homogenization in the global economy. An ontology based on *différance*, however, renders economy as relational. It integrates market, state and social economies and denies the possibility of a single fixed entity. Rather, an understanding of one economy (e.g., market) is not possible without reference to its other (e.g., social). This is a radical alteration from an essentialist dualistic ontology. *Différance* frees the social economy from its subordinated positioning *vis-à-vis* the market economy and state economy.

Third, the social economy forms a heterotopic space. The knowledge emanating from the social economy may not conform to existing capitalist practices and knowledge. This is not to be minimized, but instead should be viewed as a necessary definition of an economy-in-relation. The social economy is not only a site for the production of goods, services and other intangibles (e.g., social capital) but is also a space with its own order, logic and dynamic. Consequently, the social economy, along with its output, requires independent inquiry and policy not as capitalism-lite or capitalism's burden but as a distinct and interrelated economy. The articulation of an unessential economy provides the framework for the empirical portion of this book.

5   Methodology and case study

Study objectives

The social economy is not only generative of employment, but also reflective of a larger transition from Employment to Work. As discussed in Chapter 2, the paradigm shift to Work reflects the lived reality of the contemporary global political economy.[1] The transition to Work, however, is not a voluntary liberal bourgeois sentiment. Individuals are compelled to engage differentially in the post-Employment era in order to address the crisis of social reproduction.[2]

This crisis is constituted by contradictions between the power of capital over the social as well as alterations within the social itself. In terms of the former, the class compromises that shaped the 'Golden Age' of welfare capitalism have been removed by the extended power of capital. Individuals and societies are more exposed to the deep oscillations of global market forces. This exposure has heightened the centrality of employment, as the inability to sell one's labour-power becomes a risk no longer mediated effectively through the Fordist welfare state.

Remedies to this manifestation of the crisis of social reproduction are expressed through the coinciding and colliding of employment generation strategies by both dominant and alternative social formations. Overlooked in this process has been employment generation within the social economy. With nearly 900,000 paid workers in the Canadian social economy, this sector represents 6 per cent of overall workers.[3] This is comparable to the size of the construction industry with its 931,000 workers, as well as the finance, insurance, real estate and leasing industries with their respective totals of 936,000 workers.[4]

Yet the social economy cannot be understood solely as an economic manifestation. Its employment potential cannot be viewed in isolation from the larger transformations in the global political economy and the challenges it presents to disciplinary neo-liberalism. As argued in Chapter 2, the metanarratives of the Employment paradigm, such as full employment, economy, growth, nation, gender and the environment, are being challenged, chosen or undermined. The inability of the institutional order to address and remedy the risks associated with their decline, exploitation and demands has led to their increased visibility in the post-Employment era as contested notions.

This becomes apparent when examining the metanarrative of employment. The ideational basis for employment, the work ethic that formed the mode of *régulation*, no longer holds sway in the post-Employment era. It is not that paid work is no longer central. Rather its centrality is heightened, as associated risks are no longer contained. However, employment itself does not provide for the removal of risks and in some cases serves to exacerbate them. The ideational rupture arises from the material basis of paid work found in the regime of accumulation, which becomes increasingly arbitrary as the delineations between what constitutes employment and what does not become ever more blurred.

This has triggered a social response. Individuals are taking action, combining with others in order to address the crisis of social reproduction that they are collectively facing. The result is the organic basis of the social economy where individuals expend their labour-power in order to address the multivariate risks that are present in the post-Employment era. Simultaneously, the social economy functions to lessen the constraints on capital and the state, as it takes over the role of social reproduction that is so necessary within the social. Nevertheless, the social economy is a unique institutional manifestation as it explicitly incorporates and acknowledges the contribution of both paid work and non-paid work.[5] Furthermore, the social economy is centred on issues of social reproduction as much as it is on issues of production and consumption.[6] The social economy therefore is both a generator of employment and an indicator of the transition to a Work paradigm. It is an expression of the Work paradigm consciousness of *being-in-the-world-with-others*.

Methodology

The case study focuses on the social economy in Toronto, Canada. To facilitate the operationalization of the argument, two surveys were developed and administered. This method was the most accurate means available to quantify both whether and to what extent there was a transition from Employment to Work. At issue was whether actual existing practices and not just theoretical possibilities within the social economy were indicative of a transition to the Work paradigm. Consequently, assessments that stemmed from those actually engaged in the day-to-day operations of the social economy formed the sole basis for these determinations.

One survey was constructed to examine the paradigm shift from a worker perspective utilizing the definition given in this study, which includes both staff and volunteers (Worker Survey). The other survey concentrated on the organizational level and was applied to executive directors (or their designated representatives) (Organization Survey).

Those who worked at the organizations were asked to provide feedback on their experiences and to consider the broader role played by the social economy in this current historical juncture. Analysis focused on distinctions based on organizational activity, work status (paid work, full-time paid work, part-time paid work, non-paid work), gender, age, childcare responsibilities, new social movement participation and educational attainment. The Organization Survey centred on the specifics of the organization that the respondents were representing. The analysis measured work generation on the basis of the organization's size, epoch, scope and primary activity.

The study therefore collected the following data:

- **basic case study demographics:** Both surveys provide quantitative data on both organizations and workers in the Toronto social economy. The Organization Survey provides information pertaining to the structure of organizations coupled with service type and delivery. The Worker Survey provides data on worker demographics and the conceptualization of the social economy both as an autonomous sector and in relation to the state and market economies.
- **work generation:** The study examines the overall trend towards the Work paradigm within Toronto social economy organizations and participants. It asked respondents of the Organization Survey to identify paid work, non-paid work, part-time work and full-time work totals for 2000 and 2003. Additionally, they were asked to project organizational requirements for paid work and non-paid work three to five years into the future. The study therefore examined work generation trends from 2000 to 2006.
- **work composition and value:** Workers, in turn, were asked to reflect on their labour-power expenditures. The study sought to test the participation, value and management of various forms of work and combined these findings to test the prevalence of the Work paradigm. Findings are discussed in Chapter 7.

Construction of surveys

The two surveys were constructed and then reviewed by experts in the field as well as by other Social Science researchers (See Appendices A and B). The surveys were evaluated on five criteria:

1   Were the questions straightforward?
2   Did the questions fit the Canadian social economy?
3   Could the questions be timed so that the suggested approximate time of 20 minutes could be tested independently?
4   Is the online format accessible and easily read?
5   Did the questions test for the hypothesis?

This evaluation led to alterations due to the discovery of a number of shortcomings. Most prominently the surveys' use of the term 'work' to include all forms of labour expenditure in the production of a good or service required clearer articulation.

The final version of the Worker Survey was therefore divided into four sections:

1 worker typology, engagement in various forms of work;
2 conceptualization of social economy and policy preferences;
3 social economy and relation to state and market;
4 worker demographics.

The final version of the Organization Survey was divided into five sections:

1 organizational demographics;
2 organizational size and structure;
3 organizational finances;
4 policies to enhance work;
5 respondent data.

The study was also influenced by recent scholarship in the field, specifically Sigrid Betzelt's excellent study of the social economy in Germany.[7] Betzelt was responsible for the development and implementation of the German portion of a three-nation study commissioned by the European Union (EU) entitled, 'New Employment Opportunities in the Third Sector' (NETS).[8]

The EU study is a welcome development in the theorization of the sector and reveals a shift in scholarly research towards viewing the social economy as generative of employment.[9] However, while the shift to employment generation is a critical development, the continued practice of bifurcating labour into paid/non-paid is a significant limitation. The social economy is predicated on both paid and non-paid work. To map the paid/non-paid bifurcation onto the social economy places it once again within the *capitalocentric* trap discussed in Chapter 3. The social economy, as an economy, operates separate from and with divergent logics to those contained within the market and state economies. By not theorizing this difference studies continue to replicate and confirm the hegemony of the previous paradigm of Employment, thereby curtailing the full potential and significance of the social economy.

Indeed the social economy cannot be framed in isolation to the social world and political economy. Its actual form, practices and functions must be theorized. Not to do so represents a significant opportunity for co-option within the classical liberal framework of nineteenth-century charity. Framing it in this larger context reveals that the social economy is only a symptom and not an antidote to the crisis of social reproduction. The central issue remains work, and the power to define and account for it.

Online surveys

Both the Organization and Worker Surveys were constructed as online surveys. They were written into HTML and tagged to conform to a set of established and potential database queries. The surveys were uploaded to workingalternatives.net, a website that was created with several built-in measures to ensure confidentiality and security.[10]

First, the site utilized Secure Sockets Layer (SSL) protocol, which required 128-bit encryption of both the sending and receiving data. Furthermore, the SSL connection provided a mechanism to detect tampering when data was transferred. Second, the Organization Survey had an additional measure of security with login and password protection. Directors were provided with their login and password information in a separate e-mail just prior to the launch of the data collection process. Without the proper login information the survey was not accessible. Third, when participants completed the online survey and clicked the 'Submit' button, the responses were immediately submitted to a database based on a pre-defined system of tags and codes. Personal information, apart from that required for demographic purposes, was not collected, thus ensuring an added degree of anonymity. Fourth, this process centralized all responses into a single file, which not only facilitated the data analysis process but also ensured that all entries were tabulated.

This online component was both the study's strength and its shortcoming. From a research perspective, the use of the Internet made the study possible in terms of financial and time considerations. It also facilitated the quick transfer of data from HTML to database formatting and subsequently to other statistical analysis software. While studies indicate that mail and, by extension, e-mail surveys receive lower rates of participation, the ability to send out e-mails enabled the study to be viewed by far more potential respondents than would otherwise have been possible.[11]

Yet, as indicated by some responses, apprehension regarding the use of new technologies negatively impacted participation in the study (i.e., confidentiality of transmitting information, browser compatibility etc). In this respect, paper versions of the surveys would have alleviated some of these concerns. A majority of respondents did, however, indicate that the online survey was the primary factor in their participation, as it provided flexibility in terms of when and at what pace they could complete the process.

Telephone survey

After consulting with industry experts and participants it was decided that the Organization Survey should not only include an online version but also a telephone interview component.[12] This was conducted in two ways:

1   **pre-arranged:** E-mails sent to case studies (totalling 500) included the

option of completing an online or telephone survey. The e-mail included the dates that the data collection would take place.

2   **cold-calling:** A further 150 organizations were contacted by telephone. After explaining the purpose of the study as well as the requirements, prospective respondents were given the option of proceeding with the survey on the phone, scheduling a more convenient time or utilizing the online version. These organizations were also encouraged to invite their workers to fill out the Worker Survey. This process was facilitated by a follow-up e-mail with the website's hyperlink and a reiteration of the research project, its importance and the affiliation with the university coupled with the confidentiality statements.

Social economy classification schema

The study required the utilization of a classification schema that focused on the primary activity of the social economy organizations in order to establish the case study population. While this represented only one of the factors assessed in the testing of the hypothesis, it has been the primary manner in which research on the sector has been conducted both within Canada and globally.

Nonetheless, research in this area remains inconsistent as a universal definition and therefore classification schema for the social economy remains undeveloped. In order to bridge this shortcoming in the existing data on the social economy, this study adopts both the classification systems utilized in Canadian research on the sector as developed by David Sharpe and the International Classification of Nonprofit Organizations (ICNPO) developed by the John Hopkins Comparative Nonprofit Sector Project.[13]

Canadian classification (CCRA)

Sharpe's study has provided a catalyst for a growing body of research on the Canadian social economy. This groundbreaking study quantified the social economy in Canada by adopting the Canada Customs and Revenue Agency (CCRA) definition of charitable organizations. In doing so a pan-Canadian inventory of organizations was established, which classified social economy organizations by activity into six fields: Benefit to Community, Education, Health, Religion, Welfare, and Other.[14] This framework is hereafter referred to in this study as CCRA.

While this classificatory system is highly useful in researching the sector, it does present researchers with a number of shortcomings. First, it operationalizes the limited definition set out by CCRA that defines the sector as organizations that are registered charities under Canadian tax law.[15] This definition has been criticized as being outdated and not conforming to contemporary Canadian society as it negates informal organizations and those that form for short durations.[16] Adhering to the definition established by the

CCRA would have effectively negated the contribution of some of this study's participating organizations.

This classification schema also reduces the perceived diversity of service delivery present in the social economy. In doing so, it restricts the social economy to the traditional norms of charity that arose from the nineteenth century.[17] The category called Community Benefit for example tends, as a result, to be a grab bag for organizations that do not conform to more traditional understandings of the term 'charity'. Furthermore, the classificatory system limits comparison to the larger global processes underway that conform to the associational revolution.

International Classification of Nonprofit Organizations (ICNPO)

The John Hopkins Comparative Nonprofit Research Project addresses many of the shortcomings of the Sharpe study. First, it develops the ICNPO, an international classificatory system, which enables a significant degree of international and comparative research on the sector.[18] Second, it identifies a more diverse typology of service delivery options within the social economy by expanding service delivery options from six to thirteen:[19]

- business and professional associations;
- culture and recreation;
- development and housing;
- education and research;
- environment;
- health;
- international activities;
- law, advocacy and politics;
- philanthropic intermediaries and voluntarism promotion;
- religion;[20]
- social services;
- unions;
- not classified elsewhere.

Adding to the ICNPO model of classification

This approach hybridizes both the definition and the classification schema developed by the John Hopkins project and adds two classifications to the expanded ICNPO: Identity, and New Information Technologies.[21] In terms of the former, identity as a function of an organization conforms to the presence of multiculturalism on the political agenda and the multicultural aspects of Toronto. The incorporation of new information technologies conforms not to the utilization of new technologies in the sector but to social economy organizations that focus on this form of service delivery. The addition of these classifications is not only appropriate for the Canadian social economy but has global application, as it focuses on identity, culture and centrality of new information technologies that have been foregrounded with the transition to the Work paradigm.

Sampling methodology

Systematic sampling was the primary methodology utilized in the selection of case study elements. This methodology is most effective when the population size is known.[22] However, in the case of the Toronto social economy no such data set exists.

A search of the CCRA listing for organizations in Toronto revealed 4,573 matches.[23] As indicated above, however, this listing remained incomplete as it only accounted for those organizations that filed a T3010 *Registered Charities Information Returns* form. This definitional problem was replicated on the national level. As of August 2003, the CCRA listed 78,000 registered charities in Canada. Jack Quarter indicated an additional 100,000 organizations not counted by the CCRA, which placed the number of organizations closer to 178,000.[24]

Taking this difference and applying it to the Toronto social economy revealed the possibility of 5,579 organizations. Yet this did not provide any certainty regarding population size as the Quarter study was completed in 1992. According to Erwin Dreeseen, CCRA registrations have been expanding by approximately 2,000 organizations per year for the last 30 years and the number of unregistered organizations was likely to be even higher.[25]

In order to address this discrepancy in the sampling frame and to ensure a representative sample of the Toronto social economy population, a multi-method comprehensive sampling frame was also utilized. This methodology requires seeking social economy organizations through a variety of sources, including the Internet, phonebooks, umbrella organization listings as well as experts in the field and government registries.[26] Online sources included www.211.ca, a comprehensive listing of community, social, health and government services in Toronto, as well as other web portals.[27] These sources provided an additional 4,000 organizations, some of which proved to be repetitious.[28]

Given the difficulties in finalizing the total population, the study proceeded in the following manner. It assumed that the CCRA number of 4,573 represented the lowest number of Toronto social economy organizations. Transferring the discrepancy at the national level between the CCRA and the Quarter study revealed the possibility of 5,579 organizations in Toronto. Taking the CCRA numbers and adding them to the numbers yielded by the multimethod comprehensive sampling frame suggested the possibility of 7,573 organizations. The difference was taken between the two latter results yielding a population size of 6,500 organizations. Returning to the systematic sampling procedure, every tenth organization of a specific service delivery (e.g., Social Services) was selected as a case study element.

A total of 650 organizations were contacted to seek their participation in the study.

Data collection process

An initial e-mail was sent out. This e-mail provided participants with a short overview of the project, highlighted the shortcomings in existing literature on the sector and identified how the current study would fill this gap. It solicited the participation of both the organization's directors and workers in the completion of two separate surveys and provided examples of topics and questions as well as estimated completion times.

The aim of this initial e-mail was to both inform and aid participants in their decision to participate. The e-mail ended with both an assurance of confidentiality and notification of how the findings would be distributed.

Based on the notification deadline two instructional e-mails were then sent out to all organizations that agreed to participate. One was for executive directors and provided the password and login information required to access their survey on the website. The other was sent to executive directors to be forwarded to participating workers. In both cases, a hyperlink to the website was provided as well as a reiteration of confidentiality for participants.

Participants who decided to proceed with a telephone interview were asked to provide a convenient date and time for completing the survey.

Statistical significance and rates of return

A total of 650 organizations were originally contacted to request participation in the study. Of the 650 organizations, 500 were contacted by e-mail and 150 were contacted by phone. Of those contacted, 89 organizations responded affirmatively to participate in the study with the online option. This corresponds to an 18 per cent return rate. The participation rate from the phone calls was significantly less at 8 per cent with 12 of the 150 organizations agreeing to take part.[29] The study, which comprised 101 organizations (n=101), surpassed the number required for statistical significance with +/– 10 per cent sampling error.[30]

Of the 6,765 workers found in the Toronto social economy in 2003, 123 agreed to participate in the study, comprising a 2 per cent participation rate (n=123). While this is a significantly lower response rate, which will be discussed in the next section, it replicates the +/–10 sampling error found in the Organization results.

Limitations of the research

This is an exploratory study, which requires further research to solidify its findings.[31] The lack of comparable studies and data to work from provides both its strength and weakness. In terms of the former, this study develops an innovative research programme on the transition to the Work paradigm and quantifies this by examining social economy organizations in Toronto, Canada. The focus on Toronto-based organizations coupled with the framing of the study places it in uncharted territory. The shortcomings are in the sample itself as well as the sampling methodology utilized. These do not negate the value of the study but suggest caution in generalizing its findings. This was a necessary trade-off in order to complete the study and initiate further debate and research along the lines established in this project.[32]

Sampling methodology considerations

The definitional problems that have hampered the ability of researchers to identify the social economy population in Canada and the lack of any study to do so in Toronto required this study to consider various sampling methodologies including: simple random sampling, proportionate stratified sampling and stratified sampling.

Simple random sampling was not feasible as there was a possibility that this sampling methodology would lead to a heavy bias towards a single type of service delivery. The type of service delivery was only one factor under consideration in the study, which also included epoch, scale, scope and size of organization. However, focusing heavily on a single factor would jeopardize the diversity that exists within the Toronto social economy. This is critical to the bivariant analysis, which combines factors in order to better understand work generation and potential policies to aid the emerging Work paradigm.

Proportionate stratified sampling presented its own shortcomings. The only data available that provides a breakdown of the social economy in Canada is the Sharpe study. This study, beyond the issue of representing only those organizations within the CCRA definition, represents a national calculation. Transposing this onto the Toronto social economy population distorted the study's findings and undermined its innovativeness. For example, are there distinctions between social economy organizations in rural and Northern Canada as opposed to urban and Southern Canada? In addition, a proportionate stratified sample would have conferred responses from non-respondents while under-representing actual responses from those who participated.

Stratified sampling presented similarities to systematic sampling. However, it did not provide an adequate means of selecting organizations. Once organizations were categorized into activity, it was necessary to develop a method of determining which organizations would be selected as potential participants in the study. Using systemic sampling, every tenth organization was selected. However, the issue of sample bias cannot be overlooked in the study.

The inability to provide an accurate account of the total social economy population in Toronto renders the study findings susceptible to bias in the form of coverage errors.[33] This remains the case even with calculation of the +/– 10 per cent sampling error with the sample size. An attempt has been

made in this study to limit the potential of bias with the sampling methodology chosen and by improving external validity. Wherever possible, the case
study findings are contextualized within the broader Canadian economy
and society by drawing on research findings of other researchers.

The study is also limited by the non-return bias. In terms of the Organization Survey, the results may not be representative of those who did not
complete the survey since non-returns were not necessarily evenly distributed
throughout the sample population. The Worker Survey presents a related
shortcoming due to the low return rate. Furthermore partial non-response
error is present, as respondents throughout the sample did not answer every
question.[34]

The following steps were taken to reduce the non-return bias:

- pre-testing the surveys;
- stating the importance of the study;
- the use of follow-up and reminder e-mails mentioning affiliation with a
  reputable research university (York University).

The survey was also simple, thorough and easy to read with directors
receiving the option of completing them online or over the telephone. To
induce participation, directors were also informed that research findings
would be shared with the community.

Case study introduction: Toronto social economy organizations

Characteristics of organizations

Questions regarding organizational characteristics centred on the following
five factors: historical periodization, geographical scope, number of branches
and primary field of activity (according to both the CCRA and ICNPO
categorizations).

Historical periodization of organizations

A significant proportion of respondent organizations (69 per cent) were
formed between 1980 and 2003, which places them within the post-
Employment era. The remaining 27 per cent of respondent organizations
were formed between 1946 and 1979, which conforms to the Employment
paradigm.[35] While precise dates of transition between these phases of development are erroneous, as each is indicative of moments, ascendancy and
displacement of modes of development are clearly discernable.[36]

This study uses 1979 as the year of demarcation as it symbolizes the introduction of neo-liberal structural reforms in Canada. It saw the election of a
minority government under the leadership of the Progressive Conservative
party, whose mandate was to address the crisis of the termination of the

Employment paradigm.[37] The political structure increasingly shifted to neo-liberal responses, which sought to reduce the size of government and eliminate inflationary pressures.[38]

This resulting weighting of organizations also conforms to the transition in modes of development. It was not until the end of the 1970s that the social economy re-emerged as an important organizational form and analytical category. Historically, as Eric Shragge and Jean-Marc Fontan argue, the social economy emerges in times of crisis and transition.[39] The structural reforms introduced at the end of the 1970s therefore made social economy expansion both 'necessary and possible'.[40] The 1945–79 and the 1980–2003 divisions correspond to the epoch classificatory scheme utilized in the bivariant analysis.

Geographical scope

58 per cent of respondent institutions carried out their activities within the greater Toronto metropolitan area. Thirty-two per cent delivered their services within Canada (18 per cent as provincial and 14 per cent as national). The activities of the remaining 12 per cent were concentrated outside Canada. Of these, 3 per cent were focused on North America with the remaining 9 per cent operating at a global scale. These results indicate an inverse relationship with service delivery and scope as the number of organizations declines with the broadening of the scope of activity. While the social economy is a global force, its centrality is as a local force, embedded in and through the local.

The high proportion of local organizations within this study is, in part, indicative of the sampling procedure that focused on organizations within Toronto and, specifically, the type of organizations excluded from previous studies of the sector due to factors such as size and informal organizational structuring. However, the proportion of small organizations can also be accounted for as being indicative of the dialectic of reflexive development and risk society characteristic of the post-Employment era and the Work paradigm. The burgeoning of risks that are characteristic of the intensification of disciplinary neo-liberalism has necessitated a social response in the form of new social economy organizations. The crisis of social reproduction that was more readily associated with the global South is now increasingly a global phenomenon.

Nonetheless, while organizations operating beyond Canada constitute a small percentage of overall respondents, these organizations are more overtly indicative of processes of globalization. At a basic level, they are indicative of a broader patterning, which has seen the expansion of the social economy globally. These organizations are able to extend their reach as a result of the shifts brought about by the communications, transportation and cultural transformations that constitute the multidimensional processes of globalization. This is most often discussed under the rubric of non-governmental movements and development.[41] The combining element for the scalar dimensions is the nature of the current historical juncture, with structural reforms and risks triggering a crisis of social reproduction globally. The scalar levels identified here will be used in the bivariant analysis.

Number of branches

Eighty-four per cent of the institutional respondents indicated that they had one to three branches. Sixteen per cent had four or more with 9 per cent of these reporting ten or more branches. The overwhelmingly small size of organizations is a result of the structuring of the sector and sampling procedures. In terms of the former, 70 per cent of organizations within the Canadian social economy are characterized as small. Only health and educational organizations have a tendency to be larger.[42] Beyond this structural consideration, the survey required detailed and specific responses to questions regarding financing and changes in work from 2000 to 2003. This precluded participation by some of the larger organizations contacted as substantial oversight and understanding were required to complete the survey. This presented logistical questions, for example, such as the added step of contacting someone who had this knowledge or could easily access it.

The survey could more readily be answered by organizations that had the necessary information in one central location and could be accessed by the institutional representative. As such, smaller organizations, while also pressured in terms of resources, responded in larger numbers. Additionally as the case studies were drawn from Toronto-based organizations, the sample lent itself to smaller organizations whose service focus was more local than global.

Primary fields of activity (CCRA) and percentage growth

Figure 5.1 reveals that the highest return rates for the study came from Social Service organizations, comprising 52 per cent of the case study. Organizations whose primary activity was Benefit to Community comprised the second largest grouping with 24 per cent. The remaining quarter identified their primary activities as Education (16 per cent), Health (6 per cent) and Other (2 per cent). The lack of data to indicate the service delivery composition within Toronto makes it difficult to contextualize this distribution to determine its representative quality. However, comparing the results to the Sharpe study reveals some conformity in results.

A deviation occurs when examining the number of respondents who indicated Social Services and Benefit to Community as their primary fields of activity. Both activity classifications represent a significantly higher composition of the Toronto social economy. Beyond the unavailability of data on the Toronto social economy and the limited definitional methodology employed by the Sharpe study, the subject matter of this study may have also

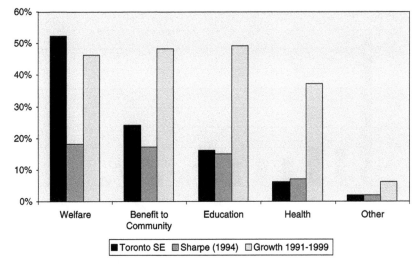

Figure 5.1 Primary fields of activity (CCRA) and percentage growth.

Adapted from Sharpe, 2001

been a factor in the response rates. The political nature of the survey, particularly in regards to policy and the role of the corporate and state sectors, may have deterred some organizations from participating while encouraging others.[43] Restructuring within Toronto has placed a tremendous degree of strain on both social service and community benefit agencies. The issue of work, both paid and non-paid, therefore may be more pressing for these organizations.

Primary fields of activity (ICNPO)

The ICNPO provides a more comprehensive breakdown of the case study. While the Social Services category remains intact and the largest at 39 per cent of respondents, three differentiated categories are highlighted with the ICNPO classification. Law, Advocacy and Politics along with Arts, Recreation and Leisure each represent 10 per cent of institutional respondents. Environment and Animal Welfare represents 7 per cent. These three classifications are significant as they highlight divergent elements of the social, reflecting the transition from the Employment paradigm to that of the Work paradigm. Specifically, these categorizations indicate the foregrounding of reflexivity and reflexive development as opposed to charity and technocratic government. The argument is not that Social Services is a residual classification but that it conforms to the dominant imaginary of the social economy as charity. The latter three therefore challenge the categorization and association of the social economy as charity.

Organizations focusing on Law, Advocacy and Politics are increasingly

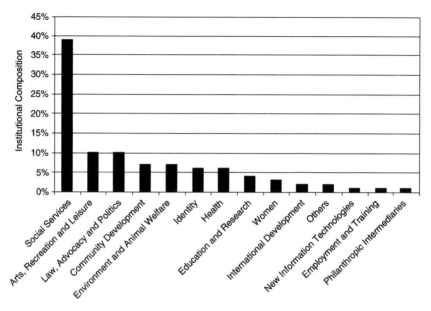

Figure 5.2 Primary fields of activity (ICNPO).

central to communities under structural reform, as they are indicative of the shift to subpolitics. The advocacy role of organizations, however, is highly contentious in terms of receiving both public and government legitimation.[44] It was only in 2003 that the CCRA changed the so-called 10 per cent rule that had limited advocacy spending to only 10 per cent of a charity's revenue and clarified the definition of charitable and political activity.

Arts, Recreation and Leisure, while widespread, is also beyond the traditional imaginary of charity. As pollster Allen Gregg writes, '[a]sk Canadians about their priorities for government spending, and *funding* for the arts and culture will turn up near the bottom of their hit parade (it routinely wrestles for last place with foreign aid)'[45] [original emphasis]. The underlying reasons for this are beyond the scope of this chapter. However, its existence reflects the residual basis of welfare provision in Canada, which divides provision into worthy and unworthy. Art as a form of expression may also present cultural production that is beyond those that the society subscribes to and in doing so brings questions of legitimacy to the fore. As a result, financing of this sector has become increasingly political.[46]

Nevertheless, in 2001, the Arts, Recreation and Leisure sector had the highest amount of non-paid work events at 23 per cent and the highest amount of non-paid work hours at 26 per cent.[47] With 351,000 Canadians engaging in non-paid work in this sector, its presence cannot be denied.[48]

The next largest grouping of respondents is Environment and Animal Welfare, representing 7 per cent of all organizational respondents.[49] Ecological crises coupled with the inability of the institutional order to address these concerns has manifested in the growth of a green identity and green movements.[50] The politicization of many environmental organizations against the institutional order has placed these organizations outside the CCRA definition of charitable organizations. Yet participation in environmental events increased from 11 per cent to 16 per cent in the year 2000.[51]

These three categorizations challenge the restricting definition of the social economy. Both the CCRA and the ICNPO classifications schemes are utilized in the bivariant analysis. Specific focus will be placed on the three categories discussed above.

Organizational finances

Questions regarding organization finances centred on the following five factors: annual budget; revenue sources: average contribution and frequency; revenue sources: institutional composition; average composition of institutional expenses; and composition of expenses. Each criterion is described further in the following sections.

Annual budget

The respondent institutions were divided into three size categories, which formed the size classification schema utilized in the bivariant analysis. The basis of the groupings derived from earlier research conducted by Linda Roberts.[52] That study found organizations of $100,000 were able to employ staff and run a small office.[53] The results found nearly half of the sample (49 per cent) has a budget above $300,000 per annum. The remaining half has budgets of $0 to $100,000 (23 per cent) and $100,000 to $300,000 (28 per cent). Many of the organizations, irrespective of size classification, identified undercapitalization as the most critical constraint on work generation in the sector.[54] The disproportionate reliance on other forms of capital, such as social and cultural capital, has not curtailed the precariousness felt throughout the sector.

Revenue sources

Figure 5.3 reveals the average contribution and frequency of revenue sources. The data indicates that the primary sources of funding in this sector are private institutions and donors (36 per cent) with 74 per cent of institutional respondents identifying this as a source of revenue. Various levels of government constitute 38 per cent of funding with an average of 36 per cent of institutional respondents. In terms of the latter, the provincial contribution amounted to 20 per cent while the federal contribution amounted to 11 per cent. The city of Toronto contributed 7 per cent of all accrued revenue. The remaining sources contributed a total of 26 per cent of organizational

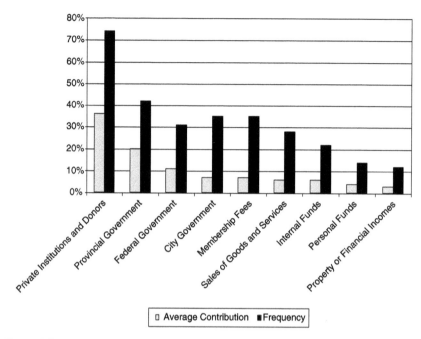

Figure 5.3 Revenue sources: average contribution and frequency.

funding. These included membership fees (7 per cent), sales of goods and services (6 per cent), internal funds (6 per cent), personal funds (4 per cent) and property or financial incomes (3 per cent).[55]

A recent study of funding of Canadian non-profits revealed a significantly different distribution with government funding totaling 60 per cent, earned income representing 26 per cent and private giving constituting 14 per cent of total funding.[56] While the discrepancy in totals suggests that the use of the CCRA-determined non-profit definition provides a different understanding of the sector, in both instances the contribution of earned income should be noted.[57] In part this is reflective of the changes that the sector has undergone with continued government restructuring and cutbacks. Most notably, the shift from core- to project-based funding has served to increase precariousness in the sector and compelled organizations to seek alternative sources of funding.[58]

Figure 5.4 provides a closer examination of funding sources by showing the relationship between the various sources of funding and the contribution made by percentage. Respondents identify private institutions as providing a substantial portion of funding as 29 per cent of organizations indicate that they receive 61 per cent to 100 per cent of their funding from this source. Nineteen per cent of organizations indicate that 61 per cent to 100 per cent of their funding derives from the three levels of government with the provincial government representing the largest share (12 per cent).

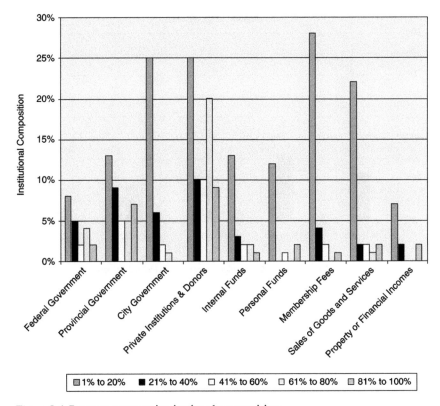

Figure 5.4 Revenue sources: institutional composition.

Average composition of institutional expenses

Respondents identified human resources as constituting the highest portion of annual budgets (51 per cent). Operational and financial costs constituted 42 per cent and 8 per cent on average. Sixteen per cent of respondents did not respond to this question. Telephone respondents indicated that the numbers were not easily available and would require calculation. While it is unclear whether the same rationale applied for online respondents, it may be fair to conclude that the difficulty in answering the question influenced the lower response rate.

Composition of expenses

Figure 5.5 indicates that 25 per cent of respondents identified operational costs as constituting 61 per cent to 100 per cent of annual budgetary allocations while financial costs were constrained to between 1 per cent and 40 per cent of the annual budgets. The low financial costs are associated with the lack of availability of credit to the sector. A closer examination of expenses reveals

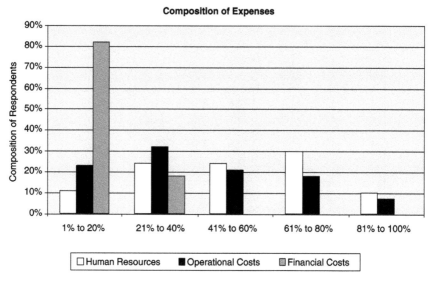

Figure 5.5 Composition of expenses.

that 40 per cent of institutions accord 61 per cent to 100 per cent of the institution's annual budget to costs pertaining to human resources. The composition of human resource costs reflects the labour intensity of the sector. The significance of labour in the sector's output is discussed with the findings of the Worker Survey.

Characteristics of staff respondents

Characteristics of workers

Questions regarding worker demographics centred on the following five factors: gender, age, childcare responsibilities, educational attainment, and engagement in a social movement.

Gender composition of workers

The gender composition of respondents is weighted significantly towards females (78 per cent) with men constituting only 22 per cent of workers sampled. These findings are highly biased in relation to the overall composition of paid work in the Canadian labour market, which is composed of 43 per cent female and 57 per cent male and the overall composition of non-paid work in Canada with 53 per cent female and 47 per cent male participation.[59] This discrepancy is attributable in part to the sampling methodology, which included organizations that did not conform to the CCRA definition and the combining of paid work and non-paid work into the single classification of work.

However, gender differentiation in paid work is revealed upon closer inspection of the paid work service sector in Canada where the ratio of women to men is 1.98, which is above the OECD average of 1.77.[60] Additionally, Norah McClintock states, '[t]o the extent that there is a typical Canadian volunteer, she is between 35 and 54 years old, is married, has some post-secondary education, is employed, has a household income of over $60,000, and a religious affiliation'.[61] Other studies also indicate the gender imbalance in work within Canadian social economy organizations. McMullen and Schellenberg find that women constitute 75 per cent of paid work in the sector and 68 per cent of managers.[62] Louise Mailloux *et al.* find that social economy organizations that focus on health and social services may be as much as 80 per cent to 90 per cent female.[63]

Age composition of workers

Figure 5.6 reveals that the highest proportion of workers in the sector range in age from 25 to 44 (61 per cent). The heavier weighting of 25 to 34 year olds does not conform to the overall Canadian paid-work labour market, which indicates a higher proportion of older workers.[64] However, this weighting may be attributable to the sample in terms of the sector studied, the distinction between paid work and non-paid work as well as the urban focus, which would support a higher participation rate for younger Canadians. In terms of the age distribution of non-paid work in Canada, Hall *et al.* (2001) provide a participation rate within age groups: 29 per cent for ages 15–24, 24 per cent for 25–34, 30 per cent for those aged 35–44 and 45–54, with 28 per cent for those aged 55–64 and 18 per cent for those 65 and older.[65] The 'Canadian social economy non-paid work' in Figure 5.6 derives from this calculation, measuring instead participation against total population. In

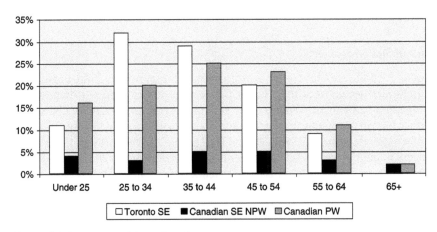

Figure 5.6 Age composition of workers.

Adapted from Hall *et al.*, 2001, 34 and Statistics Canada, 2003 doing so, we see that non-paid work is more evenly distributed throughout age groupings and is a significant portion of the Canadian population overall.

Childcare responsibilities

Forty per cent of respondents indicated that they had childcare responsibilities. This conforms to research done nationally, which indicates that 38 per cent of non-paid workers are parents/guardians.[66] Parents aged 45 to 54 had the highest participation rate, at 46 per cent for female parents and 51 per cent for male parents.[67] However, children have differential impacts on non-paid work. As Rose Anne Devlin indicates, the decision to engage in non-paid work is dependent on the age of the child(ren).[68] Parents with children aged five and younger are less inclined to engage in non-paid work in the non-profit sector as the work required in the form of housework and family expands. Once their children are older and hence more self-reliant, the amount of family-related work changes, and appears to exert a positive influence on this decision.

The necessity of caretakers to realign their engagement in work to conform to the age and needs of their children requires a closer examination. In order to do this, the study asked respondents to identify the age(s) of their children. The ensuing bivariant analysis combined the first and last categories and retained the *7–12 year old* classification.

Nineteen per cent of respondents identified having children aged six years and younger. The decision to have the range include children up to age six represented an acknowledgement of a shift in education in Canada with Kindergarten being typically a half-day. Eleven per cent of respondents identified having children aged 7 to 12 while 21 per cent indicated childcare responsibilities for children aged 13 to 18+ years of age. A child's age played a role in determining parental work strategies, which in turn impacted parents' other forms of work, including paid work.[69]

Educational attainment

Figure 5.7 indicates that a high proportion of respondents hold university degrees (69 per cent) with a Bachelor's degree as the largest component, comprising 42 per cent. Twenty-three per cent of respondents indicated some form of formal education beyond a high school diploma. These findings conform to research done in the sector. Hall *et al.* (2001) report that those with university degrees comprise 39 per cent of non-paid workers in the Canadian social economy.[70] McMullen and Schellenberg indicate that 58 per cent of paid workers in the social economy have post-secondary credentials.[71] According to these researchers, the highest levels of education are found in health, education and social services (62.9 per cent). The OECD provides similar conclusions, stating that the ratio of university-educated to non-university-educated workers in the service sector is higher than that of the

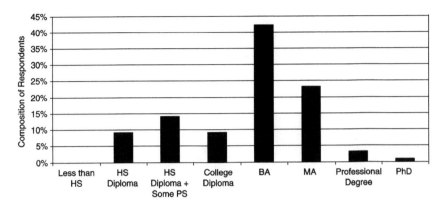

Figure 5.7 Educational attainment.

goods producing sector (0.29 to 0.09).[72] Social services have the highest ratio at 0.53, revealing the knowledge intensity of the sector.

Engagement in a social movement

Nearly a quarter of respondents (24 per cent) indicated involvement in a social movement. Half of these respondents pointed out that their involvement was as a result of their work in the social economy. The composition of individuals involved in a social movement may be correlated to the large-scale mobilizations and protests referred to as the 'Days of Action' and the 'Citizens for Local Democracy Movements' that developed after provincial elections in 1996.[73] The ensuing structural reforms, including the amalgamation of Toronto, led to a reinvigoration of civil society. This double movement has provided for the substantive growth of the Toronto social economy.

Work structuring of staff respondents

Workers in the social economy were asked to submit information on the structure of their work. Responses can be classified according to the following four factors: primary field of organizational activity, split into CCRA or ICNPO; paid work and non-paid work; and full-time paid work with part-time paid work.

Primary field of organizational activity (CCRA)

Figure 5.8 is similar to Figure 5.1, as the category of Welfare constitutes a significant portion of worker respondents (43 per cent). Workers involved in Education constituted the next largest grouping at 26 per cent. Organizations classified as Benefit to Community constituted 18 per cent with Health and Other representing 9 per cent and 4 per cent of social economy workers. The

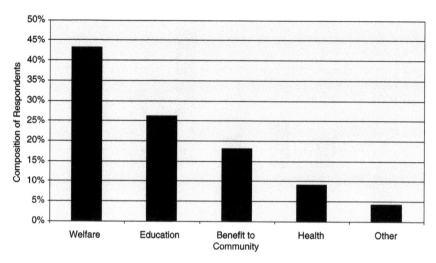

Figure 5.8 Primary fields of organizational activity (CCRA).

significantly higher rate of Welfare organizations while reflective of the research design can also be attributable to structural reforms in Toronto. Welfare is the second largest component of the CCRA with a 46 per cent organizational growth rate from 1991 to 1999.[74]

Primary field of organizational activity (ICNPO)

Figure 5.9 indicates that 58 per cent of respondents identified Social Services (40 per cent) along with Arts, Recreation and Leisure (18 per cent) as the primary work activity. These findings conform to the high levels of non-paid work found in these social economy sectors. Hall *et al.* (2001) found that the most non-paid work events and hours occurred in Arts, Recreation and Leisure (23 per cent and 26 per cent) followed by Social Services (20 per cent and 20 per cent).[75] The remaining classifications constitute a range from 2 per cent to 9 per cent of respondents. Nonetheless, Social Services along with Arts, Recreation and Leisure are discussed further in the bivariant analysis, as they represent seemingly diametric elements of the social economy in regards to the traditional definitions of 'charity' as discussed in previous sections.

Paid work and non-paid work

80 per cent of respondents indicated that they received some sort of paid income in the social economy sector. This is the inverse of the overall composition of paid work and non-paid work in the sector. In 2000, 6.5 million Canadians engaged in non-paid work in the non-profit sector.[76] In 1999, Workplace and Employee Survey (WES) data indicated paid work as totaling 900,000 in the sector.[77] This indicates that paid work comprises 12 per cent

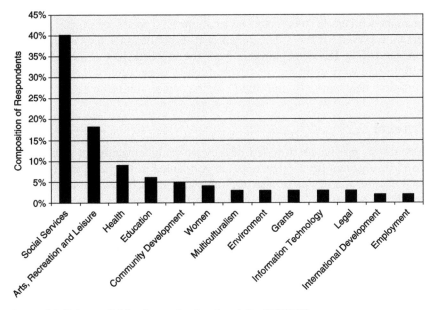

Figure 5.9 Primary fields of organizational activity (ICNPO).

of the Canadian social economy while non-paid work is equivalent to 88 per cent.

The smaller representation of non-paid work in the population sample is in part a result of the study dates and method. A number of organizations indicated the impossibility of worker participation, particularly when it came to non-paid worker participation, as September was normally a time when new non-paid workers were screened to join the respective organizations. Furthermore while directors were offered the opportunity to participate through a telephone interview, workers were not. The only option available to those who worked in the sector was through the online survey.

Despite these limitations, this is a representative sample as this study focuses on work with paid work and non-paid work representing only one factor in the analysis. Other forms of work examined in the bivariant analysis include family, self, political, school and housework.

Full-time and part-time work

Nearly one-third of respondents (28 per cent) indicated that their paid work in the social economy was part-time.[78] This is significantly higher than the overall paid work labour market, in which only 13 per cent of the labour force works part-time.[79] However, this conforms to levels of part-time paid work within the overall social economy at 26 per cent.[80]

The overall paid work labour market trend towards non-standard work arrangements is also characterized by the increasing numbers of workers engaged in two or more forms of paid work. Overall, 5 per cent of surveyed Canadian workers in 2000 held two or more paid forms of work.[81] Of the workers surveyed for this study, 26 per cent responded that they held two or more paid jobs. Part-time workers were the most likely to be engaged in multiple paid work at 45 per cent. Nevertheless, 16 per cent of those engaged in full-time paid work also indicated holding two or more paid jobs.

Afterword

These results provide an overview of the case study. Indicative of similarities to and divergences from other research conducted in the field, the Toronto social economy provides a basis for the elaboration of the paradigm shift from Employment to Work. This research follows existing studies in their focus on the voluntary sector. It diverges however in its broader definition of the social economy to include, for example, the household. This definitional discrepancy is critical as this study aims to embed the social economy within economies. That is, it builds on the unessential definition of economy developed in Chapter 4. As a consequence, unlike other studies that focus on either voluntary efforts or paid work within the social economy, this study eliminates this produced bifurcation. Focusing on the characteristics discussed in this chapter, the following chapter utilizes bivariant analysis to elaborate on the structure of work in the Toronto social economy.

6 Structuring the Work paradigm

The consumption of labour-power

An analysis of the consumption of labour-power within the social economy reveals the emergence of the Work paradigm, that is, a paradigm character-ized by the extensive and intensive growth of a sector that is simultane-ously generative of and reliant upon both paid work and non-paid work. Nevertheless, the social economy sector has largely gone unnoticed and under-utilized as a site for the origination of paid work. As discussed in Chapters 3 and 4, this is largely due to the privileged position the market economy holds as the sole legitimate initiator of paid work within dominant economic discourses. Yet the social economy sector is one of the fastest grow-ing employers within the Canadian economy. However, the generation of paid work is not uniform but uneven, as the case study reveals that organiza-tions classified as engaged in benefit to community, provincial in scope, medium-sized and originating within the Employment paradigm show the highest concentration of paid work generation.

Capitalocentric metanarratives deterritorializing work, defined in this research as the production of labour, and reterritorializing it solely as employ-ment simultaneously marginalize the generation of non-paid work as some-thing contrary to the function of paid work altogether. In short, non-paid work is conceived within the dualism of employment/not employment. Within dominant discourses therefore, non-paid work is not defined as a manifest-ation of labour-power, but instead contained both in function and mean-ing within the normative and depoliticizing discourses of 'housework' and 'volunteering'.[1] Yet the ensuing case study analysis points to the centrality of non-paid work to social economy growth, as the proportion of non-paid work expansion is significantly higher than that of paid work. Similar to paid work, non-paid work growth is nevertheless uneven with highest rates of growth in organizations classified as engaged in health, local in scope, small in size and originating within the post-Employment era.

The central empirical findings of this chapter challenge the essentialized conceptions and consequent enactment of economy that forcibly delimits work as employment and renders its others invisible. Social economy growth cannot be restricted to either the expansion in non-paid work or paid work. Instead, social economy growth is irreducibly predicated upon work in its full definition, as the enactment of reflexively engaged labour-power. Labour-power is vital to an elaboration of the social economy and an emergent Work paradigm. Unlike machinic or dead labour, labour-power is a necessary but contingent social relation. As Marx put forward in his discussion of labour-power and dead labour, labour-power is imbued with agency and is therefore variable.[2] This disturbs economics-as-usual, as labour-power becomes the subject of production rather than its object revealing the arbitrariness of these essentialist classifications. In terms of a further elaboration of the Work paradigm, this necessitates a re-reading of the basis of production as labour-power produces while capital consumes.

In adopting this alternative imaginary, a critical step is taken towards subverting the hegemonic conception of economy and work that was brought about during the Employment paradigm. The shift is from an essential economy to one that is critically unessential, from the paradigm of Employment to that of Work. In other words, the growth in work is not measured within the restrictive and unrepresentative confines of employment. With the expenditure of labour-power as the basis of analysis, the contribution of non-paid work is explicitly brought into deliberations on social economy growth and its future potentials. With the elimination of the either/or construction of paid work and/or non-paid work, what emerges is work. This forms the starting point for an analysis of work generation possibilities in the social economy. This chapter therefore analyzes the emergence of the Work paradigm by focusing on work generation within organizations in the Toronto social economy.

Overall changes in work, 2000 to 2003: single-variant analysis

Figure 6.1 illustrates the percentage change in work within the social economy from 2000 to 2003. According to this data, the social economy generated work in all of its manifestations, including paid work (13 per cent) and non-paid work (11 per cent). However, the most significant rate of growth came in the area of part-time paid work (21 per cent).

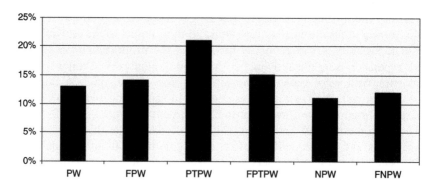

Figure 6.1 Changes in work generation 2000–3.

The growth of paid work

Between 2000–3, paid work within the social economy sector grew faster than in any other sector of the Canadian economy over the same time period. At 13 per cent growth, paid work within the social economy surpassed the rate of growth in construction (12 per cent); utilities (11 per cent); and business, building and other support services (11 per cent), as indicated in Table 6.1.

The significance of this rate of growth is enhanced when we consider the distribution of paid work within the Canadian economy. Overall, the Canadian social economy accounts for 6 per cent of all paying jobs in the country, which is comparable in size to that provided by the finance, insurance, real estate and leasing sector (6 per cent); and the construction industry (6 per cent). This represents the ninth largest sector for national paid work, making the social economy a core sector of the Canadian economy.[3]

Many of these paying jobs involve female participation. According to Figure 6.1, female paid work grew by 14 per cent from 2000 to 2003. Female participation in the Canadian labour market has steadily increased from 40 per cent in 1960 to 72 per cent in 2000.[4] This increasing participation rate has been nearly universal, including women with preschool children, whose participation has risen from 61.2 per cent in 1988 to 66.8 per cent in 1998.[5] The lower rate of participation in the earlier part of the century reveals a clear adherence to the Employment paradigm when paid work was perceived

Table 6.1 Change in paid work, 2000–3

Industry	Paid work growth 2000–3	Distribution of paid work
All industries	5%	100%
Goods-producing sector	3%	25%
Construction	12%	6%
Utilities	11%	1%
Forestry, fishing, mining, oil and gas	2%	2%
Manufacturing	1%	15%
Agriculture	−9%	2%
Services-producing sector	6%	75%
Business, building and other support services	11%	4%
Health care and social assistance	9%	11%
Finance, insurance, real estate and leasing	7%	6%
Educational services	7%	7%
Public administration	7%	5%
Information, culture and recreation	6%	4%
Accommodation and food services	6%	7%
Trade	6%	16%
Professional, scientific and technical services	5%	6%
Other services	2%	5%
Transportation and warehousing	−2%	5%

Source: Statistics Canada, 2003

as part of the masculine domain. Alterations in the gendered composition of the labour market since then have effectively challenged the male-breadwinner and female-carer model that underwrote social reproduction in the Employment paradigm.

However, the gendered division of labour still exists and the growth rate of female paid work within the social economy conforms to the gendered division of labour within the larger labour market. Forty per cent of women who work in the Canadian labour market for a wage or salary are actively engaged in some sort of care work, that is, community, social and personal services.[6] These occupations are characterized by low pay and the social economy is no exception to this. McMullen and Schellenberg factor median earnings for paid work in the social economy to be $2.00CAD to $4.00CAD per hour lower than their counterparts in the market economy.[7]

The growth of part-time paid work

According to survey respondents, the highest rate of growth in the social economy sector in 2000–3 was in the area of part-time paid work. As evidenced in Figure 6.1, this type of work increased by 21 per cent during this time period. This is slightly less than the national average for the social economy, which is 25 per cent.[8]

The intense growth of part-time paid work reflects labour's increased flexibility within a world that has reduced the 'standard employment relationship' that once existed within the Employment paradigm.[9] This increase is fraught with risks to individual workers, employers and the larger society. Workers struggle to make ends meet in a world where the majority of part-time paid work implies economic and social hardship. Employers struggle with a workforce that is fleeting and temporary. In terms of the larger society, the increase in part-time paid work has contributed to a marked polarization in the incomes, institutional access, and life chances of its citizenry. Such vast polarization undermines the legitimacy of the existing institutional order as it triggers a crisis in social reproduction.

As Beck posits, the distinction increasingly in the post-Employment era is not between blue and white-collar jobs but between standardized full-time paid work and a 'risk-fraught system of flexible, pluralized, decentralized underemployment'.[10] In Canada, this is evidenced by the exclusion of non-standard workers from non-statutory benefits, such as extended health plans, dental care, paid sick leave, long-term disability benefits and pension plans. These benefits are extended to 58 per cent of workers engaged in full-time paid work and only 17 per cent of workers engaged in part-time paid work.[11]

Figure 6.2 provides an overview of part-time paid work within the Canadian labour market. The percentage of part-time paid work is growing, having increased from 13 per cent of the Canadian labour force in 1975 to 19 per cent in 2002. Despite this, part-time paid work remains a highly contentious issue. For some workers, the additional time provided by part-time paid work

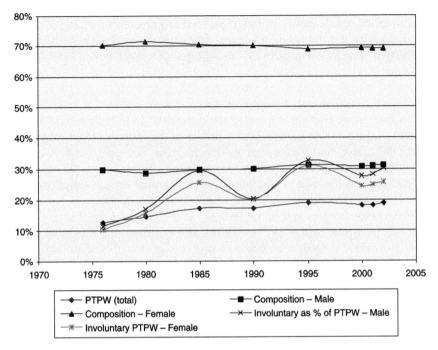

Figure 6.2 Part-time paid work, 1975–2002.

Source: OECD, 2004

enables their participation in other pursuits. For others, the income part-time paid work provides acts to supplement their household income. In these respects, the flexibility of part-time paid work is deemed by some as a positive choice. However, with full-time paid work identified as the standard form of paid work in Canada, part-time paid work is defined as non-standardized work and subject to the limitations that entails. The choices for many, therefore, are highly constrained. Part-time paid work may be the only option available with increasing capitalist rationalization of full-time paid work. Furthermore, the abandoning of the male-breadwinner model and its curtailment of the associated family wage sets the impetus to increase family income as a potential necessity rather than a choice, an attempt to simply maintain living standards rather than improve them.

As we see in Figure 6.2, part-time paid work is clearly a gendered phenomenon, with women comprising 70 per cent of part-time paid work participants over the last 27 years. This number has remained constant despite economic fluctuations. More critical factors in the creation of part-time paid work are industry and occupational characteristics, along with local unemployment levels. This is evidenced within the Canadian social economy. The precariousness associated with funding in particular, such as project funding versus organizational funding, contributes to the rise of part-time paid work in this sector. The existence of organizational funding makes it possible for organizations to tailor labour-power to organizational requirements forming just-in-time-paid work. Project funding, in turn, reinforces the need for labour-power flexibility as funding is project-driven, uneven and short term in duration. This flexibility comes at a cost for the Canadian social economy, as the sector is plagued by poor worker retention. According to Hall *et al.* (2001), this remains a key inhibitor to capacity building.[12]

This discussion highlights a necessary distinction in part-time paid work between voluntary and involuntary part-time paid work. According to Figure 6.2, involuntary part-time paid work also increased from 1975 to 2002: from 11 per cent to 30 per cent for males and 10 per cent to 26 per cent for females. This increase in involuntary part-time paid work is significant as there is a considerable earnings loss, of approximately $3.00CAD per hour ($2.55CAD for females and $3.19CAD for males), between involuntary and voluntary part-time paid work.[13] While this rise in involuntary part-time paid work is constant it should be noted that it is also exacerbated during economic recessions, particularly for men. Men are less likely to choose part-time paid work and therefore are more likely to be involved in this type of work on an involuntary basis. For example, in the recessionary period from 1990 to 1995 the number of men involved in involuntary part-time paid work increased from 20 per cent to 30 per cent, even higher than that of females involved in involuntary part-time paid work.

Studies indicate that despite the higher incidence of part-time paid work in the social economy, the rate of involuntary part-time paid work remains the same across all economies: social, market, and state.[14] Since women make up the vast majority of participants in part-time paid work, I suggest that the gender imbalance that currently exists in the social economy sector towards the feminization of labour may be a contributing factor to the lower incidences of involuntary part-time paid work within it.

In any case, part-time paid work in the social economy is emblematic of the Work paradigm, as it is increasingly the only way individuals can engage in the labour market. For those with increased work commitments, such as family work resulting from the restructuring of the state's social commitments, part-time paid work may be the only way to maintain these commitments while still earning an income. For others, such as those seeking entry or maintained involvement in the waged-labour market, part-time paid work may simply be the only job available.

The common denominator between both of these circumstances is the shifting of risks from the social to the individual. The social compromise of the Employment paradigm, which consisted of full employment, a family wage and social insurance, has been hollowed out. It has not been eliminated, as the Employment paradigm remains institutionally dominant, but it has been vacated of the benefits that once provided it with more balance.

A paradigm shift from Employment to Work challenges this state of affairs – not as an attempt to revert back to the full-time paid-work utopia of the Employment paradigm, but instead to shift to the multiwork heterotopia of the Work paradigm. The issue is not the elimination of part-time paid work, but the elimination of the precariousness associated with it. The expansion of part-time paid work within the labour market, and specifically within the social economy, does not necessarily point to a shortage of work. Rather, it is an indication of the expansion of work as individuals increasingly bear the risks associated with the post-Employment era. As I will argue in Chapter 7, individuals are forced to re-evaluate paid work in juxtaposition with their other forms of work, including those of family, house, voluntary and political work. Paid work, and increasingly part-time paid work, becomes but one manifestation of labour-power, a circumstance that is better explained by the transition to a Work paradigm.

The growth of non-paid work

Another manifestation of labour-power that is indicative of the transition to the Work paradigm is non-paid work. According to Figure 6.2, this form of work increased by 11 per cent from 2000 to 2003.[15] The proportion of workers engaged in non-paid work as opposed to paid work within the Toronto social economy is 5:1.[16] Additionally, 8 per cent of institutional respondents indicated that there were no paid workers in their organizations at all. This is significantly less than the national average, which depending on the study utilized ranges from 15 per cent to 42 per cent.[17] For these reasons the contribution of non-paid work to the development of the social economy and its social output cannot be discounted nor underestimated.

In fact, the growth and subsequent impact of non-paid work emanating from the social economy has been noticed both nationally and globally. Globally, the United Nations General Assembly acknowledged the role of non-paid work with its 1997 declaration proclaiming 2001 as the International Year of Volunteers. Canada joined in this effort by emphasizing five objectives in the promotion of volunteer work: a celebration of volunteerism, the promotion of volunteerism for all, an expansion of the definition of volunteerism in Canada, the improvement of voluntary organizational infrastructures, and the development of the voluntary sector knowledge base.[18] While these are welcome developments they retain an essentialist ontology of economy, as work remains forcibly constrained to the seemingly disparate acts of employment and volunteering.

Nonetheless, underlying these acknowledgements is the understanding that non-paid work is essential to development strategies and a critical dimension of active citizenship.[19] In Toronto, non-paid work provided the full-time paid work equivalent of 74,900 jobs in 1997.[20] Organizations within the Toronto social economy case study projected serving 368,534 individuals in 2003, which represents a 32 per cent increase from 2000. This production of labour-power in conjunction with its social output highlights a consciousness of *being-in-the-world-with-others*. This is the sole means of understanding why non-paid work growth is so significant within the social economy. The labour-power supplied is the antithesis of *homo economicus*, as motivation cannot be reduced to the one-dimensional consideration of self-interest guided on the basis of contractual social relations. Instead, it may be the crisis of social reproduction and the social provisioning responses inherent in the social economy that account for extensive and intensive growth.

On a national scale, conservative estimates indicate that social economy organizations contribute 4 per cent to the Canadian GDP.[21] Notwithstanding that GDP is an incomplete measure of value creation, Table 6.2 places the social economy contribution above industries, such as mining, oil and gas extraction (3.5 per cent), agriculture, fishing and hunting (2.3 per cent) and accommodation and food services (2.2 per cent).[22]

The single-variant analysis of the Toronto social economy provides the basis for the conclusion that the social economy is generative of work. However, work generation within the social economy is uneven. A more precise understanding of work generation emerges through the utilization of bivariant analysis.

For the purposes of a bivariant analysis, organizations were examined along four dimensions: activity (both CCRA and ICNPO), scope, budget and epoch. This analysis reveals that to the extent that we can construct an ideal

Table 6.2 Gross domestic product composition

Industry	GDP Composition
All industries	100%
Finance, insurance, real estate, renting, leasing and management of companies and enterprises	20%
Manufacturing	17.5%
Wholesale trade	6.2%
Health care and social assistance	6%
Public administration	5.7%
Retail trade	5.6%
Construction industries	5.4%
Educational services	4.5%
Transportation and warehousing	4.5%
Professional, scientific and technical services	4.4%
Information and cultural industries	4.1%
Mining, oil and gas extraction	3.5%
Utilities	2.5%
Other services (except public administration)	2.4%
Agriculture, fishing and hunting	2.3%
Accommodation and food services	2.2%
Administration, support, waste management and remediation services	2.2%
Arts, entertainment and recreation	0.9%

Source: Statistics Canada, 2003

type of organization for work generation, this organization is composed of the following characteristics:

• it is engaged in community benefit or welfare activities;
• it is local in scope;
• it is small in size;
• it was founded within the post-Employment era.

Overall changes in work, 2000 to 2003: bivariant analysis

While the previous section indicated that the social economy was generative of work, this section will reveal the uneven nature of this work generation. It assesses this information based on four key factors: activity, scope, budget, and size.

Activity and work: 2000–3

As indicated in Chapter 5, there is no current categorization of social economy organizations for researchers to use. As a result, this research has made use of both the CCRA and ICNPO categorizations to organize social economy players and assess numbers.

Figure 6.3 reveals the uneven work generation pattern within the Toronto social economy community based on CCRA categorizations.[23] Between 2000 and 2003, organizations within the Benefit to Community category showed the greatest increase in paid work at 22 per cent. This was followed by Welfare

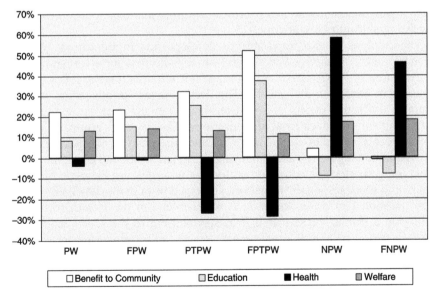

Figure 6.3 CCRA and changes in work generation 2000–3.

at 13 per cent. These gains suggest that organizations whose activities are more class-based have expanded their service delivery, which is reasonable when considering social policies during the time period under study. Welfare, in particular, has been subject to government cutbacks, devolution and ideological assaults. At the same time, communities have seen the birth of a variety of organizations to aid and advocate for those impacted by such cuts. In this sense, the social economy has not simply filled a vacuum left as a result of the state's apparent withdrawal from this form of service delivery. It has also become an initiator of welfare delivery alternatives. A conventional example of a service that attempts to fill a service vacuum is the food bank. Food banks were originally thought to be temporary measures that would be scaled back once government welfare programmes and the overall economy shifted from recession and restructuring. An innovative delivery system has been the development of programmes specific to ethnic and cultural communities such as those that service the First Nations communities. These programmes have replaced state welfare programmes but have also instituted programmes that are specifically geared towards the communities they serve.

Within the same time period, Health organizations showed the greatest increase in non-paid work (58 per cent) while also having the greatest decline in paid work (–4 per cent). The increase in non-paid work may be attributable to long-term or objective factors, such as the survey's focus on Toronto (the centre for healthcare delivery for the province) and the fact that the overall population is aging. Yet the dramatic increase suggests a more immediate rationale. Indeed, such an increase may, like that seen in the area of welfare, be attributable to a social response on the part of individuals to deep and persistent cuts in Canada's universal healthcare system. These cutbacks have been highlighted in federal and provincial elections and therefore continue to receive significant public attention.

This analysis is also applicable to developments in Education. While Welfare and Community Benefit were among the first social programmes restructured by the Conservative government in Ontario, this was followed by changes in education and health. The deep cutbacks in education within Ontario sparked a variety of social responses ranging from protest to the establishment of educational organizations. The drop in non-paid work (–9 per cent), as indicated in Figure 6.3, may therefore be an indication of occupational fatigue. The accompanying rise in paid work and part-time paid work suggests that the education sector has moved along the cycle of cutbacks and social responses to again create waged work in the social economy. The question that arises therefore is whether or not the Health sector is following a similar pattern of increasingly shifting to the social economy. After a period of high non-paid work growth, will it also generate waged work again?

While Figure 6.3 analyzed social economy organizations based on the CCRA categorizations, Figures 6.4a and 6.4b do so based on the ICNPO categorizations. The illustrations exemplify the unevenness of work generation

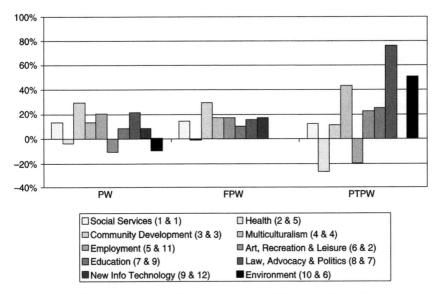

Figure 6.4a ICNPO and changes in work generation 2000–3 (paid work).

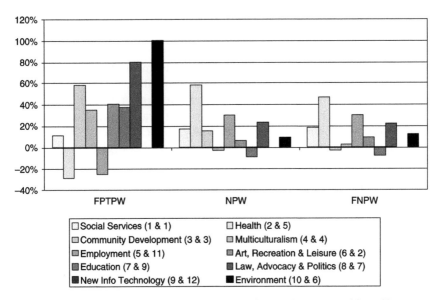

Figure 6.4b ICNPO and changes in work generation 2000–3 (non-paid work).

within the social economy as they provide both an ICNPO breakdown of percentage growth in work as well as an absolute numeric ranking of paid work and non-paid work. In terms of the latter, the largest numbers of paid workers from 2000 to 2003 were engaged in Social Services (rank 1) and Health organizations (rank 2). However, in terms of non-paid work, the greatest benefactors of this form of labour-power were the Social Services (rank 1) and Arts, Recreation and Leisure organizations (rank 2).

The increased production of labour-power in Social Services organizations lends itself most readily to the risk society thesis. Its growth is the result of welfare state restructuring along with a simultaneous organic response to try and meet unmet social needs. The high rates of non-paid work within Arts, Recreation and Leisure, are also indicative of the Work paradigm as they point to the existence of multiwork strategies that go beyond utilitarian measures.

In terms of paid work, organizations whose primary activities were Community Development (29 per cent), Legal, Advocacy and Politics (21 per cent) and Employment (20 per cent) had the largest increases according to the research data. Legal, Advocacy and Politics also had the highest percentage growth in part-time paid work (76 per cent) and non-paid work (23 per cent).

The growth of Legal, Advocacy and Politics suggests a characteristic strategy shift on the part of community groups to expand their activities beyond the norm, in this case advocating at legislatures. The emergence of this form of subpolitics indicates both a technocratic approach to issues of advocacy as well as the operationalization of individuation as social justice is potentially reached through individual cases.

Scope and work: 2000–3

Figure 6.5 illustrates why social economy dynamism must be viewed through the lens of work rather than the lens of employment. By differentiating organizations according to the scope of their activities, ranging from local through to global, universal increases in paid work are revealed. Provincial (16 per cent) and national (15 per cent) organizations have the largest increases followed by local (8 per cent) and global (7 per cent). The higher rate of paid work growth for provincial and national organizations highlights the centrality of the institutional structure and the significance of

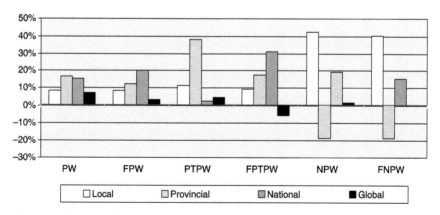

Figure 6.5 Scope and changes in work generation 2000–3.

path-dependent development. These organizations may benefit from their economies of scale. Their breadth of scope may heighten their perceived legitimacy within the funding community, including governmental sources. This reinforces a path-dependency as the perception of legitimacy for larger organizations leads to a renewal of funding which in turn augments their legitimacy.

The work generation dynamics at the local level reinforce this as these organizations have the smallest rate of paid work growth (8 per cent) while having the highest amounts of non-paid work (42 per cent). As the federal and provincial governments provide the bulk of public funding for the sector, local organizations may be at an institutional disadvantage.

However, the ability of organizations to deliver goods and services is dependent upon the availability of both paid work and non-paid work. While provincial organizations have the highest rate of paid work growth, they also have the sharpest decline in both non-paid work and female non-paid work (19 per cent). The imbalance identified here, and other similar imbalances (see Education and Art, Recreation and Leisure in Figure 6.4), indicates the potential that exists for organizations to undermine their own capacity over time. As the ratio is approximately 5:1 of non-paid workers to paid workers, productive capacity is finite and it is based on both paid work and non-paid work. If there is an over-emphasis on paid work, the organization may suffer by losing its available non-paid work.[24]

When analyzing the social economy sector from the perspective of the Work paradigm rather than the Employment paradigm, local and national organizations distinguish themselves as the most dynamic generators of work. This increased utilization of labour-power points towards further intensive and extensive social economy activity.

Budget and work: 2000–3

Within the frame of the Employment paradigm, Figure 6.6 would suggest that medium-sized organizations are the most dynamic. However, this is an incomplete vantage point as these organizations show the highest rate of part-time paid work growth (39 per cent). On a broad level, drawing attention to paid work without the requisite focus on the type of work does not address the issues of precariousness for both labour and the sector, which set off growing risks within the Canadian labour market. The rising levels of part-time paid work are triggered by the vulnerability of medium-sized organizations to alterations in their operating environments.

The imposition of *just-in-time* principles, developed in the post-Employment era *vis-à-vis* funding predicated on a project-by-project basis, renders medium-sized organizations vulnerable to alterations in the operating environment. The rising levels of part-time paid work are responses to these pressures. Large organizations, on the other hand, have a greater tendency to diversify their activities and are therefore able to shift as necessary to changing circumstances without endangering the organization. Their size

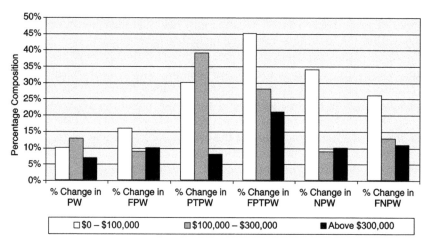

Figure 6.6 Budget and changes in work generation 2000–3.

and name recognition also enhance their fundraising prospects, which is critical to organizational success with increasing numbers of organizations seeking limited sources of funding.

Similarly, small organizations are also likely to adapt to the emergent meaning structures associated with risk society and the organizational flexibility requirements imposed by post-Fordist development. With productivity dependent upon labour-power, which cannot be reduced to paid work or non-paid work, social economy organizations must remain relevant for the sake of their own production. In other words, social economy organizations must be meaningful. However, as meanings are structured in the here and now, rather than being transcendental, issues come to the fore while others recede. The high rate of non-paid work growth within small organizations as displayed in Figure 6.6 suggests that small organizations are a critical organizational form possibly due to their very relevance. This relevancy to issues of the day becomes an attractor of labour-power. Small organizations also tend to be active in niche areas, which provide them with an initial head start in developing the skills and programmes to supply this unmet demand.

These small organizations epitomize the 'ideal type' post-Fordist organization, as they most closely resemble market economy start-ups. Within the market economy, start-ups are considered to be the centre of entrepreneurship and innovation. In terms of form, these organizations tend to lack a formal division of labour and instead require multitasking. This lack of a formal structure and requisite division of labour also contributes to a lessening of inertia that allows the organization to shift more rapidly. Finally, the limitations of size curtail the possibility of projecting for medium and long-term environmental shifts. Instead, as indicated earlier, small organizations must be more resourceful and imaginative than medium or large organizations since organizational resources are scarcer.

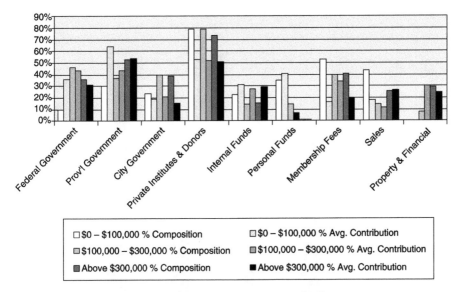

Figure 6.7 Size: budgetary composition and average contribution.

Figure 6.7 further highlights the linkages that exist between organizational size and the risks present in the Work paradigm. It displays both the percentage composition of various funding sources and their average composition. According to the data, medium and large organizations are more likely to receive funding from government. On average, medium and large organizations receive 40 per cent and 42 per cent of their budgets from the three levels of government while small organizations receive only 21 per cent. Smaller organizations, as a result, are required to seek funding in other forms, including membership fees (52 per cent), sales (43 per cent) and personal funds (34 per cent).

The reliance on personal funds by smaller organizations is not insignificant since the average contribution to annual budgets measures 45 per cent. This indicates both the precariousness associated with the post-Employment era for such organizations and reaffirms the requisite criterion that participants in such organizations may have a consciousness of *being-in-the-world-with-others*. Individuals may take on the creation and maintenance of these organizations in order to address risks that have eluded existing institutions. In doing so, they shift the location of the political from legislatures to subpolitics since their organizational manifestation challenges the power of others to determine what issues are significant and how to address them.

Epochs and work: 2000 and 2003

In Figure 6.8, organizations are classified according to the epoch in which they were founded. These classifications conform to the distinction drawn

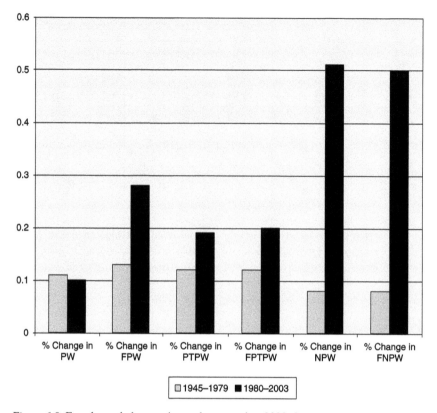

Figure 6.8 Epochs and changes in work generation 2000–3.

between the Employment and Work paradigms and reaffirm the unevenness of work generation within the social economy more broadly. Both epochs are similar in their consumption of paid work, with 11 per cent and 10 per cent growth. Organizations formed within the ascendancy of the Work paradigm though are more dynamic in terms of overall work generation as they have significantly higher levels of part-time paid work (19 per cent) and non-paid work (51 per cent).

The growth of these non-standard forms of work in organizations that were founded in the post-Employment era, however, foreground issues of precariousness and flexibility as the mechanisms for socializing risk, such as employment insurance, remain wedded to the Employment paradigm. The dynamism of organizations founded from 1980–2003 is attributable neverthe-less to confluence between the organizational structure and post-Fordist accumulation along with their closer connection to issues germinating within the social.

When analyzing the distribution of organizations according to budget-ary size and corresponding epoch, we see that a higher proportion of organizations created from 1980–2003 are small in size. Organizations created from 1945–1979, on the other hand, are more heavily concentrated amongst the largest category. As Mary K. Foster and Agnes G. Meinhard conclude, newer organizations within the Canadian social economy have proven to be highly adaptable.[25] Not only do these organizations employ a wider range of options to deal with recent disciplinary neo-liberal cutbacks, they are also more likely to view the results of change more positively. This has not necessarily resulted in success. Many respondents indicated that while they were attempting to employ a variety of strategies, they were also finding it increasingly difficult to secure additional funding sources precisely due to the perceived lack of legitimacy associated with their relatively recent arrival.

Yet this late arrival also points to the organic growth of the social economy sector as labour-power is increasingly drawn to the relevancy of the issues addressed by its organizations. Non-paid work shows a significant increase in organizations formed within the post-Employment era (50 per cent). As discussed earlier this is, in part, reflective of the subordinated character of the social economy to modes of development. Social economy organizations have incorporated the industrial form associated more closely with the dominant regime of accumulation within the respective epochs.

Organizations founded from 1945–1979 more readily adopted the prevailing organizational form that underpinned capitalist accumulation within the Employment paradigm: large-scale, centralized, and composed of hierarchical bureaucratic controls. Paradoxically this worked to progressively disconnect these organizations from the civil society they hoped to serve in terms of goods and services and organizational mandate. The separation between these organizations and the arising social needs of their constituencies is compounded by the difficulties presented by their organizational form. The combination of both issues have contributed largely to the slow rate of overall work generation in these organizations. This pattern is exemplified when comparing two social economy activities: Social Services and Arts, Recreation and Leisure.

Epochs and work 2000–3: Social Services and Arts, Recreation and Leisure

Figure 6.9 expands on the uneven work generation discussion emanating from Figure 6.8 by considering epochal distinctions for the Arts, Recreation and Leisure, and Social Services sectors. These sectors are significant as both were supported by the Keynesian Fordist state and have subsequently been subject to cutbacks and partial disentanglement from government. Work generation within Social Services substantiates the position that organizations created within the post-Employment era show higher levels of work generation. Paid work growth, for instance, is 29 per cent more in organizations founded from 1980–2003. While female paid work is 42 per cent higher

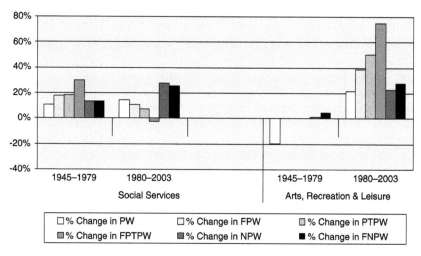

Figure 6.9 Epochs: Social Services and Arts, Recreation and Leisure.

for organizations created between 1945–79, both non-paid work and female non-paid work are increasing at approximately twice the rate for organizations founded from 1980–2003.

Organizations within the Arts, Recreation and Leisure sector provide a clearer confirmation of this uneven work generation. While paid work has decreased by 20 per cent for organizations that derive from the Employment paradigm, those that were established subsequently have had an increase of 23 per cent. Of critical significance within paid work is the rate of increase in female paid work (38 per cent) and part-time paid work (50 per cent). Non-paid work growth also demonstrates disparities between the two epochs, as organizations derived in the post-Employment era have an 85 per cent higher rate of growth.

Working futures

The survey given to organizational respondents included questions pertaining to future work generation. The projections analyzed point to continued growth, but uneven growth in the type of work generated within the social economy. These projections are based on a three to five year outlook from 2003–8.

CCRA futures

According to survey respondents, all sectors within the social economy will increase work generation over the next three to five years. This is illustrated in Figure 6.10. Over half of the respondents in Welfare (55 per cent), Benefit to Community (57 per cent) and Health (67 per cent) organizations anticipate

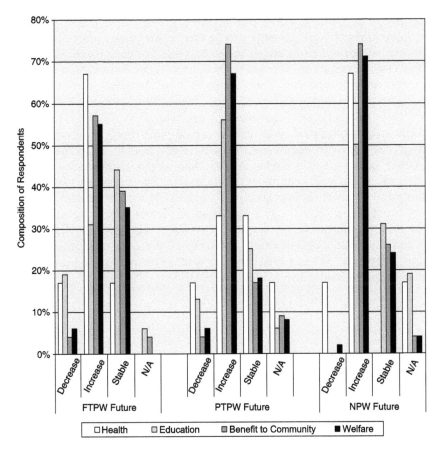

Figure 6.10 CCRA futures.

increases in full-time paid work. Education presents a more muted outlook with a larger percentage of respondents indicating that full-time paid work will only remain stable (44 per cent).

When asked about part-time paid work and non-paid work, respondents showed significant disparities depending on their organization's activity as determined by CCRA categorization. For example, respondents within Benefit to Community organizations (74 per cent) and Welfare organizations (67 per cent) projected significant increases in their consumption of part-time paid work. All sectors indicated considerable enlargement of non-paid work. This leads us to the conclusion that while the utilization of labour-power in its various manifestations underpins social economy dynamism without the requisite ontological shift to conceiving the economy as non-essentialized, uneven work generation will continue to contribute to increased risk and precariousness within the Canadian political economy.

Epoch futures

The unevenness of work generation is further substantiated when organizations are categorized along epoch, scope and size. For example, Figure 6.11 shows that organizations founded within either epoch have similar growth forecasts for full-time paid work. Organizations founded from 1945–79 reported a projected growth rate of 52 per cent while organizations founded from 1980–2003 reported a projected growth rate of 50 per cent. However, growth in part-time paid work and non-paid work point to divergences. Nearly one-third of organizations originating from 1945–79 indicate that part-time paid work will remain stable, while 52 per cent foresee growth. Conversely, only 16 per cent of organizations established between 1980–2003 project that the levels of part-time paid work would remain the same, while 69 per cent foresee growth. The likelihood of second epoch organizations to increase positions is further substantiated when analyzing the projections for non-paid work. For this type of work, 52 per cent of organizations founded between 1945 and 1979 expect growth, as opposed to 76 per cent of organizations formed between 1980 and 2003.

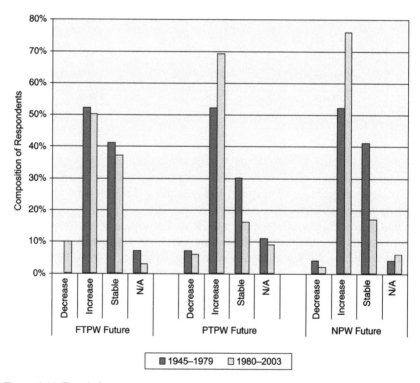

Figure 6.11 Epoch futures.

Afterword

Social economy projections of work generation in conjunction with actual changes in work from 2000–3 attest to the emergence of a Work paradigm. Single-variant analysis reveals significant growth in all forms of work. Of critical note is the rise in part-time paid work and non-paid work. Part-time paid work is structured into the Canadian social economy to a large extent by the use of project funding. This may, to some extent, address issues of accountability and fiscal responsibility but it also contributes to significant levels of precariousness and further hinders social innovation.

Non-paid work growth, and its numerical dominance over those engaged in paid work within the social economy, points to the centrality of this form of labour-power. The significance, however, is not simply measured in numbers but in the rationale for its existence. The continued growth of non-paid work within the social economy is attributable to the ongoing crisis of social reproduction and a consciousness of *being-in-the-world-with-others*. This is highlighted by small organizations that required individuals to contribute personal finances in order to ensure the organization's operations.

The bivariant analysis though provided a more nuanced and a complete understanding of work generation. By revealing patterns of uneven work generation, this analysis provides empirical evidence to the benefits of an analysis that begins its assessments from the perspective of the Work paradigm. As social economy capacity is predicated on the provision of labour-power irrespective of whether it is paid or not, this necessitates an analysis that begins with work rather than either paid work or non-paid work. In short, it is the consumption of labour-power that underpins social economy dynamism.

As social economy organizations project continued growth in the consumption of labour-power, the issue of how it is possible to produce labour-power will remain central to their possibilities of success. Chapter 7 therefore expands on this notion of labour-power within the social economy by focusing on its production from the standpoint of a multiactivity society. In doing so, a different articulation of the Work paradigm emerges, centred explicitly on the reflexive production of labour-power.

7 Structuring the Work paradigm
(Re)production of labour-power

Chapter 6 examined the transition in the Canadian economy from the Employment paradigm to the Work paradigm from the perspective of social economy organizations. In this chapter, the lens of analysis is shifted from the organization onto the worker.[1] The aim is to assess the extent to which the Work paradigm permeates and structures the daily lives of workers. Operationalizing of the epistemic and ontological frame developed in Chapters 3 and 4 forms the basis of the analysis. In general terms worker participants were asked questions relating to their paid or non-paid work in the social economy, their lifestyles and their attitudes about work.

The survey results support the thesis of a transition to the Work paradigm. Workers conceptualize economies existing in *différance*. That is, the social economy forms an economy distinct from the market and state economies. Second, the decision of respondents to engage their labour-power within the social economy sector is formulated reflexively, as workers acknowledge the higher costs associated with social economy sector participation. Third, the responses may also indicate that labour-power manifests in a heterotopic field of work where rules, functions and purposes are dissimilar to those that respondents experience in the market and state economies.

It is the lack of formal institutional acknowledgement and the necessity to address emergent risks that manifest as the crisis of social reproduction that situates respondents within the interregnum between the paradigms of Employment and Work. Respondents indicate significant levels of constraint as paradigmatic traces hail, but are unable to sustain, individuals and the broader society, which are engaged in addressing the crisis of social reproduction.

Conceptualizing the Work paradigm: economies in *différance*

A key component of the Work paradigm is the recognition of economies in *différance*. As argued in Chapter 4, *différance* is juxtaposed with dualisms whereby economy is hierarchically conceptualized as either a market economy or not a market economy. The subordinated other within this essentialist ontology is the social economy. *Différance* instead posits distinct economies co-constituted and always in-relation-with, but not in subordination to, the other. Two questions were developed to determine whether respondents conceptualized the social economy as a distinct and separate economy from that of the market economy and state economy. The first question asked whether respondents viewed the social economy as a temporary manifestation. The second question focused on whether respondents viewed the social economy as a transitory phase toward the market economy. Combined, these questions quantified the extent to which respondents identified the social economy as a heterotopic site.[2]

Is the social economy a temporary manifestation?

As indicated in Figure 7.1, single-variant analysis reveals that respondents overwhelmingly deny the conceptualization of the social economy as a temporary manifestation. Instead, 92 per cent of them view the social economy as an embedded economy within the Work paradigm.

This conceptualization of the social economy as a component of economy challenges the capitalocentrism of both Keynesian and neo-classical economics. As discussed in Chapter 3, both theorizations fail to recognize the social economy as a unique economy. At best, they consider it an addendum to the market economy. Neo-classical economics for example views the social economy solely as a charitable endeavour. But it is clear from Figure 7.1 that participants in the social economy view it differently. Respondents may more readily identify the social economy as a sector with significance and potential permanence. By distinguishing it from the market and state economies, respondents also indicate that they identify with the notion of heterotopic economies rather than that of a single utopic economy.

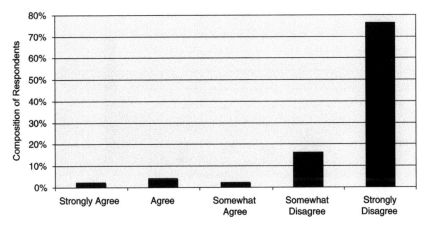

Figure 7.1 Social economy as a temporary manifestation.

Social economy exists to assist transition to market economy

When asked if the social economy exists to transition workers into the market economy, a broad consensus of respondents – 92 per cent of paid workers and 96 per cent of non-paid workers – indicate that it does not. This is consistent with the high numbers of respondents who believe that the social economy is a permanent phenomenon, thus underlying the social economy's normative status as particularly distinct from the market economy.

While the high level of support from paid workers may not be overly surprising, the high level of support by non-paid workers is significant, as it challenges the capitalocentric view that the market economy functions as a centripetal force subsuming potential alternatives.

Non-paid workers contribute approximately 364 hours per year to the social economy, correlating to a substantial time commitment. However, they also explicitly 'work' elsewhere in that the majority of non-paid workers in the social economy are employed in either the market economy or state economy. In this sense, they are an explicit example of labourers who distribute their labour-power in multiple sites. While the labour-power they make available to the social economy underpins the sector's potential for production, it is complementary to the labour produced by those engaged in paid work.

Bivariant analysis by age groupings reaffirms the strong consensus that the social economy does not exist as a means of transition to the capitalist market economy. As indicated in Figure 7.2, there is a negative correlation between age and strong disagreement with the question. Respondents aged 34 and under had the starkest opposition to the question with 62 per cent of those under 25 strongly disagreeing, and 66 per cent of those aged 25 to 34 strongly disagreeing. Meanwhile, those aged 55 to 64 had the lowest levels of strong disagreement (22 per cent).

Higher levels of disagreement amongst younger respondents is attributable

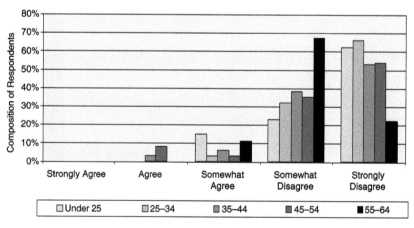

Figure 7.2 Social economy exists to assist transition to market economy: age groups.

to the overlap that exists between their entry into the paid labour market and the transition in Canada to the Work paradigm. The confluence of these two events resulted in two processes that were critical for the shift to the Work paradigm.

First, this demographic had to face the increasing rationalization of paid work in the market economy that occurred in the 1980s and 1990s. As indicated in Figure 7.3, those under 35 have consistently had higher rates of unemployment than older cohorts. However, these rates were worst during the early part of the post-Employment era.

Second, with labour rationalization, younger workers faced diminishing returns in both the quality and duration of the paid work they could find, which often resulted in the attainment of multiple jobs. For example, as part of this survey, 26 per cent of respondents indicated that they held two or more paid jobs.[3]

Echoing Gramsci who argued that 'new methods of work are inseparable from a specific mode of living and thinking and feeling', the lack of paid work or the appropriate form of paid work (i.e., underemployment) is an elemental force in shaping the mode of living.[4] The high rates of unemployment and underemployment within the market and state economies have had the unintended consequence of furthering the transition to the Work paradigm. As individuals fail to find accommodation within the market and state economies, these economies lose their privileged positions as sources of ontological security. At the same time, as individuals – particularly younger workers – increasingly secure both an income and a sense of identity within the social economy, the association of the social economy as a generator of positive outcomes, including the creation of paid work, strengthens.

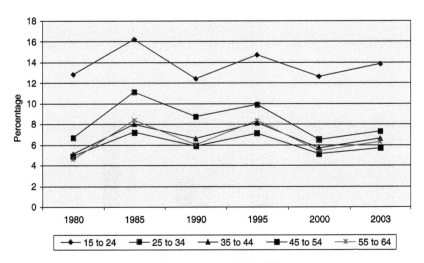

Figure 7.3 Unemployment rate by age group, 1980–2003.

Source: OECD, 2004

The under-35s entered the paid labour market at a time when the social economy was in a growth phase. From 2000 to 2003, paid work increased by 13 per cent and part-time paid work increased by 21 per cent within the Toronto social economy. As discussed earlier, in 2004 the Canadian social economy constituted 6 per cent of paid work, which is comparable in size to the finance, insurance, real estate and leasing sector, or the construction sector – representing the ninth largest sector for paid work.

Social economy exists as a result of corporate support

Finally, respondents were asked if they believed that the social economy existed as a result of corporate support. Overall, 65 per cent of respondents indicated disagreement with this statement. This was echoed in bivariant analysis that examined paid workers (94 per cent) and non-paid workers (87 per cent).

In terms of gender, a larger proportion of females – 68 per cent, compared with 58 per cent of males, disagreed with the statement. However, as indicated in Figure 7.4, these indications of broad consensus are not as straightforward as they appear.

One mitigating factor appears to be educational attainment. Analysis based on educational attainment reveals that nearly one-third of respondents who completed high school to college (32 per cent) agreed with the statement that corporate support is the basis of the social economy. This is followed by respondents who completed Bachelor's degrees (12 per cent) and post-graduate degrees (9 per cent). Disagreement with the statement is strongest amongst postgraduates, with 72 per cent, followed by respondents with Bachelor's degrees at 67 per cent, and high school to college at 56 per cent.

These findings suggest that those with higher levels of educational attainment are less inclined to view the market economy as the epicentre of production within the economy. They affirm, for some, the heterotopic status of the social economy as an alternative space that is distinct in function and purpose

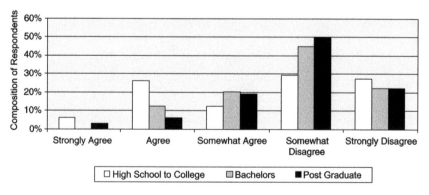

Figure 7.4 Social economy exists due to corporate support: educational attainment.

to that of the market economy. While the higher proportion of respondents within the Somewhat Disagree category may suggest that the market economy is conceived as a contributing factor to the development of the social economy, it is not viewed as the definitive source. This articulation is more closely related to a plural understanding of economies, constitutive of market, state and social.

Beyond rationalism: reflexivity and economies

In order to further quantify the shift to the Work paradigm within Canada, respondents were asked questions comparing wage levels between the state, market and social economies. Findings show that respondents challenge the neo-classical and Keynesian conceptualization of why individuals choose to engage their labour-power. While they recognize that they receive lower wages in the social economy than they would in the market and state economies, respondents choose to remain in the social economy – a decision that fails to fit within the calculus of *homo economicus*. This suggests that workers are basing their decisions on a number of factors that go beyond the unidimensional qualities of monetary compensation and utility maximization. This reflexive decision-making conforms with the Work paradigm.

Wage level comparisons between the social economy and the market economy

Overall, 68 per cent of paid workers within the social economy indicate that their incomes are below those of comparable forms of waged work in the market economy. These findings are confirmed by McMullen and Schellenberg who cite median earnings for paid work within the social economy as $4,160.00CAD to $8,320.00CAD less than those found in the market economy.[5] This relationship is further affected by factors such as educational attainment.

Figure 7.5 illustrates the impact of educational attainment on wages. While a majority of participants perceived that they earned lower wages in the social economy, the greatest perceived difference in wage levels between the social economy and market economy was seen by those respondents who answered that they held a Bachelor's degree. Approximately 74 per cent of social economy actors with Bachelor's degrees who participated in this survey felt that they were earning below the market economy rate for their position. While 18 per cent of these respondents answered that they did not know the wage differential, only 8 per cent responded that they earned more in the social economy sector.

The number of respondents with Bachelor's degrees who reported lower wages was notably higher than participants who fit in the two other educational classifications. Nearly one-fifth of those with a post-graduate degree (19 per cent) or high school to college diploma (17 per cent) indicated that

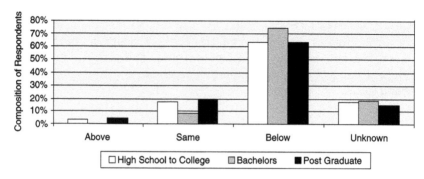

Figure 7.5 Wage level comparisons between the social economy and the market economy: educational attainment.

their wages were the same as those in the market economy. This is more than double the number of those with a Bachelor's degree (8 per cent). This is significant when considering the number of respondents who believe that the social economy is not a transition to the market economy. Over 95 per cent of those respondents hold a Bachelor's degree. This is the highest level amongst the educational categorizations. This may be explained in part by the disproportionately higher number of workers in the social economy who have post-secondary education. According to Statistics Canada, 27.9 per cent of workers within the social economy have a university degree as opposed to 15.2 per cent in the market economy.[6]

The demand for university-educated labourers within the social economy coupled with the increased rationalization of paid work within the Canadian economy has had the unintended consequence of workers increasingly identifying the social economy as a generator of paid work. Individuals with a Bachelor's degree may find that the knowledge base derived from their education is more readily utilized and valued within the social economy in comparison to the market economy.

Focusing on the ICNPO activity categorizations of Social Services and Arts, Recreation and Leisure provides further details regarding educational attainment. In the Arts sector, paid work outside the state economy is divided between the social economy (55 per cent) and the market economy (40 per cent).[7] Workers engaged in paid work within this activity classification therefore have the education required to work in the social, state or market economies. Yet 80 per cent indicate a strong preference to engage their labour-power within the social economy.

This is particularly significant when considering the wage differential between the social economy and the market economy in the Arts, Recreation and Leisure sector. The vast majority of respondents (71 per cent) recognize that the social economy pays them less for their labour. It is clear that these workers are basing their decisions on a reflexive range of factors beyond that of wage compensation and utility maximization.

While the findings suggest that survey respondents view the social economy favourably, they do not support the notion of social economy exclusivity. In other words, reflexivity suggests that individuals are not fixed within the social economy but more appropriately to what the social economy signifies. The pertinent issue is therefore whether or not the social economy can accommodate and facilitate the motivations that lead individuals to manifest their labour-power in it. As indicated elsewhere, the central issue is that of meaning and the degree of conformity to a consciousness of *being-in-the-world-with-others*. One way of measuring this is to discover whether or not the sense of achievement found in the social economy can be found elsewhere.

Sense of achievement

When participants were asked whether the sense of achievement they experienced in the social economy could be achieved elsewhere, 45 per cent of respondents answered in the affirmative. Provided with three options – state economy, market economy and other – the largest percentage of respondents (40 per cent) believed that they could achieve the same sense of achievement within the state economy. However, many respondents (32 per cent) believed that the social economy was the only economy where they could achieve a similar sense of achievement. Only 28 per cent believed that the market economy held possibilities for them.

Not only do these findings challenge the assumed hegemony of the market economy as the sole legitimate site of production, they also suggest reasons as to why workers in the social economy hold such support for the social economy and state economy. Respondents indicate that the latter two sectors present a greater likelihood to both reflect and refract the meaning that they feel is necessary to activate their labour-power. This meaning or motivation goes beyond utility maximization. It may be more readily derived from the work respondents perform and the reasons for that work. It therefore may be based on reflexive judgments and holistic reasoning rather than utility maximization and instrumental reasoning.

Reflexivity and labour-power manifestation

Figure 7.6 illustrates how respondents rank various reasons explaining why they participate in the social economy. While it focuses explicitly on paid work and non-paid work within the social economy, it is indicative of the overall complexities associated with why people choose to engage their labour-power with an activity or organization.

Those engaged in paid work (26 per cent) and non-paid work (22 per cent) cite the organization's mandate as the most important reason for their participation. This is replicated in all single-variant and bivariant analyses. There are distinctions, however, in how participants rank the other motivating factors, as indicated in Table 7.1 and Table 7.2.

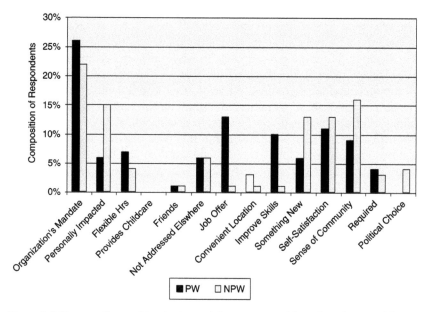

Figure 7.6 Reasons for working in the social economy: paid work and non-paid work.

Table 7.1 Top five reasons for working in the social economy: paid workers

Reason	Percentage
Organization's mandate	26%
Job offer	13%
Self-satisfaction	11%
Improve skills	10%
Sense of community	9%

Table 7.2 Top five reasons for working in the social economy: non-paid workers

Reason	Percentage
Organization's mandate	22%
Sense of community	16%
Personally impacted	15%
Something new	13%
Self-satisfaction	13%

The distinctions illustrated in Figure 7.6 are suggestive of motivations that go well beyond the detached reasoning of *homo economicus*. They combine instrumental reasons, such as self-satisfaction, with normative rationales, such as a sense of community, to trigger the exertion of labour-power within the social economy. They more aptly describe a consciousness of *being-in-the-world-with-others*.

This consciousness points to the complexity and incompatibility of subsuming reflexivity within the ontology of the Employment paradigm. Within this ontological framing, self-satisfaction, organizational mandate and a sense of community seem exclusionary. Orthodox economic theorizations posit a stark dichotomy between collectivism and individualism, as the individual is theorized as the primary agent propelling the economic system. Yet individualism and collectivism are inseparable within the social economy and both are elemental to social economy growth.

This fusion of individualism and collectivism is the process that takes place with individualization. Rationality loses its importance as a great motivator and reflexivity reigns supreme as the arbiter toward action. We cannot choose a world without other people and we cannot act in the world without impacting other people.

Adam Smith is in error when he provides us with a single-point Renaissance tableau of the butcher in the centre of the canvas as our economic subject. By drawing our gaze solely upon the butcher and away from the alterity of his *being-in-the-world*, one loses sight of the various figures and activities that made the butcher and his place possible. The butcher's dependence upon others for his paid work is not the only reality at issue. What about the other roles the butcher must perform in order to manifest his labour-power as a butcher? What about the identities that are lost in that moment of action?

Within the Work paradigm, the butcher is more aptly represented in Cubist form, an artistic language that allows us to more readily depict the complexities and embeddedness of his social relations and the multiple manifestations of his labour-power. This provides us with a more complete rendering of the individual captured within the role of the butcher without obscuring the numerous potentials that exist for his labour-power. It also expresses the primary relatedness that connects individual as well as social processes and aims.

Working economies: multiactive labour-power

The quantitative data discussed to this point reveals the conceptual emergence of the Work paradigm, as respondents indicate that they recognize both a pluralist understanding of economies and that they judge matters reflexively based on *being-in-the-world-with-others*. This section shifts the subject of analysis from respondents' conceptual understanding of the Work paradigm to the materiality of the Work paradigm. This shift is achieved by looking at labour-power.

In question after question, respondents draw attention to the fact that their labour-power is utilized in multiple sites under differing circumstances. This labour-power is always integral to and integrated with the aims of individualized social reproduction. As such, this use of labour-power is indicative of what I am calling multiactivity. Multiactivity is a key component of the Work paradigm, as labour frees itself from the constraints of employment.

Overall, respondents indicate strong acknowledgement of multiactivity (57 per cent). However, bivariant analysis highlights two additional parameters that shed light on multiactivity and the Work paradigm. These parameters are gender and participation in new social movements.

Recognition of multiactivity: gender

Figure 7.7 illustrates the differences that exist between men and women in terms of their acknowledgement of multiactivity. Over half of all women surveyed (58 per cent) strongly agreed with the notion that they lived multiactive lives. This number was somewhat reduced for men at 50 per cent.

The heightened awareness of multiactivity that exists along gendered lines may, in part, be reflective of the 'strategic silence' associated with the restructuring of the welfare state.[8] This restructuring has shifted the burden of social reproduction away from the public sphere (that is, the state economy) toward the private sphere and, therefore, particularly to women.[9] The economic demands of a society that is increasingly dependent on the market economy for its provision of goods and services has resulted in the increasing involvement of women, especially mothers, into the paid labour market. However, nothing has been done to compensate for the work that still needs to be completed at home. As indicated by the respondent survey, female respondents in particular are aware of the additional 'work' that must be done outside the parameters of paid work. As highlighted in Figure 7.8, they also do more of it.

Figure 7.8 illustrates the percentage of time respondents spend per week devoted to differing forms of work. This data is differentiated according to gender. While paid work is the largest component of multiactive engagement

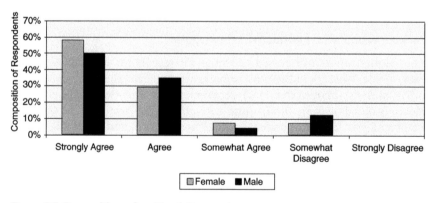

Figure 7.7 Recognition of multiactivity: gender.

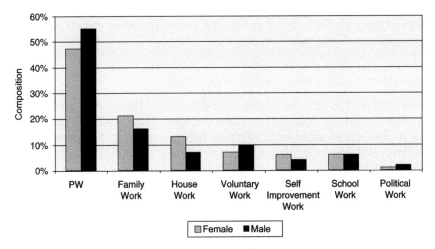

Figure 7.8 Weekly percentage composition of multiactivity: gender.

for both male and female respondents, it is more of a balanced priority for women, who spend over half of their time involved with a different work category – primarily family work and housework. Women engage 24 per cent more of their labour-power in family work than men and 46 per cent more in housework. Men exceed the energy expenditure of their female counterparts in paid work and voluntary work.

This finding is consistent with those found in other studies. As Tess Kay concludes in reference to British case studies, women are more likely to be engaged in family work outside paid work whereas men are more likely to engage in leisure.[10] Jiri Zuzanek affirms this finding within the Canadian context but also notes a shift towards increasing male participation in family work.[11]

There are various reasons that may be attributed to the increased participation of males in select forms of work outside paid work, such as family work. Many of these reasons are cultural, as societies move toward acknowledging the importance of the nurturing male. However, the most significant reason for the purposes of this research is the impact of domestic subpolitics. The curtailing of the breadwinner model toward a dual earner model has altered power relations within the household. The hierarchy of paid work and non-paid work in respect to gender no longer makes sense. Both partners earn an income and both partners return home tired. But the laundry still has to be done. As discussed in Chapter 2, this rebalancing of socially reproductive labour within the household therefore remains a sphere of cooperation, contestation and negotiation.

The recognition of multiactive lifestyles challenges and undermines the notion that individuals can clearly separate paid work from other forms of work, such as family work. The clear delineation and privileging of paid work from other forms of labour-power is integral to the premise of the Employment paradigm. This premise no longer makes sense according to the lives people are living today.

Recognition of multiactivity: new social movements

Aside from gender, the most significant differentiator between those respondents who recognized multiactivity and those who did not was their participation in new social movements. Seventy-two per cent of respondents who answered that they participated in a new social movement also strongly agreed with the notion that they lived multiactive lives. This is compared with 53 per cent of respondents who answered that they did not participate in a new social movement.

As with the issue of gender, these findings are suggestive of the unintended consequences that subpolitics presents to the Employment paradigm's employment-as-identity nexus. The Work paradigm brings risk into every aspect of social life. The inability of the existing institutional order to contain these risks brought with it new social identities and claims. Like women in the male/female dichotomy, participants engaged in new social movements are people who were asymmetrically thrust into their acknowledgment of multiactivity. Their identities are complicated by their politics, their politics by their social circumstances. These new identities sometimes conflict or collide with each other, sometimes collude or completely elide. In either case, they project identity and activity to the forefront and defy the notion that either can be static.

The argument is not that paid work is inconsequential, but rather that its pre-eminence is being challenged. Its central ontological position is being decentred by the reflexive engagement of individuals both within their existing roles (i.e., as defined by gender) and beyond these roles via the articulation of new roles (i.e., through new social movement engagement). This expanded understanding of *being-in-the-world-with-others* necessitates the expansion of the definition of work in order to (re)produce identity and social production. Multiactive engagement however reflects the complexities of heterotopia, as it introduces new conflicts and complementarities over the (re)production and distribution of labour-power.

Heterotopias at work

In order to substantiate the heterotopia of multiactivity and labour-power, respondents were asked to distinguish between seven different types of work: family work, housework, political work, paid work, self-improvement work, schoolwork and voluntary work. Their responses point to the juxtaposed forms of work as signifying not through resemblance, but as counterparts and counterpoints.

Respondents were then asked to rank each type of work according to various criteria. Their responses in this respect are enlightening in that they indicate a society irrefutably engaged in multiactivity, but an experience of multiactivity in which labour-power is strained by the irreconcilability of two paradigms.

Distinguishing between paid work and non-paid work: gender

Multiactive engagement does not denote an undifferentiated field of work. Rather, the findings indicate that labourers draw distinctions between the various manifestations of their labour-power. Participants recognize that each manifestation of labour-power is structured differently with differing logics, skill requirements, outcomes and rewards. It is in this sense that work, in its various forms, is heterotopic.

However, the experience of work as heterotopic is differentiated according to a variety of criteria. For example, Figure 7.9 illustrates this experience in terms of gender. Participants were presented with the following statement: *I distinguish between my paid work and non-paid work*. Approximately 59 per cent of the female participants either strongly agreed or agreed with the statement. This is compared with only 48 per cent of male participants who responded similarly. It is interesting to note that 28 per cent of male respondents answered that they somewhat disagreed with the statement, while only 12 per cent of female respondents answered in kind.

The differing responses based on gender suggest, again, the significance of lived experience. As evidenced earlier in this study, women are engaged in more work – both paid and non-paid – than ever before. Also, their multiactive engagement is more intensive than that of their male counterparts. For example, as illustrated in Figure 7.8, they provide a greater share of house and family work.

This gendered division of labour means that women are also more likely to engage in work trade-offs – reducing one form of work, such as paid work, in order to fulfill other work requirements, such as family work.[12] In particular,

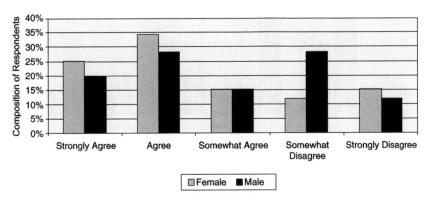

Figure 7.9 Distinguishing between paid work and non-paid work: gender.

women may more readily delineate between different forms of work since they are identified as the primary provider of labour-power to them.

It is important to note that these trade-offs speak to both the heterotopics of work and the gendered bias that exists in Canadian society when considering the provision of care. At issue within the transition to the Work paradigm is the expansion of the female identity beyond that of the socially sanctioned *wife-mother* role. The expansion of this identity along with the work required to (re)produce it is exemplary of the processes of individuation that are taking place. The decision to utilize labour-power is predicated on reflexivity; the decision to then engage in work trade-offs is as well.

As the findings indicate, work is not an undifferentiated field spatially and temporally. Rather, work exists in all three economic spaces (market economy, state economy and social economy) and shifts to correspond to the variations that arise in individual life-courses. Assorted forms of work therefore gain significance at different times in a person's life, thereby heightening the potential for conflict with other work requirements that already exist.

Distinguishing between paid work and non-paid work: part-time vs. full-time

The amount of time participants spend performing paid work also appears to affect their perception of its significance. Figure 7.10 illustrates how participants responded to the statement: *I distinguish between my paid work and non-paid work*. The information is analyzed according to the time respondents spent in paid work.

The majority of those engaged in part-time paid work (53 per cent) and full-time paid work (61 per cent) distinguish between paid work and non-paid work. Nevertheless, there are significant differences when examining

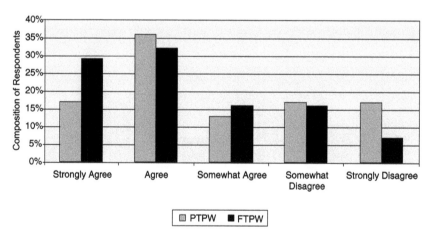

Figure 7.10 Distinguishing between paid work and non-paid work: paid work classification.

how intensely respondents agree or disagree with the statement. For example, workers engaged in full-time paid work have a 41 per cent higher rate of agreement with the statement while those engaged in part-time paid work have a 59 per cent higher rate of disagreement with the statement.

Strong support by those engaged in full-time paid work may be due to the disproportionate amount of time full-time workers spent in paid work as opposed to other forms of work. With 55 per cent of their time committed to paid work, it is possible to suggest that their identification with this form of labour-power expenditure is heightened. Paid work becomes a form of ontological security, identifying the subject in the world and to the world. The identity derived from paid work therefore is more pronounced amongst those engaged in full-time paid work and is more readily contrasted and delineated from other work activities. Workers engaged in part-time paid work, conversely, may not be able to draw upon the strong identity to paid work that arises from full-time paid work.

Triggered by the increased rationing of paid work as well as the emergence of risk society within the post-Employment era, both categorizations of workers (full-time paid work and part-time paid work) point to tensions associated with the decoupling of the employment-as-identity nexus. This tension is amplified when considering how respondents ranked their various forms of work.

Ranking work

Participants were asked to rank each of the seven forms of work from most important to least important, with 1 indicating the greatest amount of importance. Their rankings help to quantify how unevenly respondents view their multiactive engagements. Figures 7.11a and 7.11b illustrate the results according to a single-variant analysis.

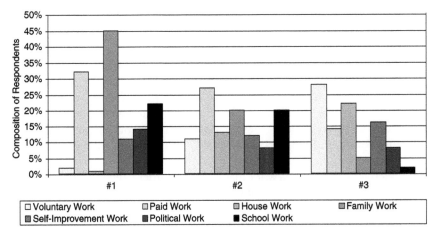

Figure 7.11a Work rankings (part 1).

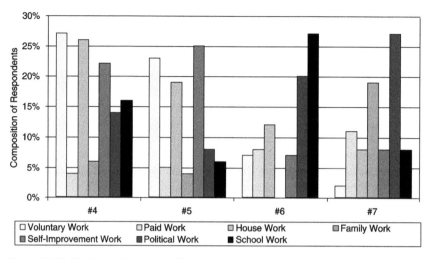

Figure 7.11b Work rankings (part 2).

Forty-five per cent of respondents ranked family work as the most import-ant form of work. This was followed by paid work at 32 per cent, then schoolwork at 22 per cent. Voluntary work ranked highest between the third and fifth ranks (28 per cent, 27 per cent and 23 per cent). Housework paral-leled this with 22 per cent, 26 per cent and 19 per cent. Political work ranked the lowest with 20 per cent and 27 per cent of respondents indicating that it was their lowest ranked form of work.

This ranking of work reveals how individuals associate divergent hierarch-ies with their multiactive engagements. When considered within the present structuring of the post-Employment era, it also points toward considerable strain.

Structuring strain: multiactivity and roles

Findings suggest that respondents are implicated by traces of both the Employment and Work paradigms. Vestiges of the Employment paradigm, such as the exclusivity of paid work to other forms of work, continue to implicate individuals. As discussed in Chapter 2, employment remains ele-mental to social reproduction. However, this hegemonic construction within an emergent Work paradigm, serves to amplify risks that individuals can only address through multiactivity.

Multiactive engagement is work that is done in order to ensure social repro-duction, as it ranges from the family, in the form of family and housework, to the broader social constituency as exemplified by voluntary and political work. Yet it is not possible to disassociate multiactive engagement from the alterations that take place in individual life courses. These alterations necessitate adjustments in the production of labour-power in conjunction with the continued dominance of paid work stemming from the Employment paradigm. As the findings indicate, caught between paradigms, respondents exhibit not only high levels of strain but schizophrenia with their consciousness of *being-in-the-world-with-others*.

Generally, the strain associated with multiactivity is most evident in individuals who are also parents.[13] Between 1992 and 1998, Canadian parents reported an increased sense of feeling rushed. This rate of increase is higher than that of non-parents. Respondents reported differing levels of strain depending on the age of their children and related childcare responsibilities. Parents with children aged 7 to 12 indicated the highest levels of strain (85 per cent) followed by parents of children aged 0 to 6 (63 per cent) and parents of children aged 13 to 18 (47 per cent).

The negative correlation in stress levels between multiactivity and the age of children is explained in part by an 'asymmetrical distribution of parental care'.[14] As children age, they require less parental supervision. For example, children aged 13 to 18 receive considerably less adult direction and care in Canadian society as they are considered to be more independent.

However, this asymmetrical distribution of parental care is only effective after a specific age. The higher rates of stress cited by respondents with children aged 7 to 12 points to the increased demand placed upon parents during this phase of a child's development. During these elementary school years, children are increasingly integrated into the community through after-school care programmes, extra-curricular sport and cultural activities. However, they remain highly dependent upon parental supervision and support.

This increasing pressure on parents of elementary school aged children to get involved with the social economy for their child's needs may account for such a disproportionate increase in social economy participation by these parents.[15] While there is a high level of stress in balancing the needs of their children at this point, there is also a greater recognition of the resources available.

Yet it is not possible to confine respondents' sense of strain solely to the expanded role of parenting. Those aged 25 to 44 indicate the highest rates of strain with their multiactivity (32 per cent and 38 per cent). Clearly, not all of these participants are parents. However, the higher rates of stress within these age groupings may be correlated to life-course expansion and the intensification of multiple working roles. These include the transition from school to work and the push to establish a solid basis of paid work; the formation of new care relationships such as young children; as well as the pursuit of individual life-paths.

The significance of multiactivity and its associated stress for individuals aged under 44 can also be viewed negatively given this demographic's lower rate of participation in the social economy. For example, 79 per cent of those aged 25 to 44 who did not engage in social economy work cited lack of time as the most pertinent factor.

Structuring strain: multiactivity and work type classification

Multiactive engagement is also constrained by the experience individuals have within their roles. Figure 7.12 illustrates this by examining the relationship individuals claimed they experienced between work and strain.

Figure 7.12 suggests that multiactive engagements not only challenge the hierarchical binary that exists between paid work and forms of non-paid work, but also force us to view the work that exists as experientially juxtaposed. For example, respondents engaged in paid work reported that they had lower levels of strain than those engaged in non-paid work (25 per cent as compared to 33 per cent). This reflects the displacement of paid work within the Work paradigm since paid work in itself is not the primary source of strain. Rather, those involved in the social economy in a non-paying or part-time capacity experience greater strain, which suggests that the strain is stemming from a factor outside paid work.

Bivariant analysis examining full-time paid work and part-time paid work illustrates how respondents experience a role and their levels of strain. Workers engaged in part-time paid work (33 per cent) indicate a much higher incidence of strain than those engaged in full-time paid work (21 per cent). On the surface, this appears counter-intuitive since people engaged in full-time paid work should have less time to trade-off for leisure activities. However, this is an analysis based on the Employment paradigm, in which the time spent completing paid employment is the only time worth measuring. When analyzing this predicament from the perspective of the Work paradigm, the entire scenario is turned on its head since work is now viewed from a social and multiactive perspective.

As such, a person engaged in non-paying or part-time 'employment' may not be working less – particularly in light of the economic risks presented by this current epoch. Rather, labourers engaged in part-time paid work are often required to stack and coordinate their allocation of time between their various work commitments – both paid and non-paid. In terms of paid work, over a quarter of the survey's respondents (26 per cent) indicated that they held two or more paid jobs. Therefore, it is possible to suggest that not

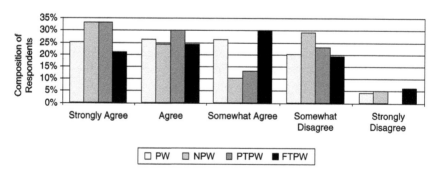

Figure 7.12 Feel strain with multiactive engagements: work type classification.

only did the increased number of jobs affect the availability of their time, but also the precariousness associated with part-time paid work in terms of lower wages and lack of benefits contributed sharply to their experience of increased strain.

The part-time phenomenon is of particular interest to women and the way in which they have structured their lives. As indicated in Figure 7.8, female respondents indicated that they spent less of their time performing paid work than their male counterparts. The percentage of time was still high – 47 per cent – but more balanced with the time they spent performing other types of work, namely housework and family work.[16] Both of these studies found that there is a distinctly gendered flavour to how individuals deal with the demands of their lives. Women are more likely to adjust their paid work in order to balance family, household, voluntary and paid work commitments. Part-time paid work therefore represents a strategy – albeit a complicated one – that uses the reality of multiactivity in an attempt to ensure social reproduction.

To summarize, these findings suggest that it is not feasible to disassociate work from the demands of individual life-courses, such as age, the number of roles occupied (i.e., parent/non-parent), and the experience within these roles (i.e., paid work – full-time paid work/part-time paid work – and non-paid work). Transcending the hierarchical binary of paid work and its others, the reality of multiactive engagements uncovers a crumpled surface of often conflicting work activities. This reality renders the projected smooth surface of paid work, as theorized by dominant discourses, as particularly exceptional and utopian.

Structuring strain: the schizophrenic subject

The transition from the Employment paradigm locates individuals in-between. Subjects are bound to the constraints of an Employment paradigm, in which economic sustenance is tied to employment, while facing the free-flowing realities of a Work paradigm that demands personal time and the expenditure of labour-power for the purposes of social reproduction. Faced with the withdrawal of the state economy and the capitalocentric require-ments of the market economy, individuals are forced to compensate for their lacks on an individual and ad-hoc basis. This societal response, along individuated circumstances, contributes not just to the constrained subject discussed earlier but more importantly to the creation of a schizophrenic subject.

Schizophrenia is conventionally discussed as a castaway categorization as it is considered to be a psychological condition characterized by delusions, hallucinations and an inability to function without being an object of clinical treatment.[17] However, my use of the term is aligned with that developed by Gilles Deleuze and Felix Guattari, which posits that radical movements can learn much from schizophrenia and the schizophrenic subject. As they argue, capitalism 'produces schizos the same way it produces Prell shampoo or Ford cars'.[18] However, capitalism and the state apparatus are incapable of normalizing the schizophrenic subject to conform to the 'accepted' codes established within society. Instead, it is only by clinical treatment and/or confinement that the schizophrenic subject can be effectively dealt with.

The significance of the schizophrenic subject, for my purposes, is in the schizophrenic's resistance to the dual processes of deterritorialization along with decoding and reterritorialization and recoding. This is pertinent in the contemporary era, which is subject to heightened claims for market employment while this form of work is increasingly subject to rationalization and uncontained risk. My contention is that the societal responses, as evidenced by workers in this case study, to activate their labour-power multiactively points to attempts to 'escape coding, scramble the codes, and flee in all directions'.[19]

The response to engage one's labour-power multiactively across workscapes and economies is not in itself constitutive of a counter hegemonic movement. As Deleuze and Guattari conclude, '[t]he schizo is not a revolutionary, but the schizophrenic process . . . is the potential for revolution'.[20] The potential is with the possibilities invoked by a prospective transition to the Work paradigm, as the multiactive engagements provide the emancipatory potential to decentre work from its straitjacket of employment in the capitalist market economy, to the broader notions of work across workscapes and economies. This is not to suggest that the respondent's multiactivity is entirely welcomed. However, this would be misinterpreting the position developed here. The issue is not whether multiactivity is chosen or imposed. Instead, drawing from the discussion on the schizophrenic subject, it is to argue that multiactivity is a flow that is ever present. The schizophrenic subject is not provided with a choice of accepting or resisting territorialization and codification. At issue therefore is the how, what and why of codification and territorialization.

The generation of the schizophrenic subject is made evident by analyzing the discrepancies that appear between how participants ranked a particular type of work versus how much time they claimed to devote to it. For example, in Figure 7.11, the majority of participants (45 per cent) revealed that they considered family work to be their most significant manifestation of labour-power. However, the amount of time engaged in this form of work fails to support its stated importance. Male respondents indicated spending 55 per cent of their work time engaged in paid work and 23 per cent combined in family work and housework. Female respondents indicated a more balanced pattern with paid work constituting 47 per cent of their time and family and housework constituting 34 per cent. Despite this attempt to balance their time between their various forms of work, female respondents indicated higher levels of strain associated with multiactivity, not less. This suggests that multiactivity alone cannot solve the pressures of social reproduction – not when individuals are choosing amongst their activities in a zero-sum game that remains tied to the Employment paradigm.

So is the situation any better then for workers engaged in full-time paid work? Such workers are more readily fixed to the economic benefits presented by the Employment paradigm but remain constrained by the pressures presented by the Work paradigm. The Work paradigm recognizes the withdrawal of the state economy from the arena of social (re)production. Workers must therefore utilize their multiactive engagement of labour-power to fill the gap.

According to Figure 7.13, full-time paid workers spend 55 per cent of their time engaged in paid work and 31 per cent of their time engaged in family and housework. Yet these workers must activate their labour in multiple settings with variable intensity over time. This possibility is at best constrained and potentially curtailed by the disproportionate amount of labour-power participants expend within paid work. Participants then experience this tension in the form of increased strain.

The tension participants experience as a result of living between two paradigms, however, is not simply an outcome of domination but part of a hegemonic process. Those engaged in full-time paid work consent to it for its monetary compensation and ontological security. Within the constraints of the Employment paradigm, these rewards are considered sufficient to ensure social reproduction since the market economy provides whatever can be purchased. But the realities of the Work paradigm cannot be bought and sold so easily. The elements of social reproduction, elements of care, provisioning and commitment depend more on a reflexive lifestyle that cannot be commodified. Workers engaged in part-time paid work may be viewed, on the

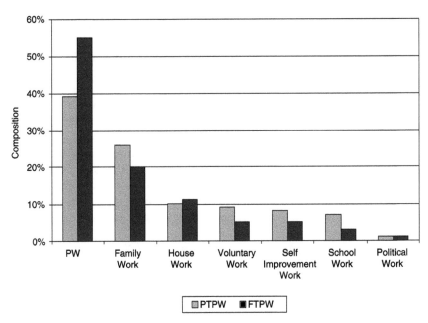

Figure 7.13 Weekly percentage composition of multiactivity: paid work classification.

other hand, as workers who are more fully integrated within the Work paradigm but constrained by the vestigial dominance of full-time paid work emanating from the Employment paradigm. While 39 per cent of their time is devoted to paid work, individuals engaged in part-time paid work display a higher proportion of time engaged in other forms of work, including family, voluntary, self-improvement and school work.

However, as illustrated in Figure 7.12, these workers report higher levels of strain than those engaged in full-time paid work. The lack of income associated both with reduced hours and lower wages serves as a constraint upon the full potential of multiactive labour-power manifestation. As this labour-power is necessary for social reproduction, the precariousness associated with part-time paid work is productive of a schizophrenic subjectivity as individuals are compelled to choose between socially necessary forms of production.

The argument here is not that schizophrenic subjectivity is limited to a specific grouping of socially constructed roles, i.e., men versus women, full-timers versus part-timers. Rather, the argument is that the schizophrenic subject is a consequence of living between two mutually exclusive paradigms. Schizophrenic subjectivity implicates and encompasses the social body democratically, without prejudice; the resources individuals have to offset it only mitigate its extent.

Afterword

Both the conceptualization of economies as well as the multiactive structuring of labour-power by respondents working in the social economy denotes the emergence of the Work paradigm. The market economy and state economy can no longer be thought of as the sole outputs of social expenditure, as labourers increasingly identify the social economy as an economy in juxtaposition to them.

This conceptualization of economic *différance* is more pronounced with workers who are younger and/or those with higher levels of educational attainment. For younger workers, rationalization of paid work within the market and state economies severely limited them from finding paid work in these economies. Additionally, the demand in the social economy for individuals with higher levels of education, coupled with the satisfaction found in the social economy, has made it an attractive option for an increasingly educated populace. As such, the decision to engage one's labour-power in the social economy sector is, in part, a rational choice.

Expanding beyond rationalism, respondents also indicate a reflexive basis for their involvement in the social economy sector. Paid workers acknowledge lower levels of wage compensation from similar positions within the market economy and state economy, but choose to remain working in the social economy sector due to reasons that are motivated beyond those of simple economic calculus. Nevertheless, this choice is not predicated on the social economy sector *per se*, but on the sense of achievement individuals garner from their participation in the sector. Similarly, non-paid workers continue to manifest their labour-power predicated on diverse motivations, including organizational conformity with their consciousness of *being-in-the-world-with-others*. In short, this suggests that while the social economy sector matches worker consciousness it cannot then be deduced that the social economy sector has a fixed signification. Instead, as respondents indicate, the state economy is also viewed as a possible replacement for the social economy. This suggests that it is the ability of the social economy sector to conform to the needs arising from the social that provides it with its capacity to encourage labour-power manifestations.

Respondents indicate that they conceptualize their broader labour-power manifestations (e.g., family work) as corresponding to the structured heterotopia of workscapes. That is, different forms of work are not only structured with different rules, functions and purposes, but are hierarchically structured. While overall the necessity to engage one's labour-power within the divergent workscapes is productive of significant strain, female respondents are disproportionately impacted. As individuals are increasingly compelled to expand and intensify their multiactive labour-power manifestations, women are forced to engage in work trade-offs. This is a result of the retained imposition of a gendered division of labour that identifies women as carers. Yet as respondents indicate, the value placed on different forms of work and the actual time available does not correspond. The result is that individuals caught between a defunct Employment paradigm and a yet to be realized Work paradigm. Hailed by both, individuals are compelled to manifest their labour-power in ways that are beyond possible.

Far from being solely an issue of work–life balance, the results of this survey point to systemic issues of meaning that cannot be captured nor resolved in such essentialist economistic calculi. It is the social nature of being and the inability of the institutional order to contain risks within the post-Employment era that compels individuals to manifest their labour-power in multiple and often schizophrenic manners. While the transition to the Work paradigm is incomplete, its pressures are clearly visible in the lived experiences of participants in the social economy sector. The way in which these individuals are addressing the crisis of social reproduction by making their decisions and attempting to cope with these new pressures is indicative of an organic response to crises. Nevertheless, unless a more systemic and proactive transformation is initiated the onerous constraints present within this interregnum point to a continuation of the crisis of social reproduction.

8 Conclusion

Towards a political economy of work

In *Paradise Lost*, John Milton wrote about 'man's' fall from heaven, as he states, 'sufficient to have stood, but free to fall'.[1] The Employment paradigm was a paradise for some in that it partially underwrote social reproduction. However it was terminated and allowed to 'fall', allowing another paradigm to enter.

The recent emergence of the social economy as a global social force and a source of contingency in current transformations is seen by some as a potential alternative to the current world order. However the social economy is also much more. The significance of the social economy rests with the expenditure of labour-power that forms its basis. The social economy relies explicitly on both paid and non-paid work. Therefore the intensive and extensive growth of the social economy is not the centrepoint for a transition to the Work paradigm. Instead, it is the way in which labour-power manifests within it that challenges the very definitions of economy and labour from which our understandings of economics are based.

Within the dominant theorizations of Keynesian and neo-classical economics, economy exists in a metonymic relationship with the market. As such, labour is conceived solely as employment within the market economy (and to a lesser extent the state economy). However, economy is constituted of not only the market and the state, but also the social. Likewise labour is not merely employment, but also an expression of social identity and meaning. More importantly, it is not the abstracted notions of market supply and demand that drive economies, but labour-power – the capacity to labour – that flows forth not from the market but from the social. In other words, it is the social that forms the (re)productive basis of economies.

With the termination of the Employment paradigm, these redefinitions have become significant, as the old order is unable to explain or reduce the risks associated with the interregnum. The recent emergence of the social economy is therefore significant in that it marks a transition from the paradigm of Employment to that of Work.

A recap of the Employment and Work paradigms

The introduction clarified the overriding question of the post-Employment era. It is no longer, 'How is it possible to generate employment?', but, 'How is it possible to ensure the (re)production of labour-power?' This question broadens the analysis from that of employment generation to the establishment, contestation and transformation of world orders. This dialectic within the recent global political economy was described as the Employment and Work paradigms.

As indicated in Chapter 1, the Employment paradigm emerged as the hegemonic mode of development after World War II. Capitalist accumulation utilizing Taylorist and Fordist mass production methodologies were matched with a set of socio-cultural compromises based on an employment-as-identity nexus. Institutionalized nationally within the Fordist welfare state and internationally with the establishment of a liberal international order under *pax-Americana*, capitalist production and social reproduction were temporarily and partially reconciled.

With employment as the central social bond, identities were normalized in reference to the idealized and gendered male-breadwinner and female-carer model. In the Canadian context, implementation of the Employment paradigm was influenced by Keynesian economics, the effects of World War II, the publication of the Beveridge and Marsh Reports, the resurgence of worker agitation and as a consequence of the (unexpected) post-war economic boom and Canada's branch plant industrialization.

However, as described in Chapter 2, the Employment paradigm is eroding. The contemporary phase of development is more readily understood as the post-Employment era or the interregnum between the paradigms of Employment and Work. Restating Gramsci, the interregnum is a consequential time marked by the withdrawal of transnational capital and the neo-liberal state from the commitment to full employment and a social wage. Different patterns and forms of resistance as well as the search for alternatives also mark it.

Within the interregnum, the Anglo-Saxon model of development, under the leadership of the United States, has been held up as the model of development. The central aim of the Anglo-Saxon model is the reassertion of the market economy as the sole means of both wealth and employment generation. Touted as a universal model that will lead to a future marked by a transition to a knowledge economy, defenders of this model have sought, by both persuasion and violent force, to enhance the hyper-power of capital over the social.

While the political commitment to full employment has been withdrawn, employment generation remains central to the legitimacy of capitalist models. Yet as discussed in Chapters 2 and 3, employment is incapable of addressing risks – specifically those of social reproduction. Instead, employment serves to exacerbate the polarization of life chances by fixing individuals within a binary structure of paid work security and non-paid work precariousness. As such, it is incapable of ensuring individual social reproduction. Employment, in this sense, does not eliminate risk but serves to amplify it.

However, the interregnum also marks the latent beginnings of a new paradigm as indicated by the dramatic intensive and extensive growth of the social economy. As analyzed in Chapter 2, the Work paradigm is predicated on the activation of the social in response to crises. As risks are increasingly thrust upon the social, individuals are compelled to manifest their labour-power reflexively. The full elaboration of labour-power as multiactive work challenges the suggestion that work is easily located within a binary structure of employment/leisure. This is a structure within the rubric of employment and the labour market.

Instead, work is more readily located in workscapes, contiguous yet porous scapes of activity that demand both energy and reflexivity. As such, this analysis broadens the issue from that of employment to that of work and from that of the market economy to that of hybrid and juxtaposed economies. As indicated in Chapter 3, workscapes are inclusive of family, house, school, self, political and voluntary work. These multiactive labour processes are inextricably social as individuals are networked in relations of dependence, mutuality, responsibility and solidarity.

This process is exampled in the social economy. Engaged in subpolitical networks ranging from the household to (trans)local communities, the social economy accommodates multiactive labour-power of divergent intensities and durations to correspond to identity structures that conform, conflict and complicate one another. Invariably though, they are based on a consciousness of *being-in-the-world-with-others*. This consciousness and its material practice of multiactive labour-power engagements across market, state and social economies refutes the hegemonic discourses that promote the market economy and market economy employment. They challenge not only how the economy and society should be organized and by whom but also the meaning systems that confer legitimacy on social practices and institutions.

Forming through subpolitical networks of various duration and scope, the social economy provides the potential to alter both the regime of accumulation and the mode of *régulation*. The social economy is a non-capitalist form of production; it is predicated on ensuring social reproduction rather than profit. Furthermore, the explicit utilization of both paid work and non-paid work in the production of the social economy challenges the existing social relations of production. As such, the social economy represents a radical possibility for altering the mode of *régulation* and also serves to moderate the polarizing effects of the regime of accumulation.

By providing access to goods and services that might otherwise not be available to individuals and communities, the social economy acts, at the least, as an escape valve or as a real, existing alternative for uneven capitalist development. Within the interregnum therefore, the critical concern is whether the social economy will become the basis for a new mode of development or be contained and co-opted to function within the existing practices of hegemonic disciplinary neo-liberalism. The social economy is already implicated in this hegemonic political project as it conforms, in part, to existing strategies that seek at best to placate growing concerns over the crisis of reproduction.

The social economy conforms to the ideological positioning within disciplinary neo-liberalism, which seeks to limit government while at the same time disciplining the social to be self-reliant. This does not, as the empirical chapters reveal, resolve the deep-seated contradictions that are a result of these radical utopian policies. Instead the social economy, within these constraints, becomes a symptom of the crisis of social reproduction rather than the means of overcoming them.

The central issue therefore remains that of labour. Who defines it, how is it defined, and for what purposes? This is the central political issue faced in the interregnum. The missing element in these debates has been a clear and coherent conceptualization of the social economy that positions it as a challenge to the hegemony of disciplinary neo-liberalism. In other words, the political nature of the social economy is absent in leading to a transition from a paradigm of Employment to Work. Table 8.1 illustrates the characteristics associated with the Employment and Work paradigms along with the post-Employment era.

While this study does not address specific policies or policy implications necessary for a transition to the Work paradigm, it does provide the necessary conceptual space for the articulation of those policies. This conceptual space arises from already existing practices within the social economy. Taking the recent emergence of the social economy as a global force signifies this potential for a paradigm shift.

Empirical findings

The empirical findings from both the Organization and Worker Surveys support the thesis of a potential transition to the Work paradigm. Organizations reveal significant increases in both the number of individuals served and the number of individuals working in the Toronto social economy. Additionally, organizations anticipate that these growth trends will continue. With a ratio of five non-paid workers for every one paid worker, the growth of the sector cannot be analyzed by isolating either of these forms of labour-power.

Worker conceptualization of the social economy as an economy, juxtaposed with the market economy and state economy, also confirmed the thesis of a transition to the Work paradigm. Viewing the social economy as forming a heterotopic space, workers indicated that the social economy provided unique and necessary goods and services apart from the market economy and state economy. Support for a transition to the Work paradigm was also indicated by the manner in which the respondents both conceived and manifested their labour-power. Workers indicated that they were aware of the necessity to be engaged multiactively across economies and across workscapes.

Table 8.1 From Employment to Work

Fields	Employment paradigm	Post-Employment era	Work paradigm
Mode of development	• Hegemonic	• Interregnum	• Yet-to-be-instituted • Possible outcome of transitive phase
Transformative forces	• Capital • Keynesian Fordist state • Pax-Americana • Organized working class	• Capital • Neo-liberal state • American domination	• Social economy • Informal subpolitical networks
Risks	• Socialized	• Individuated	• Individualized
Social Reproduction	• Gender and class compromise (latent)	• Market economy and assumed (i.e., gender roles)	• Dispersed throughout social (activated)
Subjectivity	• Employment-as-identity	• Employment-as-identity • Burgeoning identities • *Being-in-the-world-with-others* (active)	• *Being-in-the-world-with-others* (latent)
Economy	• Market economy • State economy	• Market economy • State economy • Social economies	• Market, state and social economies
Labour-power manifestations	• Labour market (single domain)	• Labour market (active) • Workscapes (latent)	• Workscapes (active)
Labour-power characteristics	• Full-time male paid work • Full-time female non-paid work	• Contingent multi-tasking paid work	• Multiactive labour-power across economies
Gendered division of labour (ideal type)	• Male breadwinner • Female carer	• Male/female paid work • Female carer	• Multiactive work engagement
Labour-power valorization	• Paid work in market and state economies	• Paid work in market economy (active) • Volunteering (latent)	• Paid work in market, social, and state economies • Non-paid work in the social economy
Economic epistemology	• Keynesian • Neo-classical synthesis	• Neo-classical • Austrian school (Hayek)	• Post-structural
Economic ontology	• Rationalism • Dualism • Metanarrative	• Contested	• Reflexivity • *Différance* • Heterotopia

Empirical findings also reaffirmed the characterization of the current era as the interregnum. Bivariant analysis of the Organization Survey indicated that work generation was highly uneven. Work generation was highest in organizations that are small, active in the fields of welfare and community development and established within the interregnum. Additionally, respondents indicated that the highest rate of growth in paid work was part-time in nature. This conforms to the precariousness that exists within the interregnum. The proliferation of non-standardized work contributes to a marked polarization in the incomes, institutional access, and life chances of citizenry.

While workers indicated support for a transition to the Work paradigm, the findings also indicated that they were caught between the paradigms of Work and Employment. Within this interregnum workers are aware of the centrality that paid work plays in their lives. They are also aware of a perceived necessity to engage their labour-power multiactively. Although paid work is a critical component to the Work paradigm, the other forms of labour-power manifestations offset its importance. However, the significance of other forms of labour-power manifestations has not been acknowledged sufficiently within the institutional order. The findings indicated that this is causing stress within survey participants. The tensions within the post-Employment era are leading to a schizophrenic subject who has to decide and prioritize between often contradictory (i.e., paid work) and non-compromisable (i.e., family work) forms of work.

Paradigms lost

Having reconceptualized economy as plural and hybrid and labour-power as multiactively engaged across economies, this project makes visible new ways of conceptualizing work within the global political economy. First, it challenges the conception of labour-power solely as employment by reframing the debate associated with capital and labour. Labour is the central issue with the extension and intensification of capitalist social relations of production. It has however become more important given the current crisis of social reproduction and given the limits reached both ecologically and socially.

Second, it pushes GPE theorization to include the social practice of labour as constitutive of identity. Work requires the assumption and performance of pluralistic identities, which are emblematic of a consciousness of *being-in-the-world-with-others*.

Third, the unintended consequences of expanding risk and the crisis of reproduction has been a burgeoning of identities beyond those mandated by employment (or the lack thereof). This burgeoning of identities was unforeseen and unintended. It is also potentially explosive as the driving force toward the Work paradigm.

Fourth, the mainstream economic theorizations of Keynesian and neoclassical economics are incapable of addressing this movement toward the Work paradigm. As indicated in Chapters 3 and 4, this is due to shortcomings in their epistemological frameworks and ontology. Unless the social imaginary moves beyond the constraints of Keynesian and neo-classical economics, the full potentials of the Work paradigm will not be realizable.

It is by engaging in what Gramsci referred to as the 'war of position' and 'war of movement' that it is possible to put forward a reappraisal of terms and policies associated with employment within the framework of the Work paradigm.[2] These form a practical basis for moving forward, but are also themselves subject to considerable debate. At issue are the following questions:

- How is labour defined?
- Who defines it?
- For what purposes is labour defined?
- How is labour to be valorized?

These are the central questions that require answering before it is possible to move forward in the Work paradigm. It must be made explicit that the transformative forces of capital, the neo-liberal state and the United States cannot define the terms of this debate over the constitution of labour. This objection has three elements:

1   Labour is a social process and must reflect its social nature.
2   Allowing these forces to define labour exposes the social to tremendous risk.
3   Addressing these risks requires the expenditure of significant social costs.

Infusing the debate with new definitions based on existing, real and potential practices is the essence of *praxis*. Unlike the current hegemonic strategies of Anglo-Saxon neo-liberal development, the language of the social economy (e.g., multiactivity, reflexivity, workscapes, and labour-power) arises from already existing strategies, which enable social reproduction.

This research invites future studies to build on both its methodology and findings. Enhancing the rigour and depth will enable a more precise and comprehensive elaboration of the possibilities presented by a transition to the Work paradigm. As Gramsci states, '[w]hat "ought to be" is therefore concrete; indeed it is the only realistic and historicist interpretation of reality, it alone is history in the making and philosophy in the making, it alone is politics'.[3] With paradigms lost, the critical question going towards the new is the contestation over how society should be organized or reorganized. This is the essence of politics. The overriding issue is that of labour and whether subpolitical networks will continue to combine and plug the lines of escape in order to establish a new mode of development predicated not on employment but work.

Appendix A
Organization Survey

TIP: For most questions it is possible to simply move your cursor over your selected response and click to register.

Section A: organization

1   In what year was this organization founded (e.g., 1990)?
2   What is the legal form of this organization? (*please select **one** item only*)

- charity
- association
- cooperative
- foundation
- federation of organizations
- other *(please specify in the space provided)*

3   Please indicate whether your organization includes any of the following *(select all that apply)*:

- members of the board
- executive staff
- paid workers
- volunteers
- clients/beneficiaries
- other *(please specify in the space provided)*

4   How many branches does your organization have?
5   What is the geographical scope of your activities? *(please select one item only)*

- global
- regional (i.e., North America)
- national (i.e., Canada)
- provincial (i.e., Ontario)
- local

6   What is your organization's primary field of activity? *(please select one item only)*

- arts, recreation, and leisure
- business, professional associations, and unions
- communication and new information technologies
- community development and housing (i.e., economic, social, and community development)
- education and research
- employment and/or training
- environment and animal welfare
- health
- identity (i.e., multiculturalism, immigration, refugees, sexual identity)
- international (i.e., promoting development)
- law, advocacy, and politics (i.e., social justice)
- philanthropic intermediaries (i.e., foundations and fundraising organizations)
- religion
- social services (i.e., services for children, youth, families, people with disabilities, and seniors)
- women
- other

7   If applicable, please select your organization's secondary field(s) of activity *(select all that apply)*:

- arts, recreation, and leisure
- business, professional associations, and unions
- communication and new information technologies
- community development and housing (i.e., economic, social, and community development)
- education and research
- employment and/or training
- environment and animal welfare
- health
- identity (i.e., multiculturalism, immigration, refugees, sexual identity)
- international (i.e., promoting development)
- law, advocacy, and politics (i.e., social justice)
- philanthropic intermediaries (i.e., foundations and fundraising organizations)
- religion
- social services (i.e., services for children, youth, families, people with disabilities, and seniors)
- women
- other

8 If you selected 'other' in question 6 and/or 7, please specify your primary and/or secondary activities:

Primary activity:
Secondary activity:

9 Please indicate how much input the following groups have in your organization's decision-making:

	1–25%	*26–50%*	*51–75%*	*76–100%*	*N/A*
Members of the board					
Executive staff					
Paid workers					
Volunteers					
Clients/beneficiaries					
Other (please specify below)					

10 If you selected 'other' in question 9, please specify who else makes decisions in your organization.

Section B: size and structure

1 How many people work for your organization in total? *(Please include board members, paid staff, all volunteers and yourself.)*

2 How many paid and non-paid workers did you have in the year 2000?

Number of paid workers in 2000:
Number of non-paid (i.e. volunteer) workers in 2000:

3 Of your paid and non-paid workers in 2000, please indicate how many were women *(If none, please enter 0.)*:

Number of female paid workers:
Number of female non-paid (i.e. volunteer) workers:

4 How many paid and non-paid workers do you currently have in the year 2003?

Number of paid workers in 2003:
Number of non-paid (i.e. volunteer) workers in 2003:

5 Of your paid and non-paid workers in 2003, please indicate how many are women *(If none, please enter 0.)*:

Number of female paid workers in 2003:
Number of female non-paid (i.e. volunteer) workers in 2003:

6 How many part-time paid workers did you have in the years 2000 and 2003? *(If none, please enter 0.)*

Number of part-time paid workers in 2000:
Number of part-time paid workers in 2003:

7 Of your part-time workers in 2000, please indicate how many were women *(If none, please enter 0.)*:

Number of female part-time workers in 2000:
Number of female part-time workers in 2003:

8 How many clients or beneficiaries did your organization serve in the years 2000 and 2003? *(If none, please enter 0.)*

Number of clients in 2000:
Number of clients in 2003:

9 Approximately how many of your full-time paid workers fit into the following age groups?

25 years and below:
26–45 years:
46–64 years:
65 years and above:
Not applicable:

10 Approximately how many of your part-time paid workers fit into the following age groups?

25 years and below:
26–45 years:
46–64 years:
65 years and above:
Not applicable:

11 Paid full-time work in the organization during the last three years has:

Decreased   Increased   Remained stable   Not applicable

12 Paid part-time work in the organization during the last three years has:

Decreased   Increased   Remained stable   Not applicable

13 Over the next few years, paid full-time work in the organization is projected to:

Decrease   Increase   Remain stable   Not applicable

14 Over the next few years, paid part-time work in the organization is projected to:

Decrease   Increase   Remain stable   Not applicable

15 On average, how many hours does a typical non-paid worker (i.e., volunteer) contribute to your organization per week?

- 1–3 hours per week
- 4–6 hours per week
- 7–9 hours per week
- 10–12 hours per week
- 13–15 hours per week
- Over 15 hours per week
- Not applicable

16 Approximately how many of your non-paid workers (i.e., volunteers) fit into the following age groups?

25 years and below:
26–45 years:
46–64 years:
65 years and above:
Not applicable:

17 Unpaid work in the organization during the last three years has:

Decreased Increased Remained stable Not applicable

18 Over the next few years, unpaid work in the organization is projected to:

Decrease Increase Remain stable Not applicable

Section C: finance

1 What is your organization's approximate total annual budget?

- Up to $10,000
- $10,000 to $25,000
- $25,000 to $50,000
- $50,000 to $75,000
- $75,000 to $100,000
- $100,000 to $125,000
- $125,000 to $250,000
- $250,000 to $300,000
- Over $300,000

2 Please indicate how much funding you receive from the following sources (in percentages):

- Federal government %
- Provincial government %
- City government %
- Private institutions and donors %
- Internal funds %

- Personal funds   %
- Membership fees   %
- Sales of goods and services   %
- Property or financial incomes   %
- Other (please specify in the space provided)   %
  Total   100%

3   Please indicate how your organization allocates its funds:

- Human resources costs (i.e., wages)   %
- Operational costs (i.e., rent)   %
- Financial costs (i.e., interest paid)   %
- Other costs (specify in the space provided)   %
  Total   100%

4   If you had a significant budgetary surplus, please indicate how your organization would choose to allocate its surplus funds:

- Investing to improve the quality of services and goods   %
- Investing to increase the quantity of services and goods   %
- Increasing the number of paid workers   %
- Paying off any outstanding organizational debts   %
- Supporting other non-profit organizations   %
- Reducing the prices of goods and services sold by
  the organization   %
- Organizing training activities   %
- Investing in infrastructure (i.e., new location)   %
- Other (please specify in the space provided)   %
  Total   100%

5   Has your organization ever tried to obtain loans from a bank, credit union, or trust company?

Yes   No

6   If yes, how would you assess the willingness of the financial institution to loan the money to your organization?

Hard   Fairly hard   Moderate   Fairly easy   Easy   Not Applicable

Section D: policies

1   In your opinion, which future policies would have a positive impact on increasing the number of paid workers in your organization? *(Please select up to five answers.)*

- increasing the demand for goods and services of the sector (i.e., government spending, increase wages throughout the economy)
- increasing the amounts eligible for tax deductible donations

- increasing access and availability of credit (i.e., bank loans)
- lowering costs for new information technologies
- increasing public awareness of the distinctness of nonprofit service delivery
- reduction and reorganization of working time (i.e., 35-hour work week, longer vacation time)
- expanding leave programs (i.e., parental, family, educational)
- lowering labour costs (i.e., lowering the minimum wage, matching wage increases with productivity gains, government wage sharing programs)
- lowering taxes on the nonprofit sector
- expanding education and training opportunities (i.e., grants, scholarships, facilities)
- providing individualized education and training guidance (i.e., counsellors)
- establishing community-based economic planning
- increasing engagement by the nonprofit sector itself in the political and policymaking process
- decreasing income support programs (i.e., lowering employment insurance benefits, shortening duration of benefits)
- expanding workfare programs to include compensation for any non-paid work performed in the nonprofit sector
- establishing a universal national daycare program
- establishing a universal national citizen's wage (i.e., a minimum income for all canadians)
- subsidizing care provided by families for the elderly

2 In your opinion, which future policies would have a positive impact on increasing the numbers of unpaid workers (i.e., volunteers) in your organization? *(Please select up to five answers.)*

- increasing demand for goods and services of the sector (i.e., government spending, increase wages throughout the economy)
- increasing the amounts eligible for tax deductible donations
- increasing access and availability of credit (i.e., bank loans)
- lowering costs for new information technologies
- increasing public awareness of the distinctness of nonprofit service delivery
- reduction and reorganization of working time (i.e., 35-hour work week, longer vacation time)
- expanding leave programs (i.e., parental, family, educational)
- lowering labour costs (i.e., lowering the minimum wage, matching wage increases with productivity gains, government wage sharing programs)
- lowering taxes on the nonprofit sector

- expanding education and training opportunities (i.e., grants, scholarships, facilities)
- providing individualized education and training guidance (i.e., counsellors)
- establishing community-based economic planning
- increasing engagement by the nonprofit sector itself in the political and policymaking process
- decreasing income support programs (i.e., lowering employment insurance benefits, shortening duration of benefits)
- expanding workfare programs to include compensation for any non-paid work performed in the nonprofit sector
- establishing a universal national daycare program
- establishing a universal national citizen's wage (i.e., a minimum income for all canadians)
- subsidizing care provided by families for the elderly

Section E: general information

1 Gender

Female   Male   Transgendered

2 Age

under 25   25–34   35–44   45–54   55–64   65+

3 Do you attend school?

Yes   No

4 What is the highest level of schooling you have completed?

- less than high school
- High school diploma
- High school diploma and some post-secondary education
- College Diploma and/or trade certification
- Bachelor's degree
- Master's degree
- Professional degree
- PhD degree

5 How long have you worked for this current organization?

0–5 mths   6–11 mths   1–2 yrs   3–5 yrs   5 yrs+

6 Do you have parental responsibilities for a child who is *(select all that apply)*:

- 2 yrs or younger
- 3–6 yrs

- 7–12 yrs
- 13–17 yrs
- 18 yrs +
- Special needs
- Not applicable

Appendix B
Worker Survey

Section A: 15 questions

1 Are you a paid or voluntary worker for this organization?

   Paid worker   Voluntary worker *(skip ahead to question 6)*

2 If you are a paid worker in this organization, do you work full-time or part-time?

   Full-time   Part-time

3 If you are a paid worker in this organization, do you also spend time volunteering for this organization?

   Yes   No

4 How would you compare your wage level in this organization to a similar position in the corporate sector?

   Above   Same   Below   Don't know

5 How would you compare your wage level in this organization to a similar position in the public sector (i.e., the government sector)?

   Above   Same   Below   Don't know

6 How many hours of work (voluntary and paid) do you engage in per week with this organization?

   1–10 hours   11–20 hours   21–30 hours   31–40 hours   40 + hours

7 Please indicate your organization's primary field of activity *(select only one item)*:

   - arts, recreation, and leisure
   - business, professional associations, and unions
   - communication and new information technologies
   - community development and housing (i.e., economic, social, and community development)

- education and research
- employment and/or training
- environment and animal welfare
- health
- identity (i.e., multiculturalism, immigration, refugees, sexual identity)
- international (i.e., promoting development)
- law, advocacy, and politics (i.e., social justice)
- philanthropic intermediaries (i.e., foundations and fundraising organizations)
- religion
- social services (i.e., services for children, youth, families, people with disabilities, and seniors)
- women
- other

8 If applicable, please select your organization's secondary field(s) of activity *(select all that apply)*:

- arts, recreation, and leisure
- business, professional associations, and unions
- communication and new information technologies
- community development and housing (i.e., economic, social, and community development)
- education and research
- employment and/or training
- environment and animal welfare
- health
- identity (i.e., multiculturalism, immigration, refugees, sexual identity)
- international (i.e., promoting development)
- law, advocacy, and politics (i.e., social justice)
- philanthropic intermediaries (i.e., foundations and fundraising organizations)
- religion
- social services (i.e., services for children, youth, families, people with disabilities, and seniors)
- women
- other

9 If you selected 'other' in question 7 and/or 8, please specify your primary and/or secondary activities.

Primary activity:
Secondary activity:

10 Do you engage in paid work elsewhere?

Yes   No

11   How many paid jobs do you currently have (e.g., 3)?

12   If you have paid work elsewhere, is this paid work:
- with another nonprofit organization
- in the corporate sector
- in the public sector (i.e., government employee)
- self-employed

13   Do you engage in volunteer work elsewhere?

Yes   No

14   Do you spend time with your co-workers from this nonprofit organization outside of work?

Yes   No

15   Were your parents/guardians involved in the nonprofit sector when you were a child?

Yes   No

Section B: 21 questions

1   I believe that I have a good balance between my paid work and the other forms of work I engage in (i.e., paid, voluntary, family, school).

Strongly agree   Somewhat agree   Agree   Somewhat disagree   Strongly disagree

2   I often feel the strain of attempting to balance my various work responsibilities (i.e., paid, voluntary, family, school work responsibilities).

Strongly agree   Somewhat agree   Agree   Somewhat disagree   Strongly disagree

3   I recognize that I have many roles in my life (e.g., worker, parent, activist, student etc.).

Strongly agree   Somewhat agree   Agree   Somewhat disagree   Strongly disagree

4   I recognize that each of these roles requires my energy, time and commitment.

Strongly agree   Somewhat agree   Agree   Somewhat disagree   Strongly disagree

5   I try not to distinguish between my paid work and the other forms of work I do (i.e., housework, childcare work, volunteer work, political work, school work, self-improvement work).

Strongly agree   Somewhat agree   Agree   Somewhat disagree   Strongly disagree

6   I am actively engaged in a social movement (e.g., Greenpeace, women's rights, Citizens for Equal Opportunity).

Yes   No   Not sure

7 If you answered 'yes' to question 6, is your participation in the social movement due to your work with this organization?

Yes   No   Not applicable

8 If you are engaged in more than one of these forms of work, please rank their importance in your life (1 through 7):

Voluntary work
Paid work
House work
Family work (i.e., taking care of the family)
Self-improvement work (i.e., taking a pottery class)
Political work
School work

9 If there weren't any negative consequences (i.e., financial, social) would you quit any of the work categories you indicated you were engaged in?

Yes   No

10 If yes, which one(s)? (select all that apply)

Voluntary work
Paid work
House work
Family work
Self-improvement work
Political work
School work

11 How many hours of work do you perform in total (perweek)?

Voluntary work	hours per week
Paid work	hours per week
House work	hours per week
Family work	hours per week
Self-improvement	hours per week
Political work	hours per week
School work	hours per week
Other	hours per week

12 Are you the main person responsible for the housework done in your home?

Yes   No

13 Please indicate the amount of housework done by the following (in terms of percentages):

Myself   %

Partner (incl. spouse)	%
Child/children	%
Roommate(s)	%
Other family members	%
Paid service	%
Total	100%

14   Does your spouse/partner engage in paid work outside the home?

Yes   No   Not applicable

15   If you have a paid job elsewhere, what makes it possible for you to participate in this nonprofit organization? *(select all that apply)*

- flexible working hours
- job sharing
- working from home
- career breaks
- unpaid leave to facilitate childcare
- shift working
- childcare notice board service
- corporate incentive program
- I simply make the time
- other (please specify in the space provided)

16   I selected my waged work because it fits my other pursuits (i.e., house-work, childcare work, volunteer work, political work, schoolwork, self-improvement work).

Strongly agree Somewhat agree Agree Somewhat disagree Strongly disagree

17   I view my paid work as a career.

Strongly agree Somewhat agree Agree Somewhat disagree Strongly disagree

18   I view my paid work merely as a source of income.

Strongly agree Somewhat agree Agree Somewhat disagree Strongly disagree

19   I believe that I can realize what I am achieving at this nonprofit organiza-tion elsewhere (i.e., sense of self-satisfaction, working for an issue etc.).

True   False   Not certain

20   If true, where?

Corporate sector
Public sector
Other (please specify in the space provided)

21   I consider the following to be characteristics of success (please select three):

- money
- making a difference
- social change
- improved self worth
- peer recognition
- balanced life
- raising children
- power

Section C: 9 questions

1   It is important to me that I work in an organization with a community focus.

    Strongly agree Somewhat agree Agree Somewhat disagree Strongly disagree

2   It is important to me that I work in an organization that effects change, whether it be social, political, cultural, etc.

    Strongly agree Somewhat agree Agree Somewhat disagree Strongly disagree

3   The work I do here satisfies my sense of responsibility for my cause/issue (i.e., arts encouragement, environmentalism, women's rights, advocacy etc.).

    Strongly agree Somewhat agree Agree Somewhat disagree Strongly disagree

4   My work at this organization has affected how I see myself.

    Strongly agree Somewhat agree Agree Somewhat disagree Strongly disagree

5   My work at this organization has affected how others see me.

    Strongly agree Somewhat agree Agree Somewhat disagree Strongly disagree

6   Please select the top three reasons why you work for this organization:

- belief in the organization's mandate
- personally impacted by the issue the organization addresses
- provides flexible hours
- provides childcare
- friends work here
- the issue the organization deals with is not addressed adequately elsewhere
- I received a job offer
- convenient location
- improving my skills
- to try something new
- a feeling of self-satisfaction
- a sense of community

- required for education and/or career enhancement
- it was a political choice

7 If you also work in the corporate or public sector, do your reasons for doing so correspond with those above?

Yes   No   Not applicable

8 If given a choice, would you rather work in the corporate or public sector?

Yes   No

9 Please indicate if any of the following would further encourage your participation in the nonprofit sector *(select up to two)*:

- flexible working hours (i.e., a choice on when to start and finish work)
- reduction and reorganization of paid working time (i.e., 35-hour work week, longer vacation time)
- establishing a universal national citizen's wage (i.e., a minimum income for all Canadians)
- expanded leave programs (i.e., parental, family, educational)
- the establishment of a universal national daycare program
- corporate incentives program (i.e., your paid job pays you to provide volunteer work in a nonprofit)
- financial compensation (i.e., the government provides you with tax credits)
- other (please specify in the space provided)

Section D: 10 questions

1 I believe that the nonprofit sector exists in Canada because Canada is a wealthy nation.

Strongly agree Somewhat agree Agree Somewhat disagree Strongly disagree

2 I believe that the nonprofit sector exists in Canada because the corporate sector has supported its growth.

Strongly agree Somewhat agree Agree Somewhat disagree Strongly disagree

3 I believe the corporate sector should be more supportive of the nonprofit sector (i.e., through corporate grant-giving etc.).

Strongly agree Somewhat agree Agree Somewhat disagree Strongly disagree

4 I believe the nonprofit sector exists in Canada to assist people transitioning into the corporate sector.

Strongly agree Somewhat agree Agree Somewhat disagree Strongly disagree

5 I believe the nonprofit sector exists in Canada because it is an efficient way to deliver goods and services.

Strongly agree Somewhat agree Agree Somewhat disagree Strongly disagree

6 I believe the Canadian nonprofit sector challenges risks and inequalities in Canada (i.e., poverty, environment).

Strongly agree Somewhat agree Agree Somewhat disagree Strongly disagree

7 I believe the nonprofit sector exists in Canada so that governments can offload their responsibilities.

Strongly agree Somewhat agree Agree Somewhat disagree Strongly disagree

8 I believe Canadian governments (local, provincial, federal) should be more supportive of the nonprofit sector.

Strongly agree Somewhat agree Agree Somewhat disagree Strongly disagree

9 I believe the nonprofit sector is a temporary sector in Canada.

Strongly agree Somewhat agree Agree Somewhat disagree Strongly disagree

10 I believe the nonprofit sector only provides goods and services to marginalized groups in Canada.

Strongly agree Somewhat agree Agree Somewhat disagree Strongly disagree

Section E: 6 questions

1 Gender

Female   Male   Transgendered

2 Age

under 25   25–34   35–44   45–54   55–64   65+

3 Do you attend school?

Yes   No

4 What is the highest level of schooling you have completed?

- less than high school
- High school diploma
- High school diploma and some post-secondary education
- College Diploma and/or trade certification
- Bachelor's degree
- Master's degree
- Professional degree
- PhD degree

5   How long have you worked for this current organization?

    0–5 mths   6–11 mths   1–2 yrs   3–5 yrs   5 yrs+

6   Do you have parental responsibilities for a child who is *(select all that apply)*:

    - 2 yrs or younger
    - 3–6 yrs
    - 7–12 yrs
    - 13–17 yrs
    - 18 yrs +
    - special needs
    - not applicable

Notes

Working alternatives: an introduction

1 ILO, *World Employment Report 1998*, Geneva: International Labour Organization, 1998, p.10 and ILO, *Global Employment Trends*, Geneva: International Labour Organization, 2004, p.1.
2 R. Reich, *The Work of Nations: Preparing Ourselves for 21ˢᵗ Century Capitalism*, New York: Vintage Books, 1992.
3 R. Florida, *The Rise of the Creative Class: And How it's Transforming Work, Leisure, Community, and Everyday Life*, New York: Basic Books, 2002.
4 J. Rifkin, *The End of Work: The Decline of the Global Labor Force and the Dawn of the Post-Market Era*, New York: G.P. Putnam & Sons, 1995. Originally published in 1995 the book was revised in 2004. I refer to the original 1995 version.
5 Ibid., pp. 69–80.
6 U. Beck, *World Risk Society*, Cambridge: Polity Press, 1999.
7 U. Beck, *The Brave New World of Work*, trans. M.A. Ritter, Cambridge: Polity Press, 2000, pp. 1–9.
8 U. Beck, *Power in the Global Age: A New Global Political Economy*, trans. K. Cross, Cambridge: Polity Press, 2005, pp. 236–248.
9 Ibid., pp. 126–134.
10 Utilization of the terms market and state is conditional, as the study examines traces for the recombination of the old and the new that may be ushering in a new moment for the constitution of work. In formal terms, it is impossible to have a capitalist market economy without the state and it is impossible to have a state that does not internalize the capitalist market economy. Additionally, in order to enhance readability I refer to the capitalist market economy as the market economy.
11 Rifkin, *End*, pp. 256–258.
12 A. Gorz, *Reclaiming Work: Beyond the Wage-Based Society*, trans. C. Turner, Cambridge: Polity Press, 1999, pp. 80–88.
13 U. Beck, *Brave*, pp. 143–145.
14 I. Bakker and S. Gill, 'Global political economy and social reproduction', in I. Bakker and S. Gill (eds) *Power, Production and Social Reproduction*, New York: Palgrave Macmillan, 2003a, pp. 3–16.
15 Gorz, *Reclaiming*, pp. 135–136.
16 M. Heidegger, *Existence and Being*, Washington D.C.: Regnery Gateway, 1988.
17 A. Gramsci, *Selections from the Prison Notebooks of Antonio Gramsci*, Q. Hoare and G. Nowell Smith (eds), New York: International Publishers, 1999, p. 276.
18 While I employ the Gramscian term 'interregnum' to suggest a paradigm shift, it remains difficult to assess the scope and depth of this change at present. As Gramsci discusses in his theorization of the potentials of an emergent Fordism issues such

as the new methods of production as well as modes of living, thinking and feeling must be considered. This would require an expanded research project. However, the aim of this book is to initiate this programme of study by pointing to the potentials of a paradigm shift from Employment to Work.

19 I. Bakker, *The Strategic Silence: Gender and Economic Policy*, London: Zed Books, 1994; I. Bakker, *Rethinking Restructuring: Gender and Change in Canada*, Toronto: University of Toronto, 1996; I. Bakker, 'Who built the pyramids? Engendering the new international economic and financial architecture', *Femina Politica: Zeitscrift fur Feministisch Politk-Wissenschaft Special Issue: Engendering der Makrookonomie*, 2002, vol. 1, 38–48; P. Armstrong and H. Armstrong, *The Double Ghetto: Canadian Women and Their Segregated Work*, Toronto: McClelland and Stewart, 1978; M. Luxton, 'Two hands for the clock: changing patterns in the gendered division of labour in the home', *Studies in Political Economy*, 1983, vol. 12, 27–44; P. Bourdieu, *Outline of a Theory of Practice*, Cambridge: Cambridge University Press, 1977a; P. Bourdieu, 'Cultural reproduction and social reproduction', in J. Karabel and A.H. Halsey (eds), *Power and Ideology in Education*, Oxford: Oxford University Press, 1977b.

20 I. Bakker and S. Gill, 'Ontology, method and hypotheses', in I. Bakker and S. Gill (eds), *Power, Production and Social Reproduction*, pp. 17–18.

21 M. Luxton and J. Corman, *Getting by in Hard Times: Gendered Labour at Home and on the Job*, Toronto: University of Toronto Press, 2001, p. 27.

22 S. Gill, 'Globalisation, market civilisation, and disciplinary neoliberalism', *Millennium*, 1995, vol. 23, no. 3, 399–423; 'European governance and new constitutionalism: economic and monetary union and alternatives to discplinary neoliberalism in Europe', *New Political Economy*, 1998, vol. 3, no. 1, 3–14.

23 J. Brodie, 'Shifting the boundaries: gender and the politics of restructuring', in I. Bakker (ed.), *The Strategic Silence*, pp. 46–60; 'Globalization and solidarity: reflections on the Canadian way', *Citizenship Studies*, 2002, vol. 6, no. 4, 377–394; 'Globalization, in/security, and paradoxes of the social', in I. Bakker and S. Gill (eds), *Power, Production and Social Reproduction*, pp. 47–65.

24 Brodie, *Shifting*, p. 57.

25 See Bourdieu, *Outline*. Also Bourdieu, 'Cultural'.

26 P. Bourdieu, *Pascalian Mediations*, Oxford: Polity Press, 2000, pp. 142–143.

27 Bourdieu discusses cultural capital as initially provided by parents and consisting of the attitude, knowledge and skills necessary to succeed. Economic capital refers to possession of economic resources. Social capital is the group membership, relationships and social networks that individuals can access. Symbolic capital refers to the accumulation of social prestige and honour. See Bourdieu, 'Cultural'.

28 Bourdieu, *Pascalian*, p. 217.

29 Bourdieu, *Outline*, p. 95.

30 The mode of *régulation* and regime of accumulation form the basis of *Régulation* theory. The mode of *régulation* refers to the institutional ensemble of laws and norms, such as those that were institutionalized to form the Fordist welfare state. Taken together, a more or less coherent regime of accumulation and mode of *régulation* form to underwrite social reproduction. An imbalance in either is therefore a trigger for a crisis of social reproduction. The critical distinction that *Régulation* theory makes is that crises are not to be understood solely as a crisis in accumulation (e.g., falling rate of profits) but as inclusive of a crises in *régulation* (e.g., inappropriate state form). For further discussion on *Régulation* theory see M. Aglietta, *A Theory of Capitalist Regulation: The US Experience*, London: Verso Press, 1979; A. Amin (ed.), *Post-Fordism: A Reader*, Cambridge: Blackwell, 1994; R. Boyer and Y. Saillard (eds), *Régulation Theory: The State of the Art*, trans. C. Shread, London: Routledge, 2002.

31 A. Gorz, *Farewell to the Working Class: An Essay on Post-Industrial Socialism*,

trans. M. Sonenscher, London: Pluto Press, 1982, p. 1. It is important to note that self-employment does not undermine this definition, but rather highlights the hegemony of the Employment paradigm. The term stems from an abstraction of the social relations of production. Individuals engaged in this form of production are direct producers of commodities and services. In this sense they are not employees. Therefore, this form of production involves a greater degree of autonomy as the production process is unified.

32 K. Marx, *Capital: A Critique of Political Economy Volume II*, New York: Vintage Books, 1981, p. 164.

33 Ibid., p. 171.

34 For a discussion of the social economy in Canada see J. Quarter, *Canada's Social Economy: Co-operatives, Non-profits and other Community Enterprises*, Toronto: James Lorimer, 1992; *Beyond the Bottom Line: Socially Innovative Business Owners*, Westport: Quorum Books, 2000; E. Shragge and J-M. Fontan (eds), *Social Economy: International Debates and Perspectives*, Montreal: Black Rose Books, 2000.

35 These form the basis of analysis in the case studies that begin in Chapter 6.

36 M.H. Hall and K. Banting, 'The nonprofit sector in Canada: an introduction', in K. Banting (ed.), *The Nonprofit Sector in Canada: Roles and Relationships*, Montreal: McGill-Queen's University Press, 2000, p. 11.

37 K.M. Day and R.A. Devlin, *The Canadian Nonprofit Sector*, Ottawa: Canadian Policy Research Networks, 1997, p. 33; and R. Saunders, *Passion and Commitment Under Stress: Human Resource Issues in Canada's Non-profit Sector*, Ottawa: Canadian Policy Research Networks Inc, 2004, p. 16.

38 E. Priller *et al.*, 'Germany: unification and change', in L.M. Salamon *et al.* (eds), *Global Civil Society: Dimensions of the Nonprofit Sector*, Baltimore: The John Hopkins Centre for Civil Society Studies, 1999, p. 101.

39 L. Landim *et al.*, 'Brazil', in L.M. Salamon *et al.* (eds) *Global Civil Society*, p. 393.

40 It may also reflect an awareness of financial strains faced by social economy organizations and the need to support capacity building if the sector is to be able to effectively respond to the increasing demands placed on it. For further discussion on funding constraints see K. Scott, *Funding Matters: The Impact of Canada's New Funding Regime on Nonprofit and Voluntary Organizations*, Ottawa: Canadian Council on Social Development, 2003.

41 The male-breadwinner/female-carer model was an idealized goal, supported materially by the state and an ideology to which bourgeois and working classes aspired.

1 The Employment paradigm

1 A. Gramsci, *Selections from the Prison Notebooks of Antonio Gramsci*, Q. Hoare and G. Nowell Smith (eds), New York: International Publishers, 1999, pp. 365–366.

2 Ibid., pp. 279–318.

3 The argument here builds on *Régulation* theory. While *Régulation* theory accepts Althusserian concepts such as social formation, overdetermination, and interpellation it also rejects Althusser's reading of *Capital*. Specifically *Régulationists* challenge Althusser's functionalist account of social and economic reproduction by introducing contingency associated with political struggle and compromises. This is accomplished by drawing on Gramsci's conception of hegemony. Hegemony is not rigid and immobile as Althusser's conception of the ideological state apparatuses. Instead, hegemony is constantly transforming as material experiences constantly remind individuals of the disadvantages of their subordination and consequently this poses a threat to the dominant class. By incorporating the

contingency associated with hegemony, *Régulation* theory therefore is able to explain both formal and informal reproduction by focusing on specific institutional forms, societal norms and patterns of strategic conduct. For overviews of *Régulation* theory, see M. Aglietta, *A Theory of Capitalist Regulation: The US Experience*, London: Verso Press, 1979; R. Boyer, *The Regulation School: A Critical Introduction*, trans. C. Charney, New York: Columbia University Press, 1990; A. Amin, (ed.), *Post-Fordism: A Reader*, Cambridge: Blackwell, 1994; R. Boyer and Y. Saillard, (eds), *Régulation Theory: The State of the Art*, trans. C. Shread, London: Routledge, 2002.

4 For further discussion of these 'compromises', see Gramsci, *Selections*, pp. 287–289 and 310–311; D. Simonton, *A History of European Women's Work: 1700 to the Present*, London: Routledge, 1998; J.A.T. Carpi, 'The prospects for the social economy in a changing world', *Annals of Public and Cooperative Economics*, 1997, vol. 68, no. 2, pp. 247–279.

5 Birgit Pfau-Effinger argues socio-cultural compromises are also understood in terms of gender cultures and orders that form gender arrangements. However, socio-cultural compromises may also be expanded to include broader notions of identity construction that were manifest within the Employment paradigm, see B. Pfau-Effinger, 'Culture or structure as explanations for differences in part-time work in Germany, Finland and the Netherlands', in J. O'Reilly and C. Fagan (eds), *Part-Time Prospects: An International Comparison of Part-Time Work in Europe, North America and the Pacific Rim*, London: Routledge, 1998.

6 The dominant discourse of development, Modernization theory, provides an indication of the application of these ideas of progress and growth as they provided the normalizing discourse of development. For further discussion, see M. Cowen and R. Shenton, 'The invention of development', in J. Crush (ed.), *Power and Development*, New York: Routledge, 1995; J. Nederveen Pieterse, *Development Theory Deconstructions/Reconstructions*, London: Sage Publications, 2001.

7 F.W. Taylor, 'Scientific management', in F. Fisher and C. Sirianni (eds), *Critical Studies in Organization and Bureaucracies*, Philadelphia: Temple University Press, 1984, p. 78.

8 F.W. Taylor, *The Principles of Scientific Management*, New York: Harper & Row, 1911, pp. 25–26.

9 Karl Polanyi provides a more thorough historical account of the emergence of the capitalist labour market of free labourers with his discussion of the separation of economy from society in Britain with the enactment of the Enclosure Acts; see K. Polanyi, *The Great Transformation: The Political and Economic Origins of Our Time*, Boston: Beacon Hill, 1957.

10 I. Bakker and S. Gill, 'Global political economy and social reproduction', in I. Bakker and S. Gill (eds), *Power, Production and Social Reproduction*, p. 21.

11 C.F. Sabel, *Work and Politics: The Division of Labour in Industry*, Cambridge: Cambridge University Press, 1982, p. 29.

12 L. Iacocca, 'Driving force: Henry Ford', *Time Magazine*, 1988, <http://www.time.com/time/time100/builder/profile/ford.html>, viewed: 12 December 2004.

13 D. Harvey, 'The geographical and geopolitical consequences of the transition from Fordist to flexible accumulation', in G. Sternlich and J.W. Hughes (eds), *America's New Market Geography: Nation, Region, and Metropolis*, New Jersey: The State University of New Jersey, 1988.

14 Ford forced workers to accept a wage cut from $7 to $4 a day in 1932 in response to falling sales during the crisis.

15 A. Kuhn, *GM Passes Ford, 1918–1938: Designing the General Motors Performance-Control System*, University Park: The Pennsylvania State University, 1986, p. 6.

16 Janine Brodie argues that the East–West national economy was firmly established by the outbreak of World War I. A second national market economy strategy would emerge after World War II that sought deeper integration with the United States. See J. Brodie, *The Political Economy of Canadian Regionalism*, Toronto: Harcourt Brace Jovanovich, 1990, pp. 136–160.

17 The establishment, in the 1880s to the 1920s, of ad hoc corporate welfare programmes hindered the development of a national welfare system.

18 N. Tudiver, 'Forestalling the welfare state: the establishment of programmes of corporate welfare', in A. Moscovitch and J. Albert (eds), *The Benevolent State: The Growth of Welfare in Canada*, Toronto: Garamond Press, 1987, p. 191.

19 John A. Garraty argues that during the seventeenth century unemployed individuals were thought to exemplify persons who had not tapped into their full potential. By the nineteenth century unemployed persons would be considered to be primarily parasitical. This understanding of unemployed persons was, in part, the genesis for the 1834 reforms of the Poor Law in England. Classifications quickly followed of just and unjust poor, and policy would be amended introducing means testing as a way in which to ensure societal discipline. See J.A. Garraty, *Unemployment in History: Economic Thought and Public Policy*, New York: Harper & Row Publishers, 1978, pp. 57–84.

20 Quoted in D. Guest, *The Emergence of Social Security in Canada*, Toronto: Garamond Press, 1987, p. 72.

21 J. Struthers, 'A profession in crisis: Charlotte Whitton and Canadian social work in the 1930s', in Moscovitch and Albert (eds), *The Benevolent State*, p. 112.

22 In the rural context relief was provided through churches and families.

23 In 1935, the federal government, under the leadership of Conservative Prime Minister Richard B. Bennett, failed in its attempts to institute a Canadian 'New Deal' as the party was defeated electorally and the Privy Council dismissed the legislation as overstepping the bounds of the British North America Act.

24 By 1943, the CCF formed the official opposition in Ontario and British Columbia and threatened the Liberal party federally.

25 A. Moscovitch and G. Drover, 'Social expenditures and the welfare state: the Canadian experience in historical perspective', in Moscovitch and Albert (eds), *The Benevolent State*, p. 20.

26 The Beveridge model was applied predominantly in the Anglo-Saxon nations. Welfare states such as Germany, Italy, Belgium, France, Sweden and Finland pursued policies that diverged considerably from the Beveridge model.

27 Chapter 2 provides a more detailed analysis of Keynesian economics. The purpose of this discussion is to establish the manner by which Keynesian economics facilitates the institutionalization of the Employment paradigm. Chapter 3, in turn, critically examines the epistemological basis of this theorization.

28 The argument here is not that Keynes signified a unique position in his assertion that unemployment could spark social revolution. Marx provides a lucid and theoretically sophisticated articulation of capitalist contradictions. The distinction is the positioning of Keynes within the capitalist system.

29 J.M. Keynes, *The Collected Works of John Maynard Keynes Vol. XI*, London: Macmillan, 1972b, p. 324.

30 Keynes defined effective demand as aggregate output (Y), which is the sum of consumption (C) and investment (I). Hence, $Y = C + I$. The Keynesian statistician Simon Kuznets developed national income accounting in the early 1940s as a way to measure Keynes's aggregate effective demand.

31 For Keynes these three concepts were integral to the level of output, which is a function of effective demand. Effective demand, in turn, is determined by expenditures identified as either consumption or investment. The marginal efficiency of capital and the rate of interest are determinants of investment in the capitalist

market economy. At issue is whether a potential investor is able to form an expectation of increasing yields from an asset over its whole life. The marginal propensity to consume refers to the level of confidence individuals have in the overall market economy, which in turn spurs consumption of goods and services rather than savings.

32 J.M. Keynes, *The General Theory of Employment, Interest and Money*, London: Macmillan, 1936, p. 164. After World War II, governments formally implemented Keynesian policies when they acknowledged their responsibility for full employment. In Britain, this coincided with the publication of the *White Paper on Employment Policy* in 1944; in Canada with the publication of the *White Paper on Employment and Income*; and in the USA with the *Employment Act* of 1946. Both Canada and the United States removed the commitment of full employment. In Canada the government committed itself to a more vague notion of a stable level of employment and income.

33 Globe and Mail, 'Britain's new social insurance plan: a comparison with the Beveridge report', *Globe and Mail*, 26 September 1944.

34 While the Beveridge Report brought together and extended existing programmes, it should be noted that the British government did not back the final report. Instead it was insisted that Beveridge alone sign as its author and bear sole responsibility for its content.

35 William H. Beveridge stated the relationship between employment and social security was analogous to coats and trousers, '[t]hey go together'. He continued to say, 'A man is not properly dressed unless he has both. I regard social security as the trousers – but he needs a coat, too'. Quoted in K.C. Cragg, 'Must publicly direct employment: Beveridge', *Globe and Mail*, 25 May 1943.

36 Guest, *Emergence,* pp. 212–213.

37 Tudiver, *Forestalling*, p. 197.

38 P.S. McInnis, *Harnessing Labour Confrontation: Shaping the Postwar Settlement in Canada, 1943–1950*, Toronto: University of Toronto Press, 2002, p. 49.

39 Guest, *Emergence*, p. 217.

40 Unlike the British legislation that it was modeled on, which provided a flat-rate benefit system, the Canadian version provided a graduated benefit based on wage levels (means-tested benefits). This conformed to an emerging North American model of capitalism that considered the market as the primary institution for both wealth and employment generation.

41 Toronto Daily Star, 'Polls and social security', *Toronto Daily Star*, 1943a.

42 Ian Mackenzie, the Minister of Pensions and National Health. Quoted in 'To bring Canada up to date', *Toronto Daily Star*, 1943b.

43 Guest, *Emergence*, p. 125.

44 Keynes's biographer Robert Skidelsky provides a recounting of Keynes's belief regarding US dominance of post-war negotiations. See R. Skidelsky, *Keynes*, Oxford: Oxford University Press, 1996.

45 The Marshall Plan was in effect from 1948 to 1952. The total amount of grants provided in 1997 dollars was $17 billion annually, which corresponds approximately to $2 billion USD in 1948 dollars.

46 This organization was the forerunner to the Organization of Economic Cooperation and Development (OECD), created in 1960.

47 R. Sivard, *World Military and Social Expenditures: 1987–1988*, Washington D.C.: World Politics, 1987, p. 37; S. Tsru, *Japan's Capitalism: Creative Defeat and Beyond*, Cambridge: Cambridge University Press, 1993, pp. 49–51.

48 L. Althusser, *Lenin and Philosophy and Other Essays*, London: New Left Books, 1971, p. 163.

49 D. Swartz, 'The limits of health insurance', in Moscovitch and Albert (eds), *The Benevolent State*, p. 255.

50 Brodie, *Political*, p. 153.
51 J. Schor, *The Overspent American: Upscaling, Downshifting and the New Consumer*, New York: Basic Books, 1998, p. 145.
52 Z. Bauman, 'Foreword: individuality together', in U. Beck and E. Gernsheim-Beck, *Individualization: Institutionalized Individualism and its Social and Political Consequences*, London: Sage Publications, 2002, p. xv.
53 U. Beck, *World Risk Society*, Cambridge: Cambridge University Press, 1998, p. 43.
54 While the subjectivity of reproduction is also class and race based, the empirical data collected in this study focuses solely on the gendered aspects. This, in part, reflects the fact that a larger portion of women are involved within the social economy (e.g., the voluntary sector).
55 Pfau-Effinger, *Culture*, p. 178.
56 Gramsci, *Selections*, p. 304.
57 H. Fraad *et al.*, *Bringing it All Back Home: Class, Gender and Power in the Modern Household*, London: Pluto Press, 1994, p. 1.
58 For an extended discussion of the gendered aspects of subjectivity creation during industrialization, see E. Zaretsky, *Capitalism, the Family and Personal Life*, New York: Harper & Row, 1976.
59 A. Carlson, *From Cottage to Work Station: The Family's Search for Social Harmony in the Industrial Age*, San Francisco: Ignatius Press, 1993, p. 38.
60 A. Picchio, *Social Reproduction: the Political Economy of the Labour Market*, Cambridge: Cambridge University Press, 1992, p. 98.
61 D. Simonton, *A History of European Women's Work: 1700 to the Present*, London: Routledge, 1998, p. 196.
62 W.H. Beveridge, *Social Insurance and Allied Service*, New York: Macmillan Company, 1942, p. 49.
63 K. Offen, 'Depopulation, nationalism and feminism in fin-de-siècle France', *The American Historical Review*, 1984, vol. 89, 648–676.
64 Beveridge, *Social*, p. 53.
65 A. Giddens, *Beyond Left and Right: The Future of Radical Politics*, Cambridge: Polity Press, 1994, pp. 176–177.
66 The breadwinner model was neither an inevitable nor universal stage of development. In making use of this ideal type, therefore, our assumptions are tempered by a recognition of national, class and cultural differences. For example, the breadwinner model has a bourgeois undertone that would not have been possible for working class families.
67 Historian Joan W. Scott provides an exemplary discussion of the gendered construction of the industrial order in France. The study undertaken by Scott focuses on the oft-cited report on the 1848 worker revolts in Paris and provides an understanding of the gendered assumptions that afflicted this period of industrialization and societal transformation. See J.W. Scott, *Gender and the Politics of History*, New York: Columbia University Press, 1988.
68 This line of argumentation has been extended by analyzing how gender orders are constituted comparatively. See A.S. Orloff, 'Gender in the welfare state', *Annual Review of Sociology*, 1996, vol. 22, 51–78; A.L. Ellingsaeter, 'Dual breadwinners between state and market', in R. Crompton (ed.), *Restructuring Gender Relations and Employment: The decline of the Male Breadwinner*, Oxford: Oxford University Press, 1999.
69 It is also important to note the class dimension of this model. For many working class families female participation within the waged economy was critical to the family's well-being. Consequently the breadwinner model may be viewed as an 'ideal type'. For a discussion of this within a Canadian context, see R. Nakhaie,

'Class, breadwinner ideology, and housework among Canadian husbands', *Review of Radical Political Economy*, 2002, vol. 34, 137–157.
70 Gramsci, *Selections*, p. 302.

2 The Work paradigm

1 A. Lingis, *The Community of Those Who Have Nothing in Common*, Indianapolis: Indiana University Press, 1994, pp. 24–25.
2 Complicit in resurrecting the power of the United States is the Lockean heartland, which consists of the (predominantly) Anglo-Saxon nations of Australia, Britain, Canada and New Zealand. This is critical as the Anglo-Saxon model is held out to be the developmental model for emulation; see K. van der Pijl, 'International relations and capitalist discipline', in R. Albritton *et al.* (eds), *Phases of Capitalist Development: Booms, Crises and Globalizations*, London: Palgrave, 2001, pp. 1–16.
3 S. Haseler, *The Super-Rich: the Unjust New World of Global Capitalism*, New York: St. Martin's Press, 2000; J. A. Tomás Carpi, 'The prospects for the social economy in a changing world', *Annals of Public and Cooperative Economics*, 1997, vol. 68, no. 2, 247–279.
4 T. Minh-ha, *Woman, Native, Other: Writing Postcoloniality and Feminism*, Bloomington: Indiana University Press, 1989; U. Beck, *The Brave New World of Work*, trans. P. Camiller, Cambridge: Polity Press, 2000.
5 United Nations, *World Economic and Social Survey 2000*, New York: United Nations, 2000.
6 Gramsci, *Selections*, p. 276.
7 Renewed forces of primitive accumulation have meant the privatization of public assets and properties along with key resources for social reproduction such as water.
8 As the institutionalization of a Work paradigm will be a political process, either passive or otherwise, it is therefore dependent upon the constitution of social forces and historical circumstances.
9 J. Brodie, 'Globalization, in/security, and the paradoxes of the social', in I. Bakker and S. Gill (eds) *Power, Production and Social Reproduction*, pp. 47–65, p. 48.
10 Karl Polanyi describes this double movement by examining the responses to the rise of haute finance and (free) market capitalism in the nineteenth century and early twentieth century. Polanyi's analysis has been extended to an analysis of the Continental and Developmental State models. These alternative arrangements have been conceived as alternatives to (free) market capitalism, which emanates from the Anglo-Saxon nations. See M. Albert, *Capitalism Against Capitalism: How America's Obsession with Individual Achievement and Short-Term Profit Has Led it to the Brink of Collapse*, trans. P. Haviland, New York: Four Walls Eight Windows, 1993; A. Amsden, *Asia's Next Giant: South Korea and Late Industrialization*, New York: Oxford University Press, 1989; A. Amsden, *The Rise of 'the Rest': Challenges to the West From Late Industrializing Economies*, Oxford: Oxford University Press, 2001; P. Hall and D. Soskice, *Varieties of Capitalism: The Institutional Foundations of Comparative Advantage*, Oxford: Oxford University Press, 2001; R. Wade, 'East Asia's economic success: conflicting perspectives, partial insights, shaky evidence', *World Politics*, 1992, vol. 44, 270–320; R. Wade, 'Japan, the World Bank, and the art of paradigm maintenance: the East Asian miracle in political perspective', *New Left Review*, 1996, vol. 217, 3–36.
   However, the intensive and extensive growth of the social economy globally is a unique development that is specific to this current era. It therefore is indicative of a new social force, which presents divergent possibilities for transforming the global system.

11 The choice is not to be confused with the voluntarism of the liberal bourgeois subject. Instead, individuals are compelled to choose. This is in part reflective of recent technological changes that allow global instantaneous communications along with increased knowledge and impactfulness of global capitalist development.

12 For an extensive discussion of subpolitics, see U. Beck, 'World risk society as cosmopolitan society? Ecological questions in a framework of manufactured uncertainties', *Theory Culture and Society*, 1996, vol. 13, no. 4, 1–32.

13 Between April 2001 and April 2004 foreign exchange markets experienced a 57 per cent increase to $1.9 trillion USD and complex derivatives grew 77 per cent to 1.2 trillion USD. See J.E. Garten, 'The global economic challenge', *Foreign Affairs*, 2005, vol. 84, no. 1, 37–48.

14 James Mittelman provides an extensive discussion of the formation of a global division of labour; see J. Mittelman, 'Rethinking the international division of labour in the context of globalisation', *Third World Quarterly*, 1995, vol. 16, no. 2, 273–295.

15 Seventeen states and one territory are currently designated as 'right to work states': Alabama, Arizona, Arkansas, Florida, Georgia, Guam, Idaho, Iowa, Kansas, Louisiana, Oklahoma, South Carolina, South Dakota, Tennessee, Texas, Utah, Virginia, Wyoming.

16 Jeffrey Sallaz documents how General Motors shifted its strategy from 'whipsawing' to actively seeking worker consent for job losses. Whipsawing refers to playing production sites off one another. In this case GM sought to force workers in the Northern US plants to accept reductions in collective bargaining claims by threatening to increase the opening of plants in the Southern parts of the United States. As these threats became less credible, GM looked to a more subtle 'war of attrition' which was aided by (1) an improvement of working conditions and worker control over the labour process; (2) distrust of the local union; (3) alienation of older workers from manual labour coupled with identification of young workers with the company. See J.J. Sallaz, 'Manufacturing concessions: attritionary outsourcing at General Motor's Lordstown, USA assembly plant', *Work, Employment and Society*, 2004, vol. 18, no. 4, 687–708.

17 OECD, *Employment Outlook*, Paris: OECD, 1989, p. 10.

18 OECD, *Employment Outlook*, Paris: OECD, 2003, p. 14.

19 Statistics Canada, *Employment by Industry and Sex*, 2003, <http://www/statcan.ca/english/pgdb/labor10a.htm>, viewed: 2 July 2004.

20 Ibid., p. 59.

21 OECD, *Women and Structural Change*, Paris: OECD, 1994; OECD, *Employment Outlook*, 2003; M. Smith *et al.*, 'Where and why is part-time work growing in Europe?', in J. O'Reilly and C. Fagan (eds), *Part-Time Prospects: An International Comparison of Part-Time Work in Europe, North America and the Pacific Rim*, London: Routledge, 1998, pp. 35–56.

22 Statistics Canada, *Employment*, p. 59.

23 S. Pinch, *Worlds of Welfare: Understanding the Changing Geographies of Social Welfare Provision*, New York: Routledge, 1997, p. 75.

24 D. McIntosh, 'UFCW airs new Wal-Mart strategy', *Northwest Labor Press*, 2003, <http://www.walmartworkerscanada.com/news.php?articleID=00046>, viewed: 27 January 2005; K. Olsson, 'Up against Wal-Mart', *Mother Jones*, 2003, <http://www.motherjones.com/news/features/2003/03/ma_276_01.html>, viewed: 19 January 2005.

25 Forbes, 'The world's richest people: special report', *Forbes*, 2004, <http://www.forbes.com/billionaires/>, viewed: 16 December 2004.

26 UNDP, *Human Development Report: Globalization with a Human Face*, New York: Oxford University Press, 1999, p. 3.

27 M. Li, 'After neoliberalism: empire, social democracy, or socialism?', *Monthly Review*, 2004, vol. 55, no. 8, 21–36.

28 P.G. Cerny, *The Changing Architecture of Politics: Structure, Agency, and the Future of the State*, London: Sage, 1990; and 'Paradoxes of the competition state: The dynamics of political globalisation', *Government and Opposition*, 1997, vol. 32, no. 2, 251–274.

29 B. Jessop, 'Towards a Schumpeterian workfare state? Preliminary remarks on post-Fordist political economy', *Studies in Political Economy*, 1993, no. 40, 7–39; 'Post-Fordism and the state', in A. Amin (ed.), *Post-Fordism: A Reader*, Oxford: Blackwell Publishers, 2004, pp. 251–279; 'Regulationist and autopoieticist reflections on Polanyi's account of market economies and the market society', *New Political Economy*, 2001, vol. 6, no. 2, 213–232.

30 It should be noted that the Competition State is not solely at the federal level but filters to other levels of government. This is evidenced for example by the publication *Get Ready Alberta: Strengthening the Alberta Advantage*, see Government of Alberta, *Get Ready Alberta: Strengthening the Alberta Advantage*, Edmonton: Government of Alberta, 2000. This provincial document identifies sixteen targets such as reduction of debt, establishment of technology networks and widening existing transportation routes as a way to ensure the province's leadership.

31 Jean Chrétien, *Speech delivered at the Indonesia-Canada Chamber of Commerce luncheon*, 1996, <http://www.tcm-mec.gc.ca/96_01_17_JCICccl-en.asp>, viewed: 17 December 2004.

32 The sport/competition metaphor continues with the creation of the "World Competitiveness Scoreboard" from the International Institute of Management Development in Switzerland, see IMD, *World Competitiveness Scorecard*, Lausanne: Institute for Management Development, <www02.imd.ch/wcc/ranking>, viewed: 22 November 2004.

33 Jessop, 'Towards', p. 9.

34 This analysis has been applied elsewhere. Jacob Torfing for example, discusses the Schumpeterian Workfare state in relation to transformations of the Danish welfare state in the 1990s, see J. Torfing, *Politics, Regulation and the Modern Welfare State*, New York: St. Martin's Press, 1997; 'Workfare with welfare', *Journal of European Social Policy*, 1999, vol. 9, no. 1, 5–28.

35 Ontario Works, *Principles for Delivery: Directive 2.0*, Toronto: Government of Ontario, 2004.

36 The 'successes' of the Canadian polity have not gone unnoticed, as Roger Martin and Michael Porter indicate when they state that Canada's turnaround has been 'nothing short of miraculous', see R. Martin and M. Porter, 'Canadian competitiveness: Nine years after the crossroads', paper presented at the Centre for Study of Living Standards Conference on The Canada-US Manufacturing Productivity Gap, Ottawa, Ontario, 22 January, Ottawa: Centre for the Study of Living Standards, 2000, p. 14. The IMF indicates that '[t]he Canadian authorities are to be highly commended for their policy accomplishments in having put in place sound macroeconomic and structural policies', see IMF, *World Economic Outlook: Fiscal Policy and Macroeconomic Stability*, New York: International Monetary Fund, 2001, p. 30. Additionally, the IMF notes an impressive turnaround in the federal deficit position from a deficit of 5.75 per cent of GDP in 1993–4 to a surplus of 1.25 per cent in 1999–2000, see Ibid., pp. 4–11.

37 W.J. Clinton, 'Presidential statement on welfare reform legislation', The White House: Office of the Press Secretary, 2000, <www.clintonpresidentialcenter.org/legacy/082200-presidential-statement-on-welfare-reform-legislation.htm>, viewed: 17 December 2004. Lawrence M. Mead writing earlier on the imposition of workfare takes President Clinton's implicit message of employment as a precondition to rights and freedoms as an explicit objective of workfare. He writes, '[w]hile

work enforcement may seem punitive, the poor must become workers before they can stake larger claims to equality'; see L.M. Mead, 'The logic of workfare: The underclass and work policy', *ANNALS*, 1989, vol. 501, 156.

38 In the Canadian context the authors of the report *Canada at the Crossroads* suggested that Canada could choose between addressing serious deficiencies in its macroeconomic foundations of competitiveness or it could accept a dramatically lower standard of living; see M.E. Porter *et al., Canada At the Crossroads: The Reality of a New Competitive Environment*, Toronto: Business Council on National Issues and Minister of Supply and Services, 1991.

39 This figure excludes off-budget costs incurred in waging war in Afghanistan and Iraq.

40 US devaluation against the German mark totaled 50 per cent between 1969 and 1973 and 28 per cent against the Japanese Yen between 1971 and 1973; see B.J. Silver and G. Arrighi, 'Polanyi's "double movement": The belle époques of British and U.S. hegemony compared', *Politics and Society*, 2003, vol. 31, no. 2, 342.

41 For a discussion of this perceived threat, see S. George, *The Debt Boomerang: How Third World Debt Harms Us All*, London: Pluto Press, 1992; W. Bello and S. Cunningham, 'Dark victory: The global impact of structural adjustment', *The Ecologist*, 1994, vol. 24, no. 3, 87–93; W. Bello *et al., Dark Victory: The Global Impact of Structural Adjustment and Global Poverty*, London: Pluto Press, 1994.

42 Critically, the demise of the Soviet system provided additional clout to the US-led reforms.

43 The policy reforms prescribed by the Washington Consensus include: (1) fiscal discipline, (2) shifting of public-expenditures and priorities towards those offering high economic returns, (3) tax reform, (4) interest-rate liberalization, (5) trade liberalization, (6) foreign direct investment liberalization, (7) implementation of competitive exchange rates, (8) deregulation, and (9) securing of private-property rights.

44 S. Gill, 'Globalisation, market civilisation, and disciplinary neoliberalism', *Millennium*, 1995, vol. 23, no. 3, 399–423; 'The constitution of global capitalism', paper presented at the International Studies Association Annual Convention, Los Angeles, 2000, pp. 1–20.

45 This claim has been articulated by a variety of sources, see R. Reich, *The Work of Nations: Preparing Ourselves for 21st Century Capitalism*, New York: Vintage Books, 1992; J. Stiglitz, *The Annual Report of the Council of Economic Advisors*, Washington: United States Government Printing Office, 1997; The Economist, 'The great American jobs machine', *The Economist*, 13 January 2000, p. 25; The Economist, 'Undecided voters and an indecisive recovery', *The Economist*, 9 October 2004, <http://www.economist.com>, viewed: 28 November 2004.

46 OECD, *Employment Outlook*, 1989 and 1995; J.D. Sachs, 'Consolidating capitalism', *Foreign Policy*, 1995, vol. 98, 50–64; N. Glazer, 'The American welfare state: exceptional no longer?' in H. Cavanna (ed.), *Challenges to the Welfare State: Internal and External Dynamics for Change*, Cheltenham: Edward Elgar, 1998, pp. 7–20.

47 These arguments have been raised by the World Economic Forum and Center for International Development and the Institute for Competitiveness and Prosperity; see World Economic Forum and Center for International Development, 'Executive summary: competitiveness and stages of development', *World Competitiveness Report 2001/2002*, New York: Oxford University Press, 2002, pp. 3–10; Institute for Competitiveness and Prosperity, *A View of Ontario: Ontario's Clusters of Innovation*, Toronto: The Institute for Competitiveness and Prosperity, 2002.

48 OECD, *Economic Surveys: Canada*, Paris: OECD, 2004, p. 8.

49 Statistics Canada, *The Canadian Labour Market at a Glance: 2003*, Ottawa: Statistics Canada, 2004, p. 92.

50 P.M. Harrison and A.J. Beck, 'Prisoners in 2002', *Bureau of Justice Statistics*

Bulletin, 2003, <http://www.ojpusdoj.gov/bjs/pubalp2.htm#Prisoners>, viewed: 7 January 2005.

51 While prisoners often perform labour that is conventionally defined as employment, their labour is not included in labour market calculations. Arbitrarily removed, prisoner labour is conceived solely as a form of punishment (e.g., chain gangs) and/or skills acquisition (e.g., work ethic).

52 D.H. Autor and M.G. Duggan, 'The rise in the disability rolls and the decline in unemployment', *The Quarterly Journal of Economics*, Feb 2003, 157.

53 The unemployment rate would also increase with a closer examination of individuals who self-identify as self-employed. In 2003 this corresponded to 9,600,000 in the United States.

54 Reich, *Work*; OECD, *The New Economy: Beyond the Hype*, Paris: OECD, 2001.

55 R.L. Florida, *The Rise of the Creative Class: And How it's Transforming Work, Leisure, Community, and Everyday Life*, New York: Basic Books, 2002.

56 Stiglitz, *Annual Report*.

57 D.F. Hecker, 'Occupational employment projections to 2010', *Monthly Labor Review*, Nov 2001, 58.

58 A. Kalleberg *et al.*, 'Bad jobs in America: standard and nonstandard employment relations and job quality in the United States', *American Sociological Review*, 2000, no. 65, 256–278. This research also indicates that non-standard employment exacerbates gender segmentation of the labour force, as women are more likely to have jobs with bad characteristics.

59 Statistics Canada, *Employment*, p. 48.

60 Statistics Canada, *Labour Force Survey*, Ottawa: Statistics Canada, <http://www.statcan.ca/english/Pgdb/labor46.htm>, viewed: 3 October 2004.

61 Ibid.

62 Statistics Canada, *Canadian Labour Market at a Glance*, p, 66. In the United States the two largest occupational groups, sales and related (10.5 per cent) and office and administrative support (17.8 per cent), pay $14.72USD and $13.42USD per hour; see Bureau of Labor Statistics, 'Occupational Employment and Wages, 2002', p. 2, <www.bls.gov.oes>, viewed: 20 October 2004.

63 Statistics Canada, *Employment*, p. 51. This corresponds to three million workers.

64 F. MacPhail, 'What caused earnings inequality to increase in Canada during the 1980s?', *Cambridge Journal of Economics*, 2000, vol. 24, 153–175.

65 M. Mendelson, *Aboriginal People in Canada's Labour Market: Work and Unemployment, Today and Tomorrow*, Ottawa: The Caledon Institute of Social Policy, 2004, p. 18.

66 G. Esping-Andersen, *Social Foundations of Postindustrial Societies*, Oxford: Oxford University Press, 1999; A. Lipietz, 'The fortunes and misfortunes of post-Fordism', in R. Albritton *et al.* (eds), *Phases of Capitalist Development: Booms, Crises and Globalizations*, London: Palgrave, 2001. Enid Arvidson describes this new pear-shaped class structure in reference to Los Angeles:

> [a]t the top is a flourishing 'yuppie' class of highly paid producer-service, high-tech and culture-producing workers; on the bottom is a growing underclass of workers in the low-paying consumer-service and low-tech manufacturing sectors; and in between is an increasingly squeezed and shrinking middle class.

See E. Arvidson, 'Los Angeles: a postmodern class mapping', in J.K. Gibson-Graham *et al.* (eds), *Class and Its Others*, Minneapolis: University of Minnesota Press, 2000, p. 163.

67 W. Hutton, *The State We're In*, London: Jonathan Cape Press, 1995, p. 14.

68 Lipietz, 'The fortunes', p. 28.

69 Subpolitical networks have also been described as 'neo-tribes' (M. Maffesoli, *The Time of the Tribes*, London: Sage Publications, 1996) and 'the multitudes' (M. Hardt and A. Negri, *Empire*, Cambridge, MA: Harvard University Press, 2000). The term 'subpolitical networks' is preferred as it provides, for example, a more accurate description of the coalescing of divergent groupings throughout the social, ranging from the personal to the broader social relations exemplified in social movements.

70 A. Giddens, *Modernity and Self-Identity*, Cambridge: Polity Press, 1991.

71 U. Beck, *Risk Society: Towards a New Modernity*, London: Sage, 1992; *Democracy Without Enemies*, Cambridge: Polity Press, 1998.

72 This does not lead to paralysis as some sort of post-structural fatalism but instead points towards reflexive modernization, whereby the institutions are open to the other.

73 U. Beck, *The Brave New World of Work*, Cambridge: Polity Press, 2000, p. 168.

74 R. Pearson, 'Renegotiating the reproductive bargain: gender analysis of economic transition in Cuba in the 1990s', *Development and Change*, 1996, vol. 28, 671–705.

75 These forms of work form the basis of analysis in Chapters 6 and 7.

76 For an extended discussion see N. Zukewich, 'Work, parenthood and the experience of time scarcity', *Research Paper – Days of Our Lives: Time Use and Transitions Over the Life Course*, Ottawa: Statistics Canada, 1998; K.L. Johnson *et al.*, *Work-Life Compendium 2001: 150 Canadian Statistics on Work, Family and Well-Being*, Guelph: Guelph University, 2001; L. Duxbury and C. Higgins, *Voices of Canadians: Seeking Work-Life Balance*, Ottawa: Health Canada, 2003; L. Duxbury and C. Higgins, *Work-Life Conflict in Canada in the New Millennium*, Ottawa: Health Canada, 2003.

77 Duxbury and Higgins, *Work-Life*, p. 63.

78 Ibid., p. xii.

79 R. Pahl, *After Success: Fin-de-Siècle Anxiety and Identity*, Cambridge: Polity Press, 1995, p. 194.

80 P. Meiksins and P. Whalley, *Putting Work in its Place: A Quiet Revolution*, Ithaca: Cornell University Press, 2002, p. 11.

81 J. Schor, 'Voluntary downshifting in the 1990s', in J. Stanford *et al.* (eds), *Power, Employment, and Accumulation: Social Structures in Economic Theory and Practice*, London: M.E. Sharpe, 2001, p. 66.

82 Ibid., pp. 68 and 113.

83 R. Frank, *Luxury Fever: Why Money Fails to Satisfy in an Era of Excess*, New York: The Free Press, 1999, p. 193.

84 In addition, these examples and the material practices that are emerging from them reveal that formal employment does not necessarily lead to social inclusion, see B. Eme, 'Legitimate orders of social participation and the logic of social change', in R. Spear *et al.* (eds), *Tackling Social Exclusion in Europe: The Contribution of the Social Economy*, Aldershot: Ashgate, 2001, pp. 301–326; C.C. Williams and J. Windebank, 'Beyond social inclusion through employment: harnessing mutual aid as a complementary social inclusion policy', *Policy and Politics*, 2000, vol. 29, no. 1, 15–28. Instead, within the post-Employment era, it may lead to social disintegration due to factors such as long hours and home/work pressures, see F. Archibugi, *The Associative Economy: Insights Beyond the Welfare State and into Post-Capitalism*, New York: St. Martin's Press Inc., 2000.

85 R. Dwyer, 'Downward earnings mobility after voluntary employer exits', *Work and Occupations*, 2004, vol. 31, no. 1, 111–139.

86 French Prime Minster Lionel Jospin quoted in B. James, 'Jospin pledges a law on 35-hour workweek', *International Herald Tribune*, 11–12 October 1997, p. 4.

87 Michael Linton established the first LETS in Courtenay, British Columbia during the 1980s.

88 See the following for a further discussion on accessibility and LETS: T. Aldridge *et al.*, 'Recasting work: the example of local exchange trading schemes', *Work, Employment and Society*, 2001, vol. 15, no. 3, 565–579; G. Seyfang, 'Working for the Fenland dollar: an evaluation of local exchange trading schemes as an informal employment strategy to tackle social exclusion', *Work, Employment and Society*, 2001, vol. 15, no. 3, 581–593.

89 Beck, 'World'.

90 G. Deleuze and F. Guattari, *Anti-Oedipus: Capitalism and Schizophrenia*, Minneapolis: University of Minnesota Press, 1983, p. 27.

91 Ibid., p. 67.

92 M. Heidegger, *Existence and Being*, Washington D.C.: Regnery Gateway, 1988, pp. 114–116.

93 Examples include Hayek, Schumpeter, and Friedman, see F.A. Hayek, *The Road to Serfdom*, Chicago: University of Chicago Press, 1944; J.A. Schumpeter, *A Theory of Economic Development*, Cambridge: Cambridge University Press, 1934; M. Friedman, *Capitalism and Freedom*, Chicago: University of Chicago Press, 1982. Joseph Schumpeter, for example, theorized oft-cited process of creative destructiveness of capitalism. In other words, his work focused on the role of competition and innovation in the renewing of the capitalist economy. He posited that entrepreneurs, who could be independent inventors or R&D engineers in large corporations, created the opportunity for new profits with their innovations. In turn, groups of imitators attracted by super-profits would start a wave of investment that would erode the profit margin for the innovation. However, before the economy could equalize, a new innovation or set of innovations, conceptualized by Schumpeter as Kondratiev cycles, would emerge to begin the business cycle over again. Nevertheless, while Schumpeter concentrated on the role played by innovation, he did not theorize the source of innovation. Social relations are discounted and/or do not enter into the realm of analysis. However, with reference to the emergence of Silicon Valley, in addition to all their Schumpeterian attributes, the new entrepreneurs relied upon ties with one another, universities and local government for their success, see C.F. Sabel, 'Flexible specialization and the re-emergence of regional economies', in A. Amin (ed.), *Post-Fordism: A Reader*, Oxford: Blackwell Publishers, 1994, pp. 227–248.

94 Beck, *Democracy Without Enemies*, p. 126.

95 This relatedness can simultaneously refer to the rise in fundamentalism, which seeks to both identify a singular idealized identity and the hybridized interpretation discussed here.

96 The association of labour with paid work is a gendered phenomenon. Women's labour has more readily been defined as consisting of paid and non-paid work. However, this lived existence is intensifying in the current era as women are increasingly engaged in paid work. Additionally, men are increasingly relied upon to activate their labour multiactively.

3 Unpacking economy

1 Z. Bauman, *Modernity and Ambivalence*, Cambridge: Polity Press, 1991, p. 276.

2 While neo-classical and Keynesian approaches have competing and contrasting bodies of research within their own theorizations, I focus on the approaches most often found in economic textbooks, as my aim is to discuss the broad and common thematics within each of these approaches. Terence W. Hutchinson, for example, distinguishes between Keynes and Keynesians. He identifies four objectives that were pursued by Keynesians that would not have met with Keynes' approval: higher than safe employment via demand expansion, full growth objective, reduced price-stability objective and income policies to counter inflation. Similarly,

the neo-classical approach is subdivided into three schools: the British school (William Stanley Jevons and Alfred Marshall), the Swiss school (Léon Walras and Vilfredo Pareto) and the Austrian school (Carl Menger, Ludwig von Mises and Friedrich A. Hayek). The British and Swiss approaches begin with Walras's notion of the market clearing or equilibrium while the Austrian school views markets as dynamic, context dependent, and imperfect. The distinction is the inclusion of *time* within the Austrian approach as equilibrium is a possible outcome of exchanges in the market economy but not a necessary prerequisite of the system. However, what remains significant for my purposes and for each of these schools is their liberal faith that the market economy (exchanges) maximizes the welfare of a society. See T.W. Hutchinson, 'Keynes versus the Keynesians . . .?', in W. Allen (ed.), *A Critique of Keynesian Economics*, New York: St. Martin's Press, 1993.

3 It is not the intent of this chapter to discuss either of these theorizations in an exhaustive manner given the space constraints and the mentioned aims of this project.

4 F. Braudel, *Structures of Everyday Life: The Limits of the Possible*, New York: Harper & Row Publishers, 1979.

5 Adam Smith expresses this when he states,

> [i]t is not from the benevolence of the butcher, the brewer or the baker that we expect our dinner, but from their regard to their self interest. We address ourselves not to their humanity, but to their self-love, and never talk to them of our necessities, but of their advantages.

See A. Smith, *Wealth of Nations*, New York: Modern Library, 1965, p. 14.

6 Equilibrium is defined as the point where forces leading to change are either absent or countervailing. Equilibrium, within neo-classical economics, is achieved when supply equals demand.

7 Jean-Baptiste Say argued that in an economic downturn production is 'misdirected'. The downturn is not as a result of demand deficiency (i.e., overproduction). According to Say's Law, once prices and costs are enabled to readjust to the demand structure, the economy will start to grow again. In this way, Say posited that production (supply) is the cause of consumption. Say illustrates this law, for example, when he states, '[t]he greater the crop, the larger are the purchases of the growers. A bad harvest, on the contrary, hurts the sale of commodities at large'. This is in contradistinction to the notion that demand drives consumption, which is the Keynesian position. See J-B. Say, *A Treatise on Political Economy: Or the Production, Distribution and Consumption of Wealth*, New York: Augustus M. Kelly, 1971, p. 135.

8 Within neo-classical economics the inverse relationship between wage rates and the quantity of labour, and the inverse relationship between leisure time and labour time, determine employment.

9 This understanding of unemployment stems, in part, from Alfred Marshall's theorization of occasional and systematic unemployment. The former refers to unemployment, which was a result of cyclical depressions while the latter refers to individuals who refuse employment. He posited that 'occasional' unemployment would eventually disappear, while systemic unemployment would remain. Marshall viewed this form of unemployment as a 'disease' that should be remedied with the de-urbanizing of life and with the application of kind but severe discipline upon the unemployed.

10 J.M. Keynes, *The Collected Works of John Maynard Keynes Vol. IX: Essays of Persuasion*, London: Macmillan, 1972b, p. 324.

11 See Figure 4.1 for an illustration of how employment generation is thought to occur within Keynesian economics.

12 R.D. Wolff and S.A. Resnick, *Economics: Marxism versus Neoclassical*, Baltimore: John Hopkins University Press, 1987, p. 102.

13 M. Hardt and A. Negri, *Labor of Dionysus: A Critique of the State-Form*, Minneapolis: University of Minnesota Press, 1994, pp. 40–41.

14 While Keynesian economics is arguably more cautious about the merits of the (free) market it still brings us full circle back to Say's Law, as Keynesianism cannot overthrow its object – the equilibrating market. Keynesian economics views the market economy as the primary economy, with the state economy as its subordinated 'other' ensuring that the market is able to maximize welfare in society.

15 Gross National Product (GNP) is defined as the value of final output of goods and services during the year. Simon Kuznets created this new statistic, enabling an empirical account of the national economy.

16 J.K. Galbraith, *The Good Society: The Human Agenda*, Boston: Houghton Mifflin Company, 1996, p. 26.

17 W.J. Baumol, 'The macroeconomics of unbalanced growth', *American Economic Review*, 1967, vol. 57, 415–426.

18 M. Granovetter, 'Economy action and social structure: the problem of embeddedness', in M. Grannovetter and R. Swedberg (eds), *The Sociology of Economic Life*, Boulder, CO: Westview Press, 1992.

19 This goes beyond the now familiar public/private cooperation schemes to a much wider field of action. In cases of large scale emergencies it has become common to expect not only governmental action (i.e., declarations of disaster zones that initiate governmental resources) and market action (i.e., corporations providing goods to affected areas such as the case with the water crisis in Walkerton Ontario in 2000) but action by social economy actors.

20 D. Elson, 'The economic, the political and the domestic: business, states and households in the organization of production', *New Political Economy*, 1998, vol. 3, no. 2, 203.

21 Ibid.

22 Ibid.

23 Ibid.

24 See A. Oakley, *The Sociology of Housework*, Bath: The Pitman Press; H. Hartman, 'The unhappy marriage of Marxism and feminism: towards a more progressive union', in L. Sargent (ed.), *Women and Revolution*, London: Pluto, 1981.

25 V. Beechey, *Unequal Work*, London: Verso, 1987, p. 126.

26 Adam Smith also recognized that labour, like capital was a produced factor. Building on the work of the earlier Physiocrats, he posited that the social division of labour was the most productive route to social reproduction.

27 I. Bakker, 'Who built the pyramids? Engendering the new international economic and financial architecture', *Femina Politica: Zeitschrift fur Feministische Politik-Wissenschaft Special Issue: Engendering der makrookonomie*, 2002, vol. 1, 38.

28 R. Pearson, 'Renegotiating the reproductive bargain: gender analysis of economic transition in Cuba in the 1990s', *Development and Change*, 1996, vol. 28, 672.

29 Ibid.

30 A. Picchio, *Social Reproduction: The Political Economy of the Labour Market*, Cambridge: Cambridge University Press, 1992, p. 8.

31 N. Folbre, *Who Pays for the Kids? Gender and the Structures of Constraint*, London: Routledge, 1994; *The Invisible Heart: Economics and Family Values*, New York: The New Press, 2001.

32 Folbre responds to Adam Smith's infamous quote that encourages men to pursue their self-interest ('It is not from the benevolence of the butcher, the brewer, or the baker that we expect our dinner but from regard to their self interest.'). She retorts, 'Just a minute. It is not usually the butcher, the brewer, or the baker who fixes dinner, but his wife or mother'. Folbre goes on to ask, 'Does she act out of

self-interest too?' See A. Smith, *Wealth of Nations*, New York: Modern Library, 1965, p. 14; Folbre, *Invisible*, p. 9.

33 Picchio, *Social*; Bakker, 'Who'.

34 Simple reproduction, according to Marx, takes place when there is a repetition of the processes of production on the same scale. In order for this to occur the capitalist must consume the entirety of surplus value produced in each productive process and not invest any of it. However, Marx argued that under simple reproduction capital becomes constrained by its internal contradictions. The capitalist is forced to assume the expanded form of reproduction by revolutionizing the technical instruments of production (i.e., technology). It is only on this scale that accumulation begins as surplus value is reconverted into capital. This capital is then invested into production. As accumulation expands so too must production. See K. Marx, *Capital: A Critique of Political Economy Volume II*, New York: Vintage Books, 1981, pp. 145–162, 468–599.

35 Picchio, *Social*, p. 98.

36 R. Skidelsky, *Keynes*, Oxford: Oxford University Press, 1996, p. 21.

37 J. Taylor, 'Sources of political conflict in the thirties: welfare policy and the geography of need', in A. Moscovitch and J. Albert (eds) *The Benevolent State: The Growth of Welfare in Canada*, Toronto: Garamond Press, 1987, p. 152.

38 Juan A. Tomás Carpi, drawing on work by Albert Hirschman, posits that 'exit' is more closely associated with the market while 'voice' is a characteristic of the political realm. See J.A.T. Carpi, 'The prospects for the social economy in a changing world', *Annals of Public and Cooperative Economics*, 1997, vol. 68, no. 2, 253.

39 Examples include the Salvation Army and the Young Man's/Woman's Christian Association (YMCA/YWCA).

40 I. Bakker, 'Introduction: engendering macro-economic policy reform in the era of global restructuring and adjustment', in I. Bakker (ed.), *The Strategic Silence: Gender and Economic Policy*, London: Zed Books, 1994.

41 See J.S. Nye Jr., 'Globalization's democratic deficit: how to make international institutions more accountable', *Foreign Affairs*, 2001, vol. 80, no. 4, 2–6.

42 For neo-classical economists, such as Walras, Pareto, Jevons and Menger, there could be no such thing as a crisis. The market was supposed to tend toward equilibrium assuring the full employment of all factors of production including labour. Thus, any movement away had to be the result of a 'shock' i.e., it had to be a phenomenon exogenous to the sphere of economic relations (e.g., a change of customs and tastes, a natural disaster, government interference).

43 Robin Murray, of Demos, posits that an intensive recycling programme headed by community enterprises would create 40,000 to 55,000 jobs in the UK economy. Murray argues that this provides a triple dividend of local regeneration, social equity and economic benefits. R. Murray, 'Transforming the "Fordist" state', in G. Albo *et al.* (eds), *A Different Kind of State? Popular Power and Democratic Administration*, Toronto: Oxford University Press, 1999, p. 81.

44 For a discussion of social entrepreneurship in the Canadian context see J. Quarter, *Beyond the Bottom Line: Socially Innovative Business Owners*, Westport: Quorum Books, 2000.

45 See Pearson, *Renegotiating* and J.A. Nelson, *Feminism, Objectivity and Economics*, London: Routledge, 1996.

46 P. Armstrong and H. Armstrong, *The Double Ghetto: Canadian Women and Their Segregated Work*, Toronto: McClelland and Stewart, 1978, pp. 55–91.

47 G.S. Becker, 'Human capital, effort, and the sexual division of labor', *Journal of Labor Economics*, 1981, vol. 3, no. 1, 33. See also *A Treatise on the Family*, Cambridge: Harvard University Press, 1981.

48 Nelson, *Feminism*, p. 69.

49 Ibid.

50 M. Power, 'Social provisioning as a starting point for feminist economics', *Feminist Economics*, 2004, vol. 10, no. 3, 7.
51 A. Sen, 'Gender and cooperative conflicts', *Persistent Inequalities: Women and World Development*, Oxford: Oxford University Press, 1990.
52 J.M. Keynes, *The Collected Works of John Maynard Keynes Vol. XI: Essays of Persuasion*, London: Macmillan, 1972a, p. 291.
53 Arlie R. Hochchild, for example, discusses this development as the 'second shift' that women had to put in at the end of the day at their wage-labour employment. See A.R. Hochchild, *The Second Shift: Working Parents and the Revolution at Home*, New York: Viking, 1989.
54 It is important to note that given this alteration in roles, men have not acted 'rationally' and taken up the vacated role of domestic labourers. This further aggravates the current crisis of reproduction and challenges the 'rational' assumptions made by both Keynesian and neo-classical theorizations. For further discussion see J. Wheelock, *Husbands at Home: The Domestics Economy in a Post-Industrial Society*, London: Routledge, 1990.
55 Evelyn N. Glenn discusses reproductive labour as both racialized and gendered in the pre-Fordist, Fordist and post-Fordist eras. See E.N. Glenn, 'Gender, race, and the organization of reproductive labor', in R. Baldoz *et al.* (eds), *The Critical Study of Work: Labor, Technology, and Global Production*, Philadelphia: Temple University Press, 2001.
56 This is exemplified in the global structural transformations initiated in the late 1970s. Examples from the North include Margaret Thatcher's infamous TINA argument – there is no alternative. Examples from the South include the conditionality attached to Structural Adjustment Programmes (SAPs).

4 Unessential economy

1 C. Mouffe and E. Laclau, *Hegemony and Socialist Strategy*, London: Verso, 1985, p. 98.
2 R. Cox, 'Social forces, states, and world orders: beyond international relations theory', *Millennium: Journal of International Studies*, 1996, vol. 10, no. 2, 87.
3 Gilles Deleuze and Felix Guattari discuss deterritorialization and reterritorialization as a two-pronged movement. The first is that of deterritorialization, which is the process of uprooting and decoding existing patterns of action. The second is a reterritorialization and (re)recording which imposes new patterns of connectivity. See G. Deleuze and F. Guattari, *Anti-Oedipus: Capitalism and Schizophrenia*, Minneapolis: University of Minnesota Press, 1983.
4 As Robert Cox argues, a problem solving approach is best suited for correcting minor incongruities. The researcher pursues a scientific method of data collection and classification, which is thought to produce objective research findings independent of the researcher. Omitted in the process is the inability to remove oneself from the social world that shapes what, how and why questions are asked. See R. Cox with M.G. Schechter, *The Political Economy of a Plural World: Critical Reflections on Power, Morals and Civilization*, London: Routledge, 2002, p. xxii.
5 For example, the Conservative government of Margaret Thatcher in Britain actively sought to instill the values of a 'self help society'. In Canada the provincial Conservative government in Ontario embarked on a similar project with its 'common sense revolution'.
6 See L. Levesque-Lopman, *Claiming Reality: Phenomenology and Women's Experience*, Ottawa: Rowman and Littlefield Publishers, 1988.
7 Reason was allocated the place formerly occupied by religion, meaning that much of the ethical pathos of religion was transferred to reason/science: the claim to authority, moral passion and salvific features. The prophetic scope of the

religious approach was deterritorialized and reterritorialized as part of the programme of rationalism. By implication reason was the way – it was light and goodness as well as truth.

8 M. Foucault, *Discipline and Punish: The Birth of the Prison*, New York: Vintage Books, 1979.

9 R. Descartes, *Discourse on Method and Other Writings*, Harmondsworth: Penguin Books, 1968, pp. 53–54.

10 The ascendancy of scientific positivism (i.e., linear progress) with its Cartesian and rationalist view of the human subject was also marked by its counterpoint. Resistance and challenge came from theorists who sought to draw attention to the role of subjective motivations. Counterpoints included myths, intuition, repressed desires and the collective consciousness – modes of thinking often viewed within a dichotomous episteme as the 'irrational'. Theorists such as Gramsci were interested in a more sophisticated and nuanced understanding of human behaviour that implicated thought and action, knowing and doing. See A. Gramsci, *Selections from the Prison Notebooks of Antonio Gramsci*, New York: International Publishers, 1999.

11 M. Weber, *Essays in Economic Sociology*, Princeton: Princeton University Press, 1999.

12 I. Hacking, 'How should we do the history of statistics?', in G. Burchell *et al.* (eds), *The Foucault Effect: Studies in Governmentality*, Chicago: University of Chicago Press, 1991, pp. 181–196.

13 Keynes himself remained hostile to econometrics as a consequence of his regard for intuition rather than sense experience, which he viewed as the foundation of knowledge.

14 The establishment of Taylorism during the Employment paradigm is precisely an attempt to eliminate reflexive practices.

15 V. Chick, *Macroeconomics After Keynes: A Reconsideration of the General Theory*, Oxford: Philip Allan Publishers, 1983, p. 15.

16 S. Bergeron, 'The nation as a gendered subject of macroeconomics', in I. Bakker (ed.), *Rethinking, Restructuring: Gender and Change in Canada*, Toronto: University of Toronto, 1996.

17 While neo-classical theorists do not question the efficiency of the market, Friedrich Hayek presents a different theorization of the market economy as a product of evolutionary processes. See J. Tomlinson, *Hayek and the Market*, London: Pluto Press, 1990.

18 As Richard D. Wolff and Stephen A. Resnick discuss, '[c]hanges in prices or incomes in a market economy do not cause changes in preferences; they are caused by them'. See R.D. Wolff and S.A. Resnick, *Economics: Marxism versus Neoclassical*, Baltimore: John Hopkins University Press, 1987, p. 52.

19 Jacques Derrida argues for a double process in the contestation of any dichotomies such as male/female or white/black, a process of reversal and one of displacement. This is the basis of Derrida's notion of deconstruction as a double science. See J. Derrida, *Of Grammatology*, Baltimore: John Hopkins University Press, 1976. See also J.D. Caputo, *Deconstruction in a Nutshell: A Conversation with Jacques Derrida*, New York: Fordham University Press, 1997, for an excellent elaboration of deconstruction.

20 J. Derrida, *Dissemination*, Chicago: University of Chicago, 1981, p. 41.

21 J.K. Gibson-Graham, *The End of Capitalism (As We Knew It): A Feminist Critique of Political Economy*, Cambridge: Blackwell Publishers, 1996, p. 6.

22 M. Foucault, 'Truth and power', in C. Gordon (ed.), *Power/Knowledge: Selected Interviews and Other Writings, 1972–1977*, Brighton: Harvester, 1980.

23 Foucault, *Discipline*, p. 183.

24 J. Derrida, *Margins of Philosophy*, Chicago: University of Chicago, 1982.

25 F. Saussure, *Course in General Linguistics*, New York: McGraw-Hill Book Company, 1966.
26 S. Lash, 'Foreword: individualization in a non-linear mode', in U. Beck and E. Gernsheim-Beck, *Individualization: Institutionalized Individualism and its Social and Political Consequences*, London: Sage Publications, 1999, pp. vii–xiii.
27 N. Thrift, *Spatial Formations*, London: Sage Publications, 1996, p. 302.
28 M. Foucault, 'Of other spaces', *Diacritics*, 1986, vol. 16, 22–27.
29 Foucault, 'Truth', p. 133.
30 J-F. Lyotard, *The Postmodern Condition: A Report on Knowledge*, Minneapolis: University of Minnesota Press, 1984.
31 Gramsci encapsulated this by employing the concept of the 'ethical state' (*stato etico*) capturing the involvement of capitalist relations and thereby displacing instrumental understandings of the state and state power. See Gramsci, *Selections*, pp. 262–263.
32 The shift out of one metanarrative cannot be accomplished without shifting into another. As such the strikethrough over the term 'metanarrative' is indicative of this post-structural positioning. Echoing Derrida's notion of a trace, this section emphasizes that the articulation of economy must proceed as a relational concept rather than a representational one. See Derrida, *Of Grammatology*.
33 For a further explanation of situated knowledges see: D. Haraway, *Simians, Cyborgs and Women: The Reinvention of Nature*, London: Free Association Books, 1990. Similarly, for a further explanation of the notion of scattered hegemonies see: I. Grewal and C. Kaplan, 'Introduction: transnational feminist practices and questions of postmodernity', in I. Grewal and C. Kaplan (eds), *Scattered Hegemonies: Postmodernity and Transnational Feminist Practices*, Minneapolis: University of Minnesota, 1994.
34 The major aim of hegemonic projects is the construction and maintenance of nodal points that form the basis of concrete social orders.
35 Gibson-Graham, *End*, p. 14.
36 Foucault, 'Of', p. 24.
37 K. Hetherington, *Expressions of Identity: Space, Performance, Politics*, London: Sage Publications, 1998, p. 132.
38 Foucault, 'Of', p. 23.
39 K. Hetherington, *The Badlands of Modernity: Heterotopia and Social Ordering*, London: Routledge, 1997, p. 53.
40 Ibid.
41 Hetherington, *Expressions*, p. 131.
42 Hetherington, *Badlands*, p. 51.

5 Methodology and case study

1 Chapter 2 discusses the ontological shift from the paradigm of Employment to the paradigm of Work, as the signification of employment is deterritorialized and reterritorialized within the post-Employment era.
2 Social reproduction, as discussed in Chapter 3, is not simply analogous to biological reproduction but also inclusive of progressive forms of social reproduction.
3 R. Saunders, *Passion and Commitment Under Stress: Human Resource Issues in Canada's Non-Profit Sector*, Ottawa: Canadian Policy Research Networks Inc., 2004, p. 16.
4 Statistics Canada, *Employment by Industry and Sex*, 2003, <http://www.statcan.ca/english/Pgdb/labor10a.htm>, viewed: 2 July 2004.
5 The argument here should not be misconstrued. The emphasis is not on the *uniqueness* of the social economy, but on its explicit relation to paid work and

non-paid work. Indeed most accounts of the sector have focused solely on non-paid workers. It is only now that academics and policymakers are increasingly foregrounding paid work.

6 As discussed in Chapter 2, disciplinary neo-liberalism views the social economy as a more productive means than the welfare state of delivering social services to those who require it while others, such as community activists, have focused on the ability of the sector to niche services to the specifics of localized communities.

7 S. Betzelt, *The Third Sector as Job Machine? Condition, Potentials, and Policies for Job Creation in German Nonprofit Organizations*, Berlin: Peter Lang, 2001.

8 The two other EU nations involved were Italy and Spain.

9 In 1999 Statistics Canada began publishing *The Workplace and Employee Survey* (WES), which provides a national database that distinguishes between for-profit and non-profit employees in Canada. Other international studies include J.A. Peck and N. Theodore, 'Beyond employability', *Cambridge Journal of Economics*, 2000, vol. 24, 729–749; C.C. Williams and J. Windebank, 'Beyond social inclusion through employment: harnessing mutual aid as a complementary social inclusion policy', *Policy and Politics*, 2000, vol. 29, no. 1, 15–28.

10 The updated website provides colour versions of all graphs as well as additional graphs that were not included in this book.

11 See M.A. Hager *et al.*, 'Response rates for mail surveys of nonprofit organizations: a review and empirical test', *Nonprofit and Voluntary Sector Quarterly*, 2003, vol. 32, no. 2, 252–267; P. Salant and D. Dillman, *How to Conduct Your Own Survey*, New York: John Wiley and Sons, 1994.

12 The estimated 20 to 30 minute completion time for each survey precluded the possibility of extending this option to the workers.

13 D. Sharpe, *A Portrait of Canada's Charities: The Size, Scope and Financing of Registered Charities*, Toronto: Canadian Centre for Philanthropy, 1994.

14 Sharpe, *Portrait*, p. 14.

15 Section 91(3) of the *Constitution Act* gives the federal government jurisdiction to establish and define the tax code. In order to qualify as a charity, organizations must fall within the legal definition of a charity and be registered.

16 Peter Broder provides an historical review of the CCRA as well as attempts to reform the definition of charity in Canada. See P. Broder, *The Legal Definition of Charity and Canada Customs and Revenue Agency's Charitable Registration Process*, Toronto: Canadian Centre for Philanthropy, 2001.

17 Helmut Anheier and Diana Leat provide an innovative discussion of the need to transform the role of philanthropic foundations from that of charity to social creativity incubators. The study discusses the origins of the charity model in Britain, which is the basis of the Canadian understanding this sector. See H.K. Anheier and D. Leat, *From Charity to Creativity: Philanthropic Foundation in the 21ˢᵗ Century*, Bournes Green, UK: Comedia in association with the Joseph Roundtree Reform Trust, 2002.

18 Nations studied include: Argentina, Australia, Egypt, France, Germany, Ghana, Ireland, Israel, Japan, Netherlands, Pakistan, Poland and South Korea.

19 L.M. Salamon and H.K. Anheier, 'Introduction: in search of the nonprofit sector', in L.M. Salamon and H.K. Anheier (eds), *Defining the Nonprofit Sector: A Cross-national Analysis*, Manchester: Manchester University Press, 1997, pp. 70–74.

20 This study omits religious service delivery when using both classificatory schemes. The key reasoning behind this omission is that religious organizations service individuals based on denomination and therefore limit service delivery. Organizations that belong to political parties, the government (i.e., universities), trade unions and corporations have also been omitted.

21 Social economy is characterized as formal, private, non-profit distributing, self-governing and voluntary, which conforms to the John Hopkins definition.

However, the work as identified in Chapter 3 as *family work* or *housework* is not included in the definition provided by the John Hopkins analysis. This would exclude 7.5 million Canadians who provided care work to sick and elderly relations beyond *housework* activities. See K. Davidman *et al.*, 'Working in the nonprofit sector: the knowledge gap', *The Philanthropist*, 1998, vol. 14. no. 3, 6.

22 A. Rubin and E. Babbie, *Research Methods for Social Work*, second edition, Pacific Grove: Brooks/Cole Publishing Company, 1993.

23 Canada Revenue Agency, *Canadian Registered Charities*, 2002, <www.ccra-adrc.gc.ca/tax/charities/online_listings/canreg_interim-e.html>, viewed: 12 June 2003.

24 The Canadian Centre for Philanthropy utilizes the same method for calculating the size of the voluntary sector in Canada. See Canadian Centre for Philanthropy, *The Voluntary Sector in Canada: Literature Review and Strategic Considerations for a Human Resources Sector Study*, Toronto: Canadian Policy Research Networks, 1998, p. 11. The study concludes that there are 175,000 non-profit organizations in Canada. This conclusion is reached by adding Jack Quarter's conclusion of 100,000 organizations and the CCRA figure of 75,455. See J. Quarter, *Canada's Social Economy: Co-operatives, Non-profits and Other Community Enterprises*, Toronto: James Lorimer, 1992.

25 Some estimates posit that there are 870,000 grassroots associations in Canada. See M.H. Hall and K. Banting, 'The nonprofit sector in Canada: an introduction', in K. Banting (ed.), *The Nonprofit Sector in Canada: Roles and Relationships*, Montreal: McGill-Queen's University Press, 2000, p. 11. See also E. Dreessen, 'What we should know about the voluntary sector but don't', *ISUMA: Canadian Journal of Policy Research*, 2001, vol. 2, no. 2, 14.

26 D.H. Smith, *Grassroots Associations*, London: Sage Publications, 2000.

27 Other sites utilized were <www.charityvillage.ca>, <http://toronto.areaconnect.ca/>, <www.toronto.com>, <www.yahoo.ca>, <www.canoe.ca>, <www.google.ca>, <www.womennet.ca>, <http://pages.interlog.com/~oaag/index.html>.

28 The site <www.charityvillage.ca>, for example, lists 2500 organizations in Toronto.

29 The low rate of response can be attributed in part to the timing of the data collection in September and October.

30 A total of 95 organizations were required in order to broach the +/− 10 per cent sampling error.

31 This study uses the term 'findings' as opposed to 'conclusions' due to the exploratory nature of this research. Keith F. Punch provides an overview of the distinctions between 'findings' and 'conclusions'. Findings are appropriate for this study, as a broad-ranging comparative survey (e.g., analysis of a variety of national settings) would have served to increase the statistical power of the study. This type of research would require a larger team of researchers coupled with significant institutional support such as that provided by the International Labour Organization. See K.F. Punch, *Survey Research: The Basics*, London: Sage Publications, 2003, pp. 73–74.

32 The York University Institute of Social Research provided invaluable assistance with the articulation of the limits of this research as well as its contribution to the field.

33 This error arises with the inability of the study frame to adequately cover the target population. It is uncertain whether certain organizations or workers in the target population were excluded thereby resulting in under-coverage.

34 Partial non-response is noted and discussed when it arises in the ensuing analysis.

35 The remaining 4 per cent constitute organizations founded between 1890 and 1945. This grouping is not discussed, as the sample is not sufficiently large enough to make definitive or preliminary conclusions. While they conform to the

1946–79 grouping in terms of fitting within the characteristics of the Employment paradigm, their formation does not coincide with the Keynesian welfare state established subsequent to World War II.

36 For example, the Royal Commission on the Economic Union and Canada's Development Prospects, also known as the Macdonald Report, concluded that Canadian development required the establishment of a continental integration laying the basis for the Canada–United States Free Trade Agreement.

37 The party itself was divided between ascendant Monetarists, who sought to replicate the Reagan and Thatcher programmes, and welfare liberals. For further discussion see W. Christian and C. Campbell, *Political Parties and Ideologies in Canada*, third edition, Toronto: McGraw-Hill Ryerson Ltd, 1990.

38 Government restraint programmes were initiated in Ontario in the late 1970s.

39 J-M. Fontan and E. Shragge, 'Tendencies, tensions and visions in the social economy', *Social Economy: International Debates and Perspectives*, Montreal: Black Rose Books, 2000, pp. 3–5.

40 Ibid., p. 5.

41 For further discussion see D. Lewis, 'Introduction: the parallel universes of third sector research and the changing context of voluntary action', *International Perspectives on Voluntary Action: Reshaping the Third Sector*, London: Earthscan Publications Ltd., 1999.

42 K. McMullen and G. Schellenberg, *Mapping the Non-Profit Sector*, Ottawa: Canadian Policy Research Networks, 2002, p. 28.

43 While this book is not embedded within policy debates, policies that could institutionalize the Work paradigm are critical. This is a future area of research.

44 For a critique as well as articulation of alternatives to the CCRA's limitation on advocacy see IMPACS, *Let Charities Speak: Report of the Charities and Advocacy Dialogue*, Vancouver: IMPACS, 2002 and R. Bridge, *The Law of Advocacy by Charitable Organizations: The Case for Change*, Vancouver: IMPACS, 2000.

45 A.R. Gregg, 'Art for everyone', *Maclean's*, 2001, vol. 116, no. 21, 40.

46 Canada Council for the Arts, 'Volunteers in arts and culture organizations in Canada', *Research Series on the Arts*, 2001, vol. 2, no. 1, 1–11.

47 M.H. Hall *et al.*, *Caring Canadians, Involved Canadians: Highlights From the 2000 National Survey of Giving, Volunteering and Participating*, Ottawa: Statistics Canada, 2001, p. 40.

48 Canada Council for the Arts, 'Volunteers in arts and culture organizations in Canada', *Research Series on the Arts*, 2003, vol. 2, no. 1, 1.

49 Community Development constitutes 7 per cent and fits into the Social Services conception of the social economy as primarily organized around issues of charity.

50 C. Eder, *The Social Construction of Nature: A Sociology of Ecological Enlightenment*, London: Sage Publications, 1996.

51 Hall *et al.*, *Caring*, p. 41.

52 L. Roberts, *Caught in the Middle: What Small, Non-Profit Organizations Need to Survive and Flourish*, Ottawa: Voluntary Sector Initiative, 2001.

53 The initial classification of 'small' was $80,000 and revised after consultation with focus groups.

54 Hall *et al.*'s national study of the sector provides similar conclusions in terms of capacity building. Namely, the lack of capital coupled with how funding is allocated has served to undermine stability and expansion of the sector. See Hall *et al.*, *Caring*, pp. 21–28.

55 An expanded survey could examine previous utilization of these resources in the state economy and compare these with their usage in the social economy. This could determine whether and to what extent the social economy can be conceived as a mechanism of privatization.

56 N. McClintock, *Understanding Canadian Donors: Using the National Survey of*

Giving, Volunteering and Participating to Build Your Fundraising Programme, Toronto: Canadian Centre for Philanthropy, 2004, p. 4.

57 Accordance with the CCRA definitions enables organizations to access governmental funds. As some organizations within this study do not conform to this definition, the lower contribution rate of government(s) is not surprising.

58 Hall *et al.* conclude that the shift from core- to project-based funding curtails the ability of organizations to secure infrastructural development. Specifically the study found organizations have suffered diminishing autonomy and independence as they are constantly seeking funds to ensure the organization's existence. This precariousness in funding has also resulted in difficulties in recruiting and retaining staff as well as engaging in long-term planning. See Hall *et al.*, *Caring*, p. 21.

59 Hall *et al.* indicates that 25 per cent of men and 28 per cent of women in Canada provide non-paid work. See Hall *et al.*, *Caring*, p. 33. Taking the population by gender and multiplying it with the Hall percentage provides the gender ratio. It is important to note that the composition of paid work in the Canadian labour market figures are from the OECD. See OECD, *Employment Outlook 2000*, Paris: OECD, 2000, p. 23.

60 OECD, *Employment Outlook 2000*, p. 94.

61 McClintock, *Understanding*, p. 4.

62 McMullen and Schellenberg, *Mapping*, pp. 35–37.

63 L. Mailloux *et al.*, *Motivation at the Margins: Gender Issues in the Canadian Voluntary Sector*, Ottawa: Voluntary Sector Secretariat, 2002, p. 17.

64 K.L. Johnson *et al.*, *Work-Life Compendium 2001: 150 Canadian Statistics on Work, Family and Well-Being*, Guelph: University of Guelph, 2001, p. 150, <http://www.uguelph.ca/cfww>, viewed: 2 July 2003.

65 Hall *et al.*, *Caring*, p. 34.

66 F. Jones, 'Volunteering parents: who volunteers and how are their lives affected?', *ISUMA: Canadian Journal of Policy Research*, 2001, vol. 2, no. 2, 70.

67 Ibid.

68 R.A. Devlin, 'Volunteers and the paid labour market', *ISUMA: Canadian Journal of Policy Research*, 2001, vol. 2, no. 2, 63.

69 Children with special needs are not part of the study as the numbers were too small to provide any conclusive findings.

70 Hall *et al.*, *Caring*, p. 34.

71 McMullen and Schellenberg, *Mapping*, p. 12.

72 OECD, *Employment Outlook 2000*, p. 96.

73 A. Vromen, 'Community-based activism and change: the cases of Sydney and Toronto', *City and Community*, 2003, vol. 2, no. 1, 53.

74 D. Sharpe, 'The Canadian charitable sector: an overview', in J. Phillips *et al.* (eds), *Between State and Market: Essays on Charities Law and Policy in Canada*, Kingston: McGill-Queens University Press, 2001, pp. 18–19.

75 The study found religious organizations (14 per cent and 16 per cent), education and research organizations (13 per cent and 11 per cent), health organizations (13 per cent and 9 per cent) and other (17 per cent and 17 per cent) comprised the next largest segments. See Hall *et al.*, *Caring*, p. 40.

76 Ibid., p. 11.

77 Paid work is equivalent to 12 per cent and non-paid work is 88 per cent of the Canadian social economy.

78 28 per cent of women and 10 per cent of men who were engaged in paid work held part-time positions.

79 Saunders, *Passion*, p. 26.

80 Temporary work is another form of paid work that is prevalent in the social economy, but is not discussed in this study.

81 Johnson *et al.*, *Work-Life*, p. 39.

6 Structuring the Work paradigm: the consumption of labour-power

1 Non-paid work includes family, household, self-improvement, school, political, and voluntary work. For the purposes of this chapter, non-paid work refers exclusively to non-paid work done within social economy organizations. Chapter 7, however, utilizes the complete definition of work as it examines the production of labour-power.

2 K. Marx, *Capital: A Critique of Political Economy Volume II*, New York: Vintage Books, 1981.

3 This figure originates from the *Workplace and Employee Survey* conducted by Statistics Canada in 1999. The figure of 900,000 paid workers therefore under-represents the current numbers. See also R. Saunders, *Passion and Commitment Under Stress: Human Resource Issues in Canada's Non-profit Sector*, Ottawa: Canadian Policy Research Networks Inc., 2004, p. 16.

4 OECD, *Economic Surveys: Canada*, Paris: OECD, 2004.

5 Ibid.

6 Another 25 per cent are engaged in the *wholesale, retail trade, hotel and restaurant* sectors. See OECD, *Economic.*

7 Annually this corresponds to between $4,160CAD and $8,320CAD. See K. McMullen and G. Schellenberg, *Job Quality in Non-profit Organizations*, Ottawa: Canadian Policy Research Networks, 2003, p. 28.

8 Saunders, *Passion*, p. 41.

9 C.J. Cranford *et al.*, 'The gender of precarious employment in Canada', *Relations Industrielles/Industrial Relations*, 2003, vol. 58, no. 3, 454–538.

10 U. Beck, *Risk Society: Towards a New Modernity*, trans. M.A. Ritter, London: Sage, 1992a, p. 143.

11 Marshall cited in R. Saunders, *Defining Vulnerability in the Labour Market*, Ottawa: Canadian Policy Research Networks Inc., 2003, p. 22.

12 M.H. Hall *et al.*, *Caring Canadians, Involved Canadians: Highlights From the 2000 National Survey of Giving, Volunteering and Participating*, Ottawa: Statistics Canada, 2001.

13 Annually this corresponds to an average of $6,240CAD for involuntary part-time paid work with part-time female paid work receiving $6,635.20 and part-time male paid work receiving $5,304CAD less. See G.F. Barrett and D.J. Doiron, 'Working part time: by choice or by constraint', *Canadian Journal of Economics*, 2001, vol. 30, no. 4, 1043.

14 See Saunders, *Passion*; McMullen and Schellenberg, *Job Quality*.

15 Non-paid work in the social economy and its use here fits within what has conventionally been regarded as volunteer work.

16 Utilizing the estimate of 900,000 paid workers and the 6.5 million identified volunteers in 2000, the overall Canadian ratio of paid to non-paid workers is 6:1.

17 G. Betcherman *et al.*, *The Voluntary Sector in Canada: Literature Review and Strategic Considerations for a Human Resource Sector Study*, Toronto: Canadian Centre for Philanthropy, 1998, p. 32.

18 This has been institutionalized with the creation of the Voluntary Sector Initiative.

19 Mandating of voluntary work by the Ontario provincial government as a prerequisite to high school graduation is an example of this shift towards the recognition of the role played by this form of work. Kathy L. Brock however points out that this strategy is potentially counter-productive, as compelling individuals to volunteer undermines the social fabric that it is intended to supplement. See K.L. Brock, 'Promoting voluntary action and civil society through the state', *ISUMA: Canadian Journal of Policy Research*, 2001, vol. 2, no. 2, 53–61.

20 As a national total, non-paid workers contributed the full-time paid work equivalent of 549,000 jobs. See Hall *et al.*, *Caring*, p. 32.

21 M.B. Evans and J. Shields, 'Neoliberal restructuring and the third sector: reshaping governance, civil society and the local relations', a paper presented to the *Annual General Meeting of the Canadian Sociology and Anthropology Association*, Edmonton: University of Alberta, 2000, p. 4.

22 GDP is at best a partial reflection of the value of the social economy. Environmental, social, cultural and political dimensions are missing, which are necessarily foregrounded in the post-Employment era.

23 PW (paid work), FPW (female paid work), PTPW (part-time paid work), FPTPW (female part-time paid work), NPW (nonpaid work) and FNPW (female nonpaid work).

24 This emphasis on paid work and therefore the potential for undermining the sector is heightened by the emphasis on professionalization of goods and service delivery brought about by the imposition of accountability mechanisms imposed by governments.

25 A.G. Meinhard and M.K. Foster, *Women's Organizations are Different: Their Response to Shifts in Canadian Policy*, Toronto: Centre for Voluntary Sector Studies, 2002.

7   Structuring the Work paradigm: (re)production of labour-power

1 Not all findings are discussed in this chapter. Instead only those that exemplify overall findings as well as those with high statistical significance are elaborated on. Both single-variant and bivariant analysis (age groupings, childcare responsibilities, educational attainment, gender, new social movement participation, organizational activity, part-time paid work, full-time paid work, paid work and non-paid work) are utilized in communicating the findings.

2 In order to more fully analyze the shift to the Work paradigm, future studies will need to evaluate the structured diversity between the market, state and social economies. For example issues of work process, the politics of the workplace along with missions and goals would provide a heightened understanding of the contours of this emergent paradigm.

3 The national average in 2000 for multiple jobholders was 5 per cent. See K.L. Johnson *et al.*, *Work-Life Compendium 2001: 150 Canadian Statistics on Work, Family and Well-Being*, Guelph: University of Guelph, 2001, p. 39.

4 A. Gramsci, *Selections from the Prison Notebooks of Antonio Gramsci*, Q. Hoare and G.N. Smith (eds), New York: International Publishers, 1999, p. 302.

5 K. McMullen and G. Schellenberg, *Job Quality in Non-profit Organizations*, Ottawa: Canadian Policy Research Networks, 2003, p. 28.

6 Statistics Canada, *Employment by Industry and Sex*, 2003, <http://www. statcan.ca/english/Pgdb/labor10a.htm>, viewed: 2 July 2004.

7 McMullen and Schellenberg, *Job Quality*, p. 41.

8 I. Bakker, 'Introduction: engendering macro-economic policy reform in the era of global restructuring and adjustment', in I. Bakker (ed.), *The Strategic Silence: Gender and Economic Policy*, London: Zed Books, 1994.

9 For further discussion on the gendered nature of restructuring see Bakker, *Strategic*; W. Michelson and L. Tepperman, 'Focus on home: what time-use data can tell about caregiving to adults', *Journal of Social Issues*, 2003, vol. 59, no. 3, 591–610.

10 T. Kay, 'Leisure, gender and family: the influence of social policy', *Leisure Studies*, 2000, vol. 19, no. 4, 247–265.

11 J. Zuzanek, 'Parenting time: enough or too little?', *Canadian Journal of Policy Research*, 2001, vol. 2, no. 2, 125–133.

12 S.F. Mennino and A. Brayfield, 'Job-family trade-offs', *Work and Occupations*, 2002, vol. 29, no. 2, 226–256.

13 For discussions see N. Zukewich, 'Work, parenthood and the experience of time scarcity', *Research Paper – Days of Our Lives: Time Use and Transitions Over the Life Course*, Ottawa: Statistics Canada, 1998; M. Tausig and R. Fenwick, 'Unbinding time: alternate work schedules and work-life balance', *Journal of Family and Economic Issues*, 2001, vol. 22, no. 2, 101–119.

14 Zuzanek, 'Parenting', 125.

15 For further discussion see F. Jones, 'Volunteering parents: who volunteers and how are their lives affected?', *ISUMA: Canadian Journal of Policy Research*, 2001, vol. 2, no. 2, 69–74; T. Rotolo, 'A time to join, a time to quit: the influence of life cycle transit on voluntary association memberships', *Social Forces*, 2000, vol. 78, 1133–1161.

16 These findings are consistent with those cited in other studies such as Mennino and Brayfield, 'Job-Family'; and Michelson and Tepperman, 'Focus'.

17 The website <http://www.schizophrenia.ca> provides a useful starting point for this understanding of schizophrenia.

18 G. Deleuze and F. Guattari, *Anti-Oedipus: Capitalism and Schizophrenia*, trans. R. Hurley *et al.*, Minneapolis: University of Minnesota Press, 1983, p. 245.

19 Ibid., p. xxi.

20 Ibid., p. 341.

8 Conclusion: towards a political economy of work

1 J. Milton, *Paradise Lost: A Poem in Twelve Books*, New York: Macmillan Publishing, 1985, p. 63.

2 A. Gramsci, *Selections from the Prison Notebooks of Antonio Gramsci*, Q. Hoare and G.N. Smith (eds), New York: International Publishers, 1999, p. 229.

3 Ibid., p. 172.

Bibliography

Aglietta, M. (1979) *A Theory of Capitalist Regulation: the US Experience*, London: Verso Press.

Albert, M. (1993) *Capitalism Against Capitalism: How America's Obsession with Individual Achievement and Short-Term Profit Has Led it to the Brink of Collapse*, trans. P. Haviland, New York: Four Walls Eight Windows.

Aldridge, T. *et al.* (2001) 'Recasting work: the example of local exchange trading schemes', *Work, Employment and Society*, vol. 15, no. 3: 565–579.

Althusser, L. (1969) *For Marx*, Harmondsworth: Penguin Books.

—— (1971) *Lenin and Philosophy and Other Essays*, London: New Left Books.

Althusser, L. and Balibar, É. (1970) *Reading Capital*, London: New Left Books.

Amin, A. (1994) 'Post-Fordism: models, fantasies and phantoms of transition', in A. Amin (ed.), *Post-Fordism: A Reader*, Cambridge: Blackwell.

—— (1999) 'An institutionalist perspective on regional economic development', *International Journal of Urban and Regional Research*, vol. 23, no. 2: 365–378.

Amin, A. *et al.* (1999) 'Welfare as work? The potential of the UK social economy', *Environment and Planning A*, vol. 31: 2033–2051.

Amsden, A. (1989) *Asia's Next Giant: South Korea and Late Industrialization*, New York: Oxford University Press.

—— (1990) 'Third world industrialization: "global Fordism" or a new model', *New Left Review*, no. 182: 5–31.

—— (2001) *The Rise of 'the Rest': Challenges to the West From Late Industrializing Economies*, Oxford: Oxford University Press.

Anheier, H.K. and Leat, D. (2002) *From Charity to Creativity: Philanthropic Foundations in the 21st Century*, Bournes Green, UK: Comedia in association with the Joseph Roundtree Reform Trust.

Archibugi, F. (2000) *The Associative Economy: Insights Beyond the Welfare State and into Post-Capitalism*, New York: St. Martin's Press Inc.

Armstrong, P. (1996) 'The feminization of the labour force: harmonizing down in a global economy', in I. Bakker (ed.), *Rethinking Restructuring: Gender and Change in Canada*, Toronto: University of Toronto.

Armstrong, P. and Armstrong, H. (1978) *The Double Ghetto: Canadian Women and Their Segregated Work*, Toronto: McClelland and Stewart.

Arvidson, E. (2000) 'Los Angeles: a postmodern class mapping', in J.K. Gibson-Graham *et al.* (eds), *Class and Its Others*, Minneapolis: University of Minnesota Press.

Autor, D.H. and Duggan, M.G. (2003) 'The rise in the disability rolls and the decline in unemployment', *The Quarterly Journal of Economics*, vol. 118, no. 1: 157–205.

Bakker, I. (1994) 'Introduction: engendering macro-economic policy reform in the era of global restructuring and adjustment', in I. Bakker (ed.), *The Strategic Silence: Gender and Economic Policy*, London: Zed Books.

—— (1996) 'Introduction: The Gendered Foundations of Restructuring in Canada', in I. Bakker (ed.), *Rethinking Restructuring: Gender and Change in Canada*, Toronto: University of Toronto.

—— (1999) 'Neoliberal governance and the new gender order', *Working Papers*, vol. 1, no. 1: 44–59.

—— (2002) 'Who built the pyramids? Engendering the new international economic and financial architecture', *Femina Politica: Zeitscrift fur Feministische Politik-Wissenschaft Special Issue: Engendering der Makrookonomie*, vol. 1: 38–48.

Bakker, I. and Gill, S. (2003a) 'Global political economy and social reproduction', in I. Bakker and S. Gill (eds), *Power, Production and Social Reproduction*, New York: Palgrave Macmillan.

—— (2003b) 'Ontology, method and hypotheses', in I. Bakker and S. Gill (eds), *Power, Production and Social Reproduction*, New York: Palgrave Macmillan.

Barrett, G.F. and Doiron, D.J. (2001) 'Working part time: by choice or by constraint', *Canadian Journal of Economics*, vol. 30, no. 4: 1042–1065.

Bauman, Z. (1991) *Modernity and Ambivalence*, Cambridge: Polity Press.

—— (1998) *Work, Consumerism and the New Poor*, Buckingham: Open University Press.

—— (2002) 'Foreword: individually together', in U. Beck and E. Gernsheim-Beck (eds), *Individualization: Institutionalized Individualism and its Social and Political Consequences*, London: Sage Publications.

Baumol, W.J. (1967) 'The macroeconomics of unbalanced growth', *American Economic Review*, vol. 57: 415–26.

Beck, U. (1986; 1992a) *Risk Society: Towards a New Modernity*, trans. M.A. Ritter, London: Sage.

—— (1992b) 'From industrial society to the risk society: questions of survival, social structure and ecological enlightenment', *Theory, Culture and Society*, vol. 9: 97–123.

—— (1995) *Ecological Enlightenment: Essays on the Politics of the Risk Society*, trans. M.A. Ritter, Atlantic Highlands: Humanities Press.

—— (1996) 'World risk society as cosmopolitan society? Ecological questions in a framework of manufactured uncertainties', *Theory Culture and Society*, vol. 13, no. 4: 1–32.

—— (1997) *The Reinvention of Politics: Rethinking Modernity in the Global Social Order*, trans. M.A. Ritter, Cambridge: Polity Press.

—— (1998) *Democracy Without Enemies*, trans. M.A. Ritter, Cambridge: Polity Press.

—— (1999) *World Risk Society*, Cambridge: Polity Press.

—— (2000) *The Brave New World of Work*, trans. P. Camiller, Cambridge: Polity Press.

—— (2005) *Power in the Global Age: A New Political Economy*, trans. K. Cross, Cambridge: Polity Press.

Beck, U. and Gernsheim-Beck, E. (1995) *The Normal Chaos of Love*, Cambridge: Polity Press.

—— (2002) *Individualization: Institutionalized Individualism and its Social and Political Consequences*, London: Sage Publications.

Becker, G.S. (1981) *A Treatise on the Family*, Cambridge, MA: Harvard University Press.

—— (1985) 'Human capital, effort, and the sexual division of labor', *Journal of Labor Economics*, vol. 3, no. 1: 33–58.

Beder, S. (2000) *Selling the Work Ethic: From Puritan Pulpit to Corporate PR*, New York: Zed Books.

Beechey, V. (1987) *Unequal Work*, London: Verso.

Bello, W. (2001) *The Future in the Balance: Essays on Globalization and Resistance*, Oakland: Food First Books and Focus on the South.

Bello, W. and Cunningham, S. (1994) 'Dark victory: the global impact of structural adjustment', *The Ecologist*, vol. 24, no. 3: 87–93.

Bello, W. *et al.* (1994) *Dark Victory: The Global Impact of Structural Adjustment and Global Poverty*, London: Pluto Press.

Berger, P.L. and Luckmann, T. (1966) *The Social Construction of Reality: A Treatise in the Sociology of Knowledge*, New York: Doubleday & Company.

Bergeron, S. (1996) 'The nation as a gendered subject of macroeconomics', in I. Bakker (ed.), *Rethinking Restructuring: Gender and Change in Canada*, Toronto: University of Toronto.

Betcherman, G. *et al.* (1998) *The Voluntary Sector in Canada: Literature Review and Strategic Considerations for a Human Resource Sector Study*, Toronto: Canadian Centre for Philanthropy.

Betzelt, S. (2001) *The Third Sector as Job Machine? Condition, Potentials, and Policies for Job Creation in German Nonprofit Organizations*, Berlin: Peter Lang.

Beveridge, W.H. (1942) *Social Insurance and Allied Service*, New York: Macmillan Company.

—— (1945) *Report on Full Employment in a Free Society*, New York: W.W. Norton & Company.

Bhabha, H.K. (1994) *The Location of Culture*, London: Routledge.

Bourdieu, P. (1977a) *Outline of a Theory of Practice*, Cambridge: Cambridge University Press.

—— (1977b) 'Cultural reproduction and social reproduction', in J. Karabel and A.H. Halsey (eds), *Power and Ideology in Education*, Oxford: Oxford University Press.

—— (2000) *Pascalian Meditations*, trans. R. Nice, Oxford: Polity Press.

Boyer, R. (1988) 'Technical change and the theory of "*régulation*" ', in G. Dosi *et al.* (eds), *Technical Change and Economic Theory*, London: Pinter.

—— (1990) *The Regulation School: A Critical Introduction*, trans. C. Charney, New York: Columbia University Press.

Boyer, R. and Saillard, Y. (eds) (2002) *Régulation Theory: The State of the Art*, trans. C. Shread, London: Routledge.

Braudel, F. (1979) *The Structures of Everyday Life: The Limits of the Possible*, trans. S. Reynolds, New York: Harper & Row Publishers.

Bridge, R. (2000) *The Law of Advocacy by Charitable Organizations: The Case for Change*, Vancouver: IMPACS.

Brock, K.L. (2001) 'Promoting voluntary action and civil society through the state', *ISUMA: Canadian Journal of Policy Research*, vol. 2, no. 2: 53–61.

Broder, P. (2001) *The Legal Definition of Charity and Canada Customs and Revenue Agency's Charitable Registration Process*, Toronto: Canadian Centre for Philanthropy.

Brodie, J. (1990) *The Political Economy of Canadian Regionalism*, Toronto: Harcourt Brace Jovanovich.

—— (1994) 'Shifting the boundaries: gender and the politics of restructuring', in I. Bakker (ed.), *The Strategic Silence: Gender and Economic Policy*, London: Zed Books.

—— (2002) 'Citizenship and solidarity: reflections on the Canadian way', *Citizenship Studies,* vol. 6, no. 4: 377–394.

—— (2003) 'Globalization, in/security, and the paradoxes of the social', in I. Bakker and S. Gill (eds), *Power, Production and Social Reproduction*, New York: Palgrave Macmillan.

Brooks, S.G. and Wohlforth, W.C. (2002) 'American primacy in perspective', *Foreign Affairs*, vol. 81, no. 4: 20–33.

Browne, P.L. (2000) 'The neo-liberal uses of the social economy: non-profit organizations and workfare in Ontario', in E. Shragge and J-M. Fontain (eds), *Social Economy: International Debates and Perspectives*, Montreal: Black Rose Books.

Bureau of Labor Statistics (2001) 'Occupations with the largest growth, 2000–2010', *Monthly Labour Review.* Available at <www.bls.gov/emp/emptab4.htm> (accessed 9 September 2003).

—— (2003) 'Occupational employment and wages, 2002'. Available at <www.bls.gov.oes> (accessed 20 October 2004).

The Macdonald Commission (1986) *Royal Commission on Economic Union and Development Prospects for Canada*, Toronto: University of Toronto Press.

Canada Council for the Arts (2003) 'Volunteers in arts and culture organizations in Canada', *Research Series on the Arts*, vol. 2, no. 1: 1–11.

Canada Revenue Agency (2002) *Canadian Registered Charities.* Available at <www.ccra-adrc.gc.ca/tax/charities/online_listings/canreg_interim-e.html> (accessed 12 June 2003).

—— (2003) *Registered Charities – Ancillary and Incidental Political Activities.* Available at <http://www.cra-arc.gc.ca/tax/charities/policy/cps/cps-022-e.html> (accessed 17 January 2004).

Canadian Centre for Philanthropy (1998) *The Voluntary Sector in Canada: Literature Review and Strategic Considerations for a Human Resources Sector Study*, Toronto: Canadian Policy Research Networks.

Caproni, P.J. (2004) 'Work/life balance: you can't get there from here', *The Journal of Applied Behavioral Science*, vol. 40, no. 2: 208–218.

Caputo, J.D. (ed.) (1997) *Deconstruction in a Nutshell: A Conversation with Jacques Derrida*, New York: Fordham University Press.

Carlson, A. (1993) *From Cottage to Work Station: The Family's Search for Social Harmony in the Industrial Age*, San Francisco: Ignatius Press.

Carpi, J.A.T. (1997) 'The prospects for the social economy in a changing world', *Annals of Public and Cooperative Economics*, vol. 68, no. 2: 247–279.

Cerny, P.G. (1990) *The Changing Architecture of Politics: Structure, Agency, and the Future of the State*, London: Sage.

—— (1997) 'Paradoxes of the competition state: the dynamics of political globalisation', *Government and Opposition*, vol. 32, no. 2: 251–274.

Chick, V. (1983) *Macroeconomics After Keynes: A Reconsideration of the General Theory*, Oxford: Philip Allan Publishers.

Chrétien, J. (1996) Speech delivered at the Indonesia-Canada Chamber of Commerce luncheon. 17 January. Available at <http://www.tcm-mec.gc.ca/96_01_17_JCICccl-en.asp> (accessed 17 December 2004).

Christian, W. and Campbell, C. (1990) *Political Parties and Ideologies in Canada*, third edition, Toronto: McGraw-Hill Ryerson Ltd.

Clinton, W.J. (2000) 'Presidential statement on welfare reform legislation', The Whitehouse: Office of the Press Secretary. Available at <www. clintonpresidentialcenter.org/legacy/082200-presidential-statement-on-welfare-reform-legislation.htm> (accessed 17 December 2004).

Cox, R. (1987) *Power, Production and World Order: Social Forces in the Making of History*, New York: Columbia University Press.

—— (1993) 'Structural issues of global governance: implications for Europe', in S. Gill (ed.), *Gramsci, Historical Materialism and International Relations*, Cambridge: Cambridge University Press.

—— (1995) 'Critical political economy', in B. Hettne *et al.* (eds), *International Political Economy: Understanding Global Disorder*, London: Zed Books.

—— (1996) 'Social forces, states, and world orders: beyond international relations theory', *Millennium: Journal of International Studies*, vol. 10, no. 2: 127–155.

Cox, R. with Schechter, M.G. (2002) *The Political Economy of a Plural World: Critical Reflections on Power, Morals and Civilization*, London: Routledge.

Cowen, M. and Shenton, R. (1995) 'The invention of development', in J. Crush (ed.), *Power and Development*, New York: Routledge.

Cragg, K.C. (1943) 'Must publicly direct employment: Beveridge', *Globe and Mail*, 25 May.

Cranford, C.J. *et al.* (2003) 'The gender of precarious employment in Canada', *Relations Industrielles/Industrial Relations*, vol. 58, no. 3: 454–538.

Davidman, K. *et al.* (1998) 'Work in the Nonprofit Sector: The Knowledge Gap', *The Philanthropist*. vol. 14, no. 3: 34–48.

Dawson, A.D. (1996) *The Two Faces of Economics*, New York: Longman.

Day, K.M and Devlin, R.A. (1997) *The Canadian Nonprofit Sector*. CPRN Working Paper No. CPRN. 02. Ottawa: Canadian Policy Research Networks.

De Angelis, M. (2000) *Keynesian, Social Conflict and Political Economy*, New York: St. Martin's Press.

Descartes, R. (1637; 1968) *Discourse on Method and Other Writings*, trans. F.E. Sutcliffe, Harmondsworth: Penguin Books.

Defourny, J. *et al.* (eds) (2001) *Tackling Social Exclusion in Europe: The Contribution of the Social Economy*, Aldershot: Ashgate.

Deleuze, G. and Guattari, F. (1983) *Anti-Oedipus: Capitalism and Schizophrenia*, trans. R. Hurley *et al.*, Minneapolis: University of Minnesota Press.

Derrida, J. (1976) *Of Grammatology*, trans. G. Spivak, Baltimore: Johns Hopkins University Press.

—— (1981) *Dissemination*, trans. B. Johnson, Chicago: University of Chicago Press.

—— (1982) *Margins of Philosophy*, trans. A. Bass, Chicago: University of Chicago Press.

Devlin, R.A. (2001) 'Volunteers and the paid labour market', *ISUMA: Canadian Journal of Policy Research*, vol. 2, no. 2: 62–68.

Dickey, S. and Adams, K.M. (eds) (2000) *Home and Hegemony: Domestic Service and Identity Politics in South and Southeast Asia*, Ann Arbor: The University of Michigan Press.

Dreessen, E. (2001) 'What we should know about the voluntary sector but don't', *ISUMA: Canadian Journal of Policy Research*, vol. 2, no. 2: 11–19.

Drew, E. (2000) 'Reconciling divisions of labour', in S. Duncan and B. Pfau-Effinger (eds), *Gender, Economy and Culture in the European Union*, London: Routledge.

Drew, E. and Emerek, R. (1998) 'Employment, flexibility and gender', in E. Drew *et al.* (eds), *Women, Work and the Family in Europe*, London: Routledge.

Drover, G. and Kerans, P. (eds) (1993) *New Approaches To Welfare Theory*, Vermont: Edward Elgar Publishing Limited.

Duxbury, L. and Higgins, C. (2003a) *Voices of Canadians: Seeking Work-Life Balance*, Ottawa: Health Canada.

—— (2003b) *Work-Life Conflict in Canada in the New Millennium*, Ottawa: Health Canada.

Dwyer, R.E. (2004) 'Downward earnings mobility after voluntary employer exits', *Work and Occupations*, vol. 31, no. 1: 111–139.

The Economist (2000) 'The great American jobs machine', *The Economist*, 13 January.

—— (2004) 'Undecided Voters and an Indecisive Recovery', *The Economist*, 9 October. Available at <http://www.economist.com> (accessed 28 November 2004).

Eder, C. (1996) *The Social Construction of Nature: A Sociology of Ecological Enlightenment*, London: Sage Publications.

Elgin, D. (1981) *Voluntary Simplicity: Toward a Way of Life That Is Outwardly Simple, Inwardly Rich*, New York: Morrow.

Ellingsaeter, A.L. (1999) 'Dual breadwinners between state and market', in R. Crompton (ed.), *Restructuring Gender Relations and Employment: The Decline of the Male Breadwinner*, Oxford: Oxford University Press.

Elson, D. (1998) 'The economic, the political and the domestic: businesses, states and households in the organization of production', *New Political Economy*, vol. 3, no. 2: 189–208.

Eme, B. (2001) 'Legitimate orders of social participation and the logic of social change', in R. Spear *et al.* (eds), *Tackling Social Exclusion in Europe: The Contribution of the Social Economy*, Aldershot: Ashgate.

Esping-Andersen, G. (1999) *Social Foundations of Postindustrial Societies*, Oxford: Oxford University Press.

Evans, M.B. and Shields, J. (2000) 'Neoliberal restructuring and the third sector: reshaping governance, civil society and the local relations', paper presented to the *Annual General Meeting of the Canadian Sociology and Anthropology Association*, Edmonton: University of Alberta, January.

Florida, R.L. (2002) *The Rise of the Creative Class: And How it's Transforming Work, Leisure, Community, and Everyday Life*, New York: Basic Books.

Folbre, N. (1994) *Who Pays for the Kids? Gender and the Structures of Constraint*, London: Routledge.

—— (2001) *The Invisible Heart: Economics and Family Values*, New York: The New Press.

Fontan, J-M. and Shragge, E. (2000) 'Tendencies, tensions and visions in the social economy', in E. Shragge and J-M. Fontan (eds), *Social Economy: International Debates and Perspectives*, Montreal: Black Rose Books.

Forbes (2004) 'The world's richest people: special report', *Forbes*. Available at <http://www.forbes.com/billionaires/> (accessed 16 December 2004).

Foucault, M. (1979) *Discipline and Punish: The Birth of the Prison*, trans. A. Sheridan. New York: Vintage Books.

—— (1980) 'Truth and power', in C. Gordon (ed.), *Power/Knowledge: Selected Interviews and Other Writings, 1972–1977*, Brighton: Harvester.

—— (1986) 'Of other spaces', *Diacritics*, vol. 16, no. 1: 22–27.

Fraad, H. *et al.* (1994) *Bringing It All Back Home: Class, Gender and Power in the Modern Household*, London: Pluto Press.

Frank, R. (1999) *Luxury Fever: Why Money Fails to Satisfy in an Era of Excess*, New York: The Free Press.

Friedman, M. (1962; 1982) *Capitalism and Freedom*, Chicago: University of Chicago Press.

Galbraith, J.K. (1996) *The Good Society: The Human Agenda*, Boston: Houghton Mifflin Company.

Gamson, W.A. (1992) *Talking Politics*, Cambridge: Cambridge University Press.

Garraty, J.A. (1978) *Unemployment in History: Economic Thought and Public Policy*, New York: Harper & Row Publishers.

Garten, J.E. (2005) 'The global economic challenge', *Foreign Affairs*, vol. 84, no. 1: 37–48.

Gerald, E. (1996) 'International capital mobility and the scope for national economic management', in D. Drache and R. Boyer (eds), *States Against Markets: The Limits of Globalization*, London: Routledge.

Gereffi, G. (1994) 'Capitalism, development and global commodity chains', in L. Sklair (ed.), *Capitalism and Development*, New York: Routledge.

George, S. (1992) *The Debt Boomerang: How Third World Debt Harms Us All*, London: Pluto Press.

Gibson-Graham, J.K. (1995) 'The economy stupid!: metaphors of totality and development in economic discourse', *Socialist Review*, vol. 25, no. 3–4: 27–63.

—— (1996) *The End of Capitalism (As We Knew It): A Feminist Critique of Political Economy*, Cambridge: Blackwell Publishers.

Giddens, A. (1991) *Modernity and Self-Identity*, Cambridge: Polity Press.

—— (1994) *Beyond Left and Right: The Future of Radical Politics*, Cambridge: Polity Press.

—— (ed.) (2001) *The Global Third Way Debate*, Cambridge: Polity Press.

Gilbert, G. (1943) 'What price Beveridge plan and who pays?', *Saturday Night*, 9 January.

Gill, S. (1995) 'Globalisation, market civilisation, and disciplinary neoliberalism', *Millennium*, vol. 23, no. 3: 399–423.

—— (1998) 'European governance and new constitutionalism: economic and monetary union and alternatives to disciplinary neoliberalism in Europe', *New Political Economy*, vol. 3, no. 1: 3–14.

—— (2000) 'The constitution of global capitalism', paper presented at the International Studies Association Annual Convention, Los Angeles, March.

Gill, S. and Law, D. (1988) *The Global Political Economy: Perspectives, Policies and Problems*, Hemel Hempstead: Harvester/Wheatsheaf.

Glazer, N. (1998) 'The American welfare state: exceptional no longer?', in H. Cavanna (ed.), *Challenges to the Welfare State: Internal and External Dynamics for Change*, Cheltenham: Edward Elgar.

Glenn, E.N. (2001) 'Gender, race, and the organization of reproductive labor', in R. Baldoz *et al.* (eds), *The Critical Study of Work: Labor, Technology, and Global Production*, Philadelphia: Temple University Press.

Glennerster, H. and Evans, M. (1994) 'Beveridge and his assumptive worlds: the incompatibilities of a flawed design', in J. Hills *et al.* (eds), *Beveridge and Social Security: An International Retrospective*, Oxford: Oxford University Press.

Globe and Mail (1944) 'Britain's new social insurance plan: a comparison with the Beveridge Report', *Globe and Mail*, 26 September.

Gorz, A. (1982) *Farewell to the Working Class: An Essay on Post-Industrial Socialism*, trans. M. Sonenscher, London: Pluto Press.

—— (1999) *Reclaiming Work: Beyond the Wage-Based Society*, trans. C. Turner, Cambridge: Polity Press.

Government of Alberta (2000) *Get Ready Alberta: Strengthening the Alberta Advantage*, Edmonton: Government of Alberta.

Gowan, P. (2004) 'Contemporary intra-core relations and World System Theory', *Journal of World-Systems Research*, vol. 10, no. 2: 471–500.

Gramsci, A. (1971; 1999) *Selections from the Prison Notebooks of Antonio Gramsci*, Q. Hoare and G.N. Smith (eds), New York: International Publishers.

Granovetter, M. (1985) 'Economic action and social structure: the problem of embeddedness', *American Journal of Sociology*, vol. 91, no. 3: 481–510.

—— (1992) 'Economic action and social structure: the problem of embeddedness', in M. Granovetter and R. Swedberg (eds), *The Sociology of Economic Life*, Boulder: Westview Press.

Gregg, A.R. (2003) 'Art for everyone', *Maclean's*. vol. 116, no. 21: 40.

Grewal, I. and Kaplan, C. (1994) 'Introduction: transnational feminist practices and questions of postmodernity', in I. Grewal and C. Kaplan (eds), *Scattered Hegemonies: Postmodernity and Transnational Feminist Practices*, Minneapolis: University of Minnesota Press.

Guest, D. (1987) 'World War II and the welfare state in Canada', in A. Moscovitch and J. Albert, *The Benevolent State: The Growth of Welfare in Canada*, Toronto: Garamond Press.

—— (1991) *The Emergence of Social Security in Canada*, second edition, Vancouver: UBC Press.

Habermas, J. (1975) *Legitimation Crisis*, Boston: Beacon Press.

Hacking, I. (1991) 'How should we do the history of statistics?', in G. Burchell *et al.* (eds), *The Foucault Effect: Studies in Governmentality*, Chicago: University of Chicago Press.

Hager, M.A. *et al.* (2003) 'Response rates for mail surveys of nonprofit organizations: a review and empirical test', *Nonprofit and Voluntary Sector Quarterly*, vol. 32, no. 2: 252–267.

Hall, M.H. *et al.* (2001) *Caring Canadians, Involved Canadians: Highlights from the 2000 National Survey of Giving, Volunteering and Participating*, Ottawa: Statistics Canada.

Hall, M. and Banting, K. (2000) 'The nonprofit sector in Canada: an introduction', in K. Banting (ed.), *The Nonprofit Sector in Canada: Roles and Relationships*, Montreal: McGill-Queen's University Press.

Hall, P. and Soskice, D. (eds) (2001) *Varieties of Capitalism: The Institutional Foundations of Comparative Advantage*, Oxford: Oxford University Press.

Hannigan, J.A. (1995) *Environmental Sociology: A Social Constructionist Perspective*, London: Routledge.

Haraway, D. (1990) *Simians, Cyborgs and Women: The Reinvention of Nature*, London: Free Association Books.

Hardt, M. and Negri, A. (1994) *Labor of Dionysus: A Critique of the State-Form*, Minneapolis: University of Minnesota Press.

—— (2000) *Empire*, Cambridge, MA: Harvard University Press.

Harrison, B. and Kelly, M.R. (1993) 'Outsourcing and the search for "flexibility" ', *Work, Employment and Society*, vol. 7, no. 2: 213–235.

Harrison, P.M. and Beck, A.J. (2003) 'Prisoners in 2002', *Bureau of Justice Statistics Bulletin*. Available at <http://www.ojp.usdoj.gov/bjs/pubalp2.htm#Prisoners> (accessed 7 January 2005).

Hartman, H. (1981) 'The unhappy marriage of marxism and feminism: towards a more progressive union', in L. Sargent (ed.), *Women and Revolution*, London: Pluto.

Harvey, D. (1988) 'The geographical and geopolitical consequences of the transition from Fordist to flexible accumulation', in G. Sternlieb and J.W. Hughes (eds), *America's New Market Geography: Nation, Region, and Metropolis*, New Jersey: The State University of New Jersey.

Haseler, S. (2000) *The Super-Rich: The Unjust New World of Global Capitalism*, New York: St. Martin's Press.

Hayek, F.A. (1944) *The Road to Serfdom*, Chicago: University of Chicago Press.

Health Canada (2002) *International Year of Volunteers*. Available at <http://www.hc-sc.gc.ca/hppb/voluntarysector/beyond/iyv.html> (accessed 1 August 2004).

Hecker, D.E. (2001) 'Occupational employment projections to 2010', *Monthly Labor Review*, vol. 124, no. 11: 57–84.

Heidegger, M. (1949; 1988) *Existence and Being*, Washington D.C.: Regnery Gateway.

Helleiner, E. (1996) 'Post-globalization: is the financial liberalization trend likely to be reversed?' in R. Boyer and D. Drache (eds), *States Against Markets: The Limits of Globalization*, London: Routledge.

Hetherington, K. (1997) *The Badlands of Modernity: Heterotopia and Social Ordering*, London: Routledge.

—— (1998) *Expressions of Identity: Space, Performance, Politics*, London: Sage.

Hewitson, G.J. (1999) *Feminist Economics: Interrogating the Masculinity of Rational Economic Man*, Cheltenham: Edward Elgar.

Himmelweit, S. (1995) 'The discovery of "unpaid work": the social consequences of the expansion of "work" ', *Feminist Economics*, vol. 1, no. 2: 1–19.

Hirschman, A.O. (1970) *Exit, Voice and Loyalty: Responses to Decline in Firms, Organizations and States*, Cambridge, MA: Harvard University Press.

Hochschild, A.R. (1989) *The Second Shift: Working Parents and the Revolution at Home*, New York: Viking.

Hutchison, T.W. (1993) 'Keynes versus the Keynesians . . .?', in W. Allan (ed.), *A Critique of Keynesian Economics*, New York: St. Martin's Press.

Hutton, W. (1995) *The State We're In*, London: Jonathan Cape Press.

Iacocca, L. (1998) 'Driving force: Henry Ford', *Time Magazine*. Available at <http://www.time.com/time/time100/builder/profile/ford.html> (accessed 12 December 2004).

ILO (1998) *World Employment Report 1998*, Geneva: International Labour Organization.

—— (2004) *Global Employment Trends*, Geneva: International Labour Organization.

IMD (2004) *World Competitiveness Scorecard*, Lausanne: Institute for Management Development. Available at <www02.imd.ch/wcc/ranking> (accessed 22 November 2004).

IMF (2001) *World Economic Outlook: Fiscal Policy and Macroeconomic Stability*, New York: International Monetary Fund.

IMPACS (2002) *Let Charities Speak: Report of the Charities and Advocacy Dialogue*, Vancouver: IMPACS.

Institute for Competitiveness and Prosperity (2002) *A View of Ontario: Ontario's Clusters of Innovation*, Toronto: The Institute for Competitiveness and Prosperity.

James, B. (1997) 'Jospin pledges a law on 35-hour workweek', *International Herald Tribune*, 11–12 October: 1, 4.

Jessop, B. (1990) 'Regulation theories in retrospect and prospect', *Economy and Society*, vol. 19, no. 2: 153–216.

—— (1993) 'Towards a Schumpeterian workfare state? Preliminary remarks on post-Fordist political economy', *Studies in Political Economy*, vol. 40: 7–39.

—— (1994) 'Post-Fordism and the state', in A. Amin (ed.), *Post-Fordism: A Reader*, Oxford: Blackwell Publishers.

—— (2001) 'Regulationist and autopoieticist reflections on Polanyi's account of market economies and the market society', *New Political Economy*, vol. 6, no. 2: 213–232.

—— (2002) *The Future of the Capitalist State*, Cambridge: Polity Press.

Johnson, K.L. *et al.* (2001) *Work-Life Compendium 2001: 150 Canadian Statistics on Work, Family and Well-Being*, Guelph: University of Guelph.

Jones, F. (2001) 'Volunteering parents: who volunteers and how are their lives affected?', *ISUMA: Canadian Journal of Policy Research*, vol. 2, no. 2: 69–74.

Kalleberg, A. *et al.* (2000) 'Bad jobs in America: standard and nonstandard employment relations and job quality in the United States', *American Sociological Review*, vol. 65: 256–278.

Kay, T. (2000) 'Leisure, gender and family: the influence of social policy', *Leisure Studies*, vol. 19, no. 4: 247–265.

Keynes, J.M. (1936) *The General Theory of Employment, Interest and Money*, London: Macmillan.

—— (1926; 1972a) *The Collected Works of John Maynard Keynes Vol. IX: Essays of Persuasion*, London: Macmillan.

—— (1925; 1972b) *The Collected Works of John Maynard Keynes Vol. XI: Essays in Persuasion*, London: Macmillan.

Klumb, P.L. and Perrez, M. (2004) 'Why time sampling studies can enrich work-leisure research', *Social Indicators Research*, vol. 67: 1–10.

Kuhn, A.J. (1986) *GM Passes Ford, 1918–1938: Designing the General Motors Performance-Control System*, University Park: The Pennsylvania State University Press.

Landim, L. *et al.* (1999) 'Brazil', in L.M. Salamon *et al.* (eds), *Global Civil Society: Dimensions of the Nonprofit Sector*, Baltimore: The Johns Hopkins Centre for Civil Society Studies.

Lash, S. (2002) 'Foreword: individualization in a non-linear mode', in U. Beck and E. Gernsheim-Beck (eds), *Individualization: Institutionalized Individualism and its Social and Political Consequences*, London: Sage Publications.

—— (1999) *Another Modernity, A Different Rationality*, Oxford: Blackwell Publishers.

Lee, E. (1996) 'Globalization and employment: is the anxiety justified?', *International Labour Review*, vol. 135, no. 5: 485–498.

Leisering, L. and Leibfried, S. (1999) *Time and Poverty in Western Welfare States:*

United Germany in Perspective, trans. J. Biet-Wilson and L. Leisering, Cambridge: Cambridge University Press.

Levesque-Lopman, L. (1988) *Claiming Reality: Phenomenology and Women's Experience*, Ottawa: Rowman and Littlefield Publishers.

Lewis, D. (1999) 'Introduction: the parallel universes of third sector research and the changing context of voluntary action', *International Perspectives on Voluntary Action: Reshaping the Third Sector*, London: Earthscan Publications Ltd.

Li, M. (2004) 'After neoliberalism: empire, social democracy, or socialism?', *Monthly Review*, vol. 55, no. 8: 21–36.

Lingis, A. (1994) *The Community of Those Who Have Nothing in Common*, Indianapolis: Indiana University Press.

Lipietz, A. (1987) *Miracles and Mirages: The Crisis of Global Fordism*, London: Verso.

—— (1992) *Towards a New Economic Order: PostFordism, Ecology and Democracy*, Cambridge: Polity Press.

—— (1993) 'From Althusserianism to "regulation theory" ', in E.A. Kaplan and M. Sprinker (eds), *The Althusserian Legacy*, New York: Verso.

—— (2001) 'The fortunes and misfortunes of post-Fordism', in R. Albritton *et al.* (eds), *Phases of Capitalist Development: Booms, Crises and Globalizations*, London: Palgrave.

Lipsey, R.G. *et al.* (1987) *Economics*, New York: Harper & Row.

Luxton, M. (1983) 'Two hands for the clock: changing patterns in the gendered division of labour in the home', *Studies in Political Economy*, vol. 12: 27–44.

Luxton, M. and Corman, J. (2001) *Getting by in Hard Times: Gendered Labour at Home and on the Job*, Toronto: University of Toronto Press.

Lyotard, J-F. (1984) *The Postmodern Condition: A Report on Knowledge*, trans. G. Bennington and B. Massumi, Minneapolis: University of Minnesota Press.

MacPhail, F. (2000) 'What caused earnings inequality to increase in Canada during the 1980s?', *Cambridge Journal of Economics*, vol. 24: 153–175.

Maffesoli, M. (1996) *The Time of the Tribes*, London: Sage Publications.

Mailloux, L. *et al.* (2002) *Motivation at the Margins: Gender Issues in the Canadian Voluntary Sector*, Ottawa: Voluntary Sector Secretariat.

Martin, R. and Porter, M. (2000) 'Canadian competitiveness: nine years after the crossroads', paper presented at the Centre for Study of Living Standards Conference on *The Canada-US Manufacturing Productivity Gap*, Ottawa, January.

Marx, K. (1867; 1981) *Capital: A Critique of Political Economy Volume II*, New York: Vintage Books.

Massey, D. (1999) 'Spaces of politics', in D. Massey *et al.* (eds), *Human Geography Today*, Cambridge: Polity Press.

Massumi, B. (1992) *A User's Guide to Capitalism and Schizophrenia: Deviations From Deleuze and Guattari*, Cambridge: The MIT Press.

McClintock, N. (2004) *Understanding Canadian Donors: Using the National Survey of Giving, Volunteering and Participating to Build Your Fundraising Program*, Toronto: Canadian Centre for Philanthropy.

McInnis, P.S. (2002) *Harnessing Labour Confrontation: Shaping the Postwar Settlement in Canada, 1943–1950*, Toronto: University of Toronto Press.

McIntosh, D. (2003) 'UFCW airs new Wal-Mart strategy', *Northwest Labor Press*. Available at <http://www.walmartworkerscanada.com/news.php?articleID= 00046> (accessed 27 January 2005).

McMichael, P. (2000) *Development and Social Change: A Global Perspective*, second edition, Thousand Oaks: Pine Forge Press.

McMullen, K. and Schellenberg, G. (2002) *Mapping the Non-Profit Sector*, Ottawa: Canadian Policy Research Networks.

—— (2003) *Job Quality in Non-profit Organizations*, Ottawa: Canadian Policy Research Networks.

Mead, L.M. (1989) 'The logic of workfare: the underclass and work policy', *ANNALS*, 501: 156–169.

Meiksins, P. and Whalley, P. (2002) *Putting Work in its Place: A Quiet Revolution*, Ithaca: Cornell University Press.

Meinhard, A.G. and Foster, M.K. (2002) *Women's Organizations are Different: Their Response to Shifts in Canadian Policy*, Toronto: Centre for Voluntary Sector Studies.

Melucci, A. (1996) *Playing for Self: Person and Meaning in the Planetary System*, Cambridge: Cambridge University Press.

Mendelson, M. (2004) *Aboriginal People in Canada's Labour Market: Work and Unemployment, Today and Tomorrow*, Ottawa: The Caledon Institute of Social Policy.

Mennino, S.F. and Brayfield, A. (2002) 'Job-family trade-offs', *Work and Occupations*, vol. 29, no. 2: 226–256.

Michelson, W. and Tepperman, L. (2003) 'Focus on home: what time-use data can tell about caregiving to adults', *Journal of Social Issues*, vol. 59, no. 3: 591–610.

Millar, J. (1999) 'Obligations and autonomy in social welfare', in R. Crompton (ed.), *Restructuring Gender Relations and Employment: The Decline of the Male Breadwinner*, Oxford: Oxford University Press.

Milton, J. (1674; 1985) *Paradise Lost: A Poem in Twelve Books*, M.Y. Hughes (ed.), New York: Macmillan Publishing.

Minh-ha, T. (1989) *Woman, Native, Other: Writing Postcoloniality and Feminism*, Bloomington: Indiana University Press.

Minister of Reconstruction (1945) *Employment and Income with Specific Reference to the Initial Period of Reconstruction*, Ottawa: The Queen's Printer.

Mirabeau, V.R. (1766; 1968) *François Quesnay: The Economical Table (Tableau Economique)*, New York: Berman.

Mittelman, J. (1995) 'Rethinking the international division of labour in the context of globalisation', *Third World Quarterly*, vol. 16, no. 2: 273–295.

Moscovitch, A. and Drover, G. (1987) 'Social expenditures and the welfare state: the Canadian experience in historical perspective', in A. Moscovitch and J. Albert (eds), *The Benevolent State: The Growth of Welfare in Canada*, Toronto: Garamond Press.

Mouffe, C. and Laclau, E. (1985) *Hegemony and Socialist Strategy: Towards a Radical Democratic Politics*, trans. W. Moore and P. Cammack, London: Verso.

Murray, R. (1993) 'Transforming the "Fordist" state', in G. Albo *et al.* (eds), *A Different Kind of State? Popular Power and Democratic Administration*, Toronto: Oxford University Press.

—— (1999) *Creating Wealth from Waste*, London: Demos Panton House.

Nakhaie, R. (2002) 'Class, breadwinner ideology, and housework among Canadian husbands', *Review of Radical Political Economics*, vol. 34: 137–157.

Nelson, J.A. (1996) *Feminism, Objectivity and Economics*, London: Routledge.

Nye, J.S. Jr. (2001) 'Globalization's democratic deficit: how to make international institutions more accountable', *Foreign Affairs*, vol. 80, no. 4: 2–6.

Oakley, A. (1974) *The Sociology of Housework*, Bath: The Pitman Press.

OECD (1989) *Employment Outlook*, Paris: OECD.

—— (1994) *Women and Structural Change*, Paris: OECD.

—— (1995) *Employment Outlook*, Paris: OECD.

—— (2000) *Employment Outlook*, Paris: OECD.

—— (2001) *The New Economy: Beyond the Hype*, Paris: OECD.

—— (2003) *Employment Outlook*, Paris: OECD.

—— (2004) *Economic Surveys: Canada*, Paris: OECD.

Offen, K. (1984) 'Depopulation, nationalism and feminism in fin-de-siècle France', *The American Historical Review*, vol. 89: 648–676.

Olsson, K. (2003) 'Up against Wal-Mart', *Mother Jones*. Available at <http://www.motherjones.com/news/feature/2003/03/ma_276_01.html> (accessed 19 January 2005).

Ontario Works (1997) *Principles for Delivery: Directive 2.0*, Toronto: Government of Ontario.

Orloff, A.S. (1996) 'Gender in the welfare state', *Annual Review of Sociology*, vol. 22: 51–78.

Pahl, R. (1995) *After Success: Fin-de-Siècle Anxiety and Identity*, Cambridge: Polity Press.

Patterson, J. (1987) 'Winding down social spending: social spending restraint in Ontario in the 1970s', in A. Moscovitch and J. Albert (eds), *The Benevolent State: The Growth of Welfare in Canada,* Toronto: Garamond Press.

Pearson, R. (1996) 'Renegotiating the reproductive bargain: gender analysis of economic transition in Cuba in the 1990s', *Development and Change*, vol. 28: 671–705.

Peck, J.A. and Tickell, A. (1994) 'Searching for a new institutional fix: the *after*-Fordist crisis and the global-local disorder', in A. Amin (ed.), *Post-Fordism: A Reader*, Oxford: Blackwell Publishers.

Peck, J.A. and Theodore, N. (2000) 'Beyond employability', *Cambridge Journal of Economics*, 24: 729–749.

Pfau-Effinger, B. (1998) 'Culture or structure as explanations for differences in part-time work in Germany, Finland and the Netherlands', in J. O'Reilly and C. Fagan (eds), *Part-time Prospects: An International Comparison of Part-Time Work in Europe, North America and the Pacific Rim*, London: Routledge.

—— (1999) 'The modernization of family and motherhood in Western Europe', in R. Crompton (ed.), *Restructuring Gender Relations and Employment: The Decline of the Male Breadwinner*, Oxford: Oxford University Press.

Picchio, A. (1992) *Social Reproduction: The Political Economy of the Labour Market*, Cambridge: Cambridge University Press.

Pieterse, J.N. (2001) *Development Theory Deconstructions/Reconstructions*, London: Sage Publications.

Pilling, G. (1986) *The Crisis of Keynesian Economics: A Marxist View*, London: Croom Helm.

Pinch, S. (1997) *Worlds of Welfare: Understanding the Changing Geographies of Social Welfare Provision*, New York: Routledge.

Piore, M and Sabel, C.F. (1984) *The Second Industrial Divide: Possibilities for Prosperity*, New York: Basic Books Inc.

Polanyi, K. (1957) *The Great Transformation: The Political and Economic Origins of Our Time*, Boston: Beacon Hill.

Porter, M.E. (1990) *The Competitive Advantage of Nations*, London: The Macmillan Press Ltd.

Porter, M.E. *et al.* (1991) *Canada at the Crossroads: The Reality of a New Competitive Environment*, Toronto: Business Council on National Issues and Minister of Supply and Services.

Power, M. (2004) 'Social provisioning as a starting point for feminist economics', *Feminist Economics*, vol. 10, no. 3: 3–19.

Priller, E. *et al.* (1999) 'Germany: unification and change', in L.M. Salamon *et al.* (eds), *Global Civil Society: Dimensions of the Nonprofit Sector*, Baltimore: The Johns Hopkins Centre for Civil Society Studies.

Punch, K.F. (2003) *Survey Research: The Basics*, London: Sage Publications.

Putnam, R. (1993) *Making Democracy Work: Civic Traditions in Modern Italy*, Princeton: Princeton University Press.

Quarter, J. (1992) *Canada's Social Economy: Co-operatives, Non-profits and other-Community Enterprises*, Toronto: James Lorimer.

—— (2000) *Beyond the Bottom Line: Socially Innovative Business Owners*, Westport: Quorum Books.

Reich, R. (1992) *The Work of Nations: Preparing Ourselves for 21st Century Capitalism*, New York: Vintage Books.

Rifkin, J. (1995) *The End of Work: The Decline of the Global Labor Force and the Dawn of the Post-Market Era*, New York: G.P. Putnam & Sons.

Roberts, L. (2001) *Caught in the Middle: What Small, Non-Profit Organizations Need to Survive and Flourish*, Ottawa: Voluntary Sector Initiative.

Rotolo, T. (2000) 'A time to join, a time to quit: the influence of life cycle transit on voluntary association memberships', *Social Forces*, vol. 78: 1133–61.

Rubin, A. and Babbie, E. (1993) *Research Methods for Social Work*, second edition, Pacific Grove: Brooks/Cole Publishing Company.

Sabel, C.F. (1982) *Work and Politics: The Division of Labour in Industry*, Cambridge: Cambridge University Press.

—— (1994) 'Flexible specialization and the re-emergence of regional economies', in A. Amin (ed.), *Post-Fordism: A Reader*, Oxford: Blackwell Publishers.

Sachs, J.D. (1995) 'Consolidating capitalism', *Foreign Policy*, vol. 98: 50–64.

Salamon, L.M. and Anheier, H.K. (1997) 'Introduction: in search of the non-profit sector', in L.M. Salamon and H.K. Anheier (eds), *Defining the Non-profit Sector: A Cross-national Analysis*, Manchester: Manchester University Press.

Salant, P. and Dillman, D. (1994) *How to Conduct Your Own Survey*, New York: John Wiley and Sons.

Sallaz, J.J. (2004) 'Manufacturing concessions: attritionary outsourcing at General Motor's Lordstown, USA assembly plant', *Work, Employment and Society*, vol. 18, no. 4: 687–708.

Sassen, S. (2000) *Cities in a World Economy*, second edition, Thousand Oaks: Pine Forge Press.

Saunders, R. (2003) *Defining Vulnerability in the Labour Market*, Ottawa: Canadian Policy Research Networks Inc.

—— (2004) *Passion and Commitment Under Stress: Human Resource Issues in Canada's Non-profit Sector*, Ottawa: Canadian Policy Research Networks Inc.

Saussure, F. (1966) *Course in General Linguistics*, trans. W. Baskin, C. Bally and A. Sechehaye (eds), New York: McGraw-Hill Book Company.

Say, J-B. (1821; 1971) *A Treatise on Political Economy: Or the Production, Distribution and Consumption of Wealth*, trans. C.R. Prinsep, New York: Augustus M. Kelly.

Schor, J.B. (1998) *The Overspent American: Upscaling, Downshifting and the New Consumer*, New York: Basic Books.

—— (2001) 'Voluntary downshifting in the 1990s', in J. Stanford *et al.* (eds), *Power, Employment, and Accumulation: Social Structures in Economic Theory and Practice*, London: M.E. Sharpe.

Schumpeter, J.A. (1911; 1934) *A Theory of Economic Development*, Cambridge: Cambridge University Press.

Schürmann, R. (1983) 'What must I do? At the end of metaphysics: ethical norms and the hypothesis of a historical closure', in W.L. McBride and C.O. Schrag (eds), *Phenomenology in a Pluralistic Context*, Albany: State University of New York Press.

Scott, J.W. (1988) *Gender and the Politics of History*, New York: Columbia University Press.

Scott, K. (2003) *Funding Matters: The Impact of Canada's New Funding Regime on Nonprofit and Voluntary Organizations*, Ottawa: Canadian Council on Social Development.

Seem, M. (1983) 'Introduction', *Anti-Oedipus: Capitalism and Schizophrenia*, trans. R. Hurley *et al.*, Minneapolis: University of Minnesota Press.

Sen, A.K. (1990) 'Gender and cooperative conflicts', *Persistent Inequalities: Women and World Development*, Oxford: Oxford University Press.

Serrano, F. (2003) 'From "static" gold to the floating dollar', *Contributions to Political Economy*, vol. 22: 87–102.

Seyfang, G. (2001) 'Working for the fenland dollar: an evaluation of local exchange trading schemes as an informal employment strategy to tackle social exclusion', *Work, Employment and Society*, vol. 15, no. 3: 581–593.

Sharpe, D. (1994) *A Portrait of Canada's Charities: The Size, Scope and Financing of Registered Charities*, Toronto: Canadian Centre for Philanthropy.

—— (2001) 'The Canadian charitable sector: an overview', in J. Phillips *et al.* (eds), *Between State and Market: Essays on Charities Law and Policy in Canada*, Kingston: McGill-Queens University Press.

Silver, B.J. and Arrighi, G. (2003) 'Polanyi's "double movement": the *belle époques* of British and U.S. hegemony compared', *Politics and Society*, vol. 31, no. 2: 325–355.

Simonton, D. (1998) *A History of European Women's Work: 1700 to the Present*, London: Routledge.

Sivard, R. (1987) *World Military and Social Expenditures: 1987–88*, Washington D.C.: World Priorities.

Skidelsky, R. (1996) *Keynes*, Oxford: Oxford University Press.

Skousen, M. (2001) *The Making of Modern Economics: The Lives and Ideas of the Great Thinkers*, New York: M.E. Sharpe.

Smith, A. (1776; 1965) *Wealth of Nations*, New York: Modern Library.

Smith, D.H. (2000) *Grassroots Associations*, London: Sage Publications.

Smith, M. *et al.* (1998) 'Where and why is part-time work growing in Europe?' in J. O'Reilly and C. Fagan (eds), *Part-Time Prospects: An International Comparison of Part-Time Work in Europe, North America and the Pacific Rim*, London: Routledge.

Snowdon, B. *et al.* (1994) *A Modern Guide to Macroeconomics: An Introduction to Competing Schools*, Brookfield: Edward Elgar Publishing.

Statistics Canada (2003) *Employment by Industry and Sex*. Available at <http://www.statcan.ca/english/Pgdb/labor10a.htm> (accessed 2 July 2004).

—— (2004a) *Labour Force Characteristics By Age and Sex*. Available at <http://www.statcan.ca/english/Pgdb/labor20a.htm> (accessed 29 June 2004).

—— (2004b) *The Canadian Labour Market at a Glance: 2003*, Ottawa: Statistics Canada. Available at <statcan.ca/english/freepub/ 71–222-XIE/71–222-XIE2004000.pdf> (accessed 8 October 2004).

—— (2004c) *Labour Force Survey*, Ottawa: Statistics Canada. Available at <http://www.statcan.ca/english/Pgdb/labor46.htm> (accessed 3 October 2004).

Stiglitz, J. (1997) *The Annual Report of the Council of Economic Advisors*, Washington: United States Government Printing Office.

Strobel, F.R. and Peterson, W.C. (1999) *The Coming Class War and How To Avoid It: Rebuilding the American Middle Class*, London: M.E. Sharpe.

Struthers, J. (1987) 'A profession in crisis: Charlotte Whitton and Canadian social work in the 1930s', in A. Moscovitch and J. Albert (eds), *The Benevolent State: The Growth of Welfare in Canada*, Toronto: Garamond Press.

Su, B.W. (2001) 'The U.S. economy to 2010', *Monthly Labor Review*, November: 3–20.

Swartz, D. (1987) 'The limits of health insurance', in A. Moscovitch and J. Albert (eds), *The Benevolent State: The Growth of Welfare in Canada*, Toronto: Garamond Press.

Tausig, M. and Fenwick, R. (2001) 'Unbinding time: alternate work schedules and work-life balance', *Journal of Family and Economic Issues*, vol. 22, no. 2: 101–119.

Taylor, F.W. (1911) *The Principles of Scientific Management*, New York: Harper & Row.

—— (1939; 1984) 'Scientific management', in F. Fischer and C. Sirianni (eds), *Critical Studies in Organization and Bureaucracy*, Philadelphia: Temple University Press.

Taylor, J.H. (1987) 'Sources of political conflict in the thirties: welfare policy and the geography of need', in A. Moscovitch and J. Albert (eds), *The Benevolent State: The Growth of Welfare in Canada*, Toronto: Garamond Press.

Thompson, E.P. (1963) *The Making of the English Working Class*, New York: Vintage Books.

Thrift, N. (1996) *Spatial Formations*, London: Sage Publications.

Tomlinson, J. (1990) *Hayek and the Market*, London: Pluto Press.

Torfing, J. (1997) *Politics, Regulation and the Modern Welfare State*, New York: St.Martin's Press.

—— (1999) 'Workfare with welfare', *Journal of European Social Policy*, vol. 9, no. 1: 5–28.

Toronto Daily Star (1943a) 'Polls and social security', *Toronto Daily Star*, 6 February.

—— (1943b) 'To bring Canada up to date', *Toronto Daily Star*, 17 March.

Toronto Dollar (2004) Available at <www.torontodollar.com> (accessed 18 December 2004).

Tsru, S. (1993) *Japan's Capitalism: Creative Defeat and Beyond*, Cambridge: Cambridge University Press.

Tudiver, N. (1987) 'Forestalling the welfare state: the establishment of programmes of corporate welfare', in A. Moscovitch and J. Albert (eds), *The Benevolent State: The Growth of Welfare in Canada*, Toronto: Garamond Press.

UNDP (1999) *Human Development Report: Globalization with a Human Face*, New York: Oxford University Press.

—— (2002) *Human Development Report: Deepening Democracy in a Fragmented World*, New York: Oxford University Press.

United Nations (2000) *World Economic and Social Survey 2000*, New York: United Nations.

van der Pijl, K. (2001) 'International relations and capitalist discipline', in R. Albritton *et al.* (eds), *Phases of Capitalist Development: Booms, Crises and Globalizations*, London: Palgrave.

van Staveren, I. (2001) *The Values of Economics: An Aristotelian Perspective*, London: Routledge.

Vromen, A. (2003) 'Community-based activism and change: the cases of Sydney and Toronto', *City and Community*, vol. 2, no. 1: 47–69.

Wade, R. (1992) 'East Asia's economic success: conflicting perspectives, partial insights, shaky evidence', *World Politics*, vol. 44: 270–320.

—— (1996) 'Japan, the World Bank, and the art of paradigm maintenance: the East Asian miracle in political perspective', *New Left Review*, vol. 217: 3–36.

Walras, L. (1874; 1877; 1954) *Elements of Pure Economics*, Homewood: Richard D. Irwin.

Web, J. (2002) *Understanding Bourdieu*, London: Sage Publications.

Weber, M. (1999) 'Modern Capitalism: Key Characteristics and Key Institutions', in R. Swedberg (ed.), *Essays in Economic Sociology*, Princeton: Princeton University Press.

Wertheim, W.F. (1974) *Evolution and Revolution: The Rising Waves of Emancipation*, Harmondsworth: Penguin Books.

Wheelock, J. (1990) *Husbands at Home: The Domestic Economy in a Post-Industrial Society*, London: Routledge.

—— (1992) 'The household in the total economy', in P. Ekins and M. Max-Neef (eds), *Real Life Economics: Understanding Wealth Creation*, London: Routledge.

Williams, C.C. (1996) 'Informal sector responses to unemployment: an evaluation of the potential of local exchange trading systems', *Work, Employment and Society*, vol. 10, no. 2: 341–359.

Williams, C.C. and Windebank, J. (2000) 'Beyond social inclusion through employment: harnessing mutual aid as a complementary social inclusion policy', *Policy and Politics*, vol. 29, no. 1: 15–28.

Wolff, R.D. and Resnick, S.A. (1987) *Economics: Marxism versus Neoclassical*, Baltimore: Johns Hopkins University Press.

World Economic Forum and Center for International Development (2002) 'Executive summary: competitiveness and stages of development', *World Competitiveness Report 2001/2002*, New York: Oxford University Press.

Wright, D.M. (1962) *The Keynesian System*, New York: Fordham University Press.

Zaretsky, E. (1976) *Capitalism, the Family and Personal Life*, New York: Harper & Row.

Zukewich, N. (1998) 'Work, parenthood and the experience of time scarcity', *Research Paper – Days of Our Lives: Time Use and Transitions Over the Life Course*, Ottawa: Statistics Canada.

Zuzanek, J. (2001) 'Parenting time: enough or too little?', *Canadian Journal of Policy Research*, vol. 2, no. 2: 125–133.

Index